THE 300

THE 300

THE INSIDE STORY OF THE MISSILE DEFENDERS GUARDING AMERICA AGAINST NUCLEAR ATTACK

DANIEL WASSERBLY

ST. MARTIN'S
PRESS
NEW YORK

First published in the United States by St. Martin's Press, an imprint of
St. Martin's Publishing Group

THE 300. Copyright © 2020 by Daniel Wasserbly. All rights reserved.
Printed in the United States of America. For information, address
St. Martin's Publishing Group, 120 Broadway, New York, NY 10271.

www.stmartins.com

Designed by Steven Seighman

Library of Congress Cataloging-in-Publication Data

Names: Wasserbly, Daniel, author.
Title: The 300 : the inside story of the missile defenders guarding
    America against nuclear attack / Daniel Wasserbly.
Other titles: Three hundred
Description: First edition. | New York : St. Martin's Press, 2020. |
    Includes bibliographical references and index.
Identifiers: LCCN 2019054414 | ISBN 9781250221841 (hardcover) |
    ISBN 9781250221858 (ebook)
Subjects: LCSH: Ballistic missile defenses—United States. | United
    States. Army. Missile Defense Brigade, 100th—History. | United States.
    Army. Missile Defense Battalion, 49th—History. | United States.
    Missile Defense Agency—History.
Classification: LCC UG743 .W37 202 | DDC 358.1/7430973—dc23
LC record available at https://lccn.loc.gov/2019054414

Our books may be purchased in bulk for promotional, educational, or business use. Please contact your local bookseller or the Macmillan Corporate
and Premium Sales Department at 1-800-221-7945, extension 5442, or by
email at MacmillanSpecialMarkets@macmillan.com.

First Edition: 2020

10   9   8   7   6   5   4   3   2   1

For Sarah

CONTENTS

CAST OF CHARACTERS

100th Missile Defense Brigade, Colorado Springs, Colorado

SUSAN FROBE-RECELLA: *original crew member*

MARCUS KENT: *original crew member*

KEVIN KICK: *brigade commander (September 2016–December 2018)*

TIM LAWSON: *brigade commander (July 2014–September 2016)*

DAVE MEAKINS: *original crew director*

RICHARD MICHALSKI: *original crew member, crew director*

MATT POLLOCK: *crew director*

GREG SIMPSON: *original crew director*

BILL SPRIGGS: *original crew member*

MICHAEL STRAWBRIDGE: *crew director*

PATRICIA YOUNG: *crew member*

MICHAEL YOWELL: *brigade commander (April 2006–May 2009)*

49th Missile Defense Battalion, Fort Greely, Alaska

RON BAILEY: *crew member*

GREG BOWEN: *battalion commander (July 2003–May 2006), brigade commander (May 2009–July 2012)*

JARROD CUTHBERTSON: *MP, battalion and brigade crew member*

BETHANY HENDREN: *MP, crew member*

ED HILDRETH: *battalion commander (May 2006–July 2008), brigade commander (July 2012–July 2014)*

MARK KIRALY: *MP, battalion and brigade crew director*

RAY MONTOYA: *crew director, MP company commander*

JEANETTE PADGETT: *MP, crew member*

JOHN ROBINSON: *MP platoon sergeant, battalion and brigade crew member*

MARK SCOTT: *MP, battalion security*

Missile Defense Agency, Arlington, Virginia (moved to Fort Belvoir, Virginia, in 2011)

RON KADISH (US AIR FORCE): *MDA director from June 14, 1999*

HENRY "TREY" OBERING III (US AIR FORCE): *MDA director from July 2, 2004*

PATRICK O'REILLY (US ARMY): *MDA director from November 21, 2008*

JAMES SYRING (US NAVY): *MDA director from November 19, 2012*

THE 300

PROLOGUE

ANY INCOMING US PRESIDENT gets briefed on the threats and options of nuclear warfare. The choices aren't good and the dynamic is particularly tricky with North Korea, with its bellicose history, long-range missiles, and nuclear weapons. Somebody has to tell the president about the limited options, and this unenviable job typically falls to the vice-chairman of the Joint Chiefs of Staff. That four-star officer must travel to the White House and first explain the choice between "preemption" and "interdiction."

Preemption would be when the intelligence community reports a possible intercontinental ballistic missile, or ICBM, being stacked on a North Korean launchpad. The president would need to decide upon a wait-and-see approach or a preemptive strike to destroy that missile. International law says a preemptive strike is an act of war, but it is more open to interpretation if that act might be justified. Legal arguments can be made either way and the context is important: Is it possibly a test launch? Could it be a satellite payload and not a warhead? Has Pyongyang been publicly threatening to turn New York City into a sea of fire? One group of government lawyers might argue that just stacking the boosters on the launchpad could be considered a hostile act, while another group of government lawyers might argue that it's not a hostile act until the missile has been launched at the United States. The president must also be warned that preemptive strikes are not guaranteed to be successful. A missile could get through and hit the United States anyway.

Interdiction is a simpler, but equally unpalatable, concept: the Pentagon steps into the fight after a missile has already been launched at the United States. This could include the president ordering a retaliatory nuclear strike, but immediately after an enemy launch the authority for self-defense is already delegated to Northern Command, which could try to destroy the hostile warheads. Intercepting the warheads sounds like a great alternative, a respite in this otherwise horrific briefing about nuclear war. Unfortunately, at this point in the president's briefing, the vice-chairman must explain how difficult ICBM intercepts are. About ninety seconds after North Korea launches, the Pentagon will know the trajectory thanks to infrared satellites overhead and radar on US Navy ships or at fixed sites in Japan. The interceptor system needs to see and track the missile at two points to plot where it is heading, and then at a crucial third point to get good enough data to triangulate an intercept. Those satellites, radar, communication networks, and computer systems all must work properly.

The missile needs about twenty-eight minutes to travel from North Korea to, say, Seattle. Within that, there will be about a seven-minute window from the time the inbound missile crosses over the interceptor system's third radar horizon, within sight of the Cobra Dane radar station on the small island of Shemya in Alaska's Aleutian chain. The first two minutes and last two minutes of that window are statistically bad for an intercept attempt, so US Army missile crews plot their launches to hit the warhead somewhere in a three-minute time frame in the middle. The sweet spot. Four or five interceptors might be launched to collide with that one incoming warhead in the sweet spot, but the interceptors' intricate components all must work properly too.

The last part of the vice-chairman's briefing is especially unhappy, because then the president is told that there might not be sensors or radars available that can see whether the interceptors actually destroyed the warhead. If the entirety of the system works, you might not know you've killed the warhead until its full twenty-eight-minute flight time has passed—the only measure of success would be that, when the countdown hits zero, Seattle *isn't* smoldering under a mushroom cloud.

The incredibly difficult mission of homeland missile defense is assigned to the US Army's 100th Missile Defense Brigade and 49th Missile Defense Battalion. Just three hundred soldiers. The small, unconventional unit calls itself "the 300," homage to the Spartans who fought at the Battle of Thermopylae in 480 BC. Except instead of using swords and shields as did the Spartans to defend the Greeks, the modern-day 300 use phased-array radars and advanced aerospace engineering (yes, it *is* rocket science) to defend three hundred million Americans. They are asked to defend the United States from nuclear missile attacks, to sit and monitor and learn and train and relearn and retrain in perpetuity, waiting for the grim day when their skills might be demanded. This is their story.

1

THE 300

THE QUICK ALERT SOUNDED, a flashing white light and a shrill *beep, beep, beep.* At Schriever Air Force Base in Colorado Springs, across town from Cheyenne Mountain, the alert warns the 100th Missile Defense Brigade that an intercontinental ballistic missile has been launched. Five army operators from Charlie crew man their consoles.

They sit in a control station known as a node, a small room with five work consoles in a horseshoe. Each console has a double-decker phone bank with two receivers and an assortment of black, blue, and red direct-dial buttons. At the front of the room, five big TVs hang from a low drop-ceiling. On the center TV, a digital globe of Earth rotates to display a red circle where the missile launch was detected. The circle is on Panghyon Aircraft Factory in North Korea. On the screen, a red "threat fan" begins to bloom out from the circle at the launch location. The fan depicts the missile's expected path and, for now, it only shows the missile is traveling east. If the fan becomes an ellipse, showing the missile's path from North Korea toward the United States, Charlie crew may be ordered to destroy the missile.

Lieutenant Colonel Richard Michalski sits in the middle of the consoles and screens and army officers. Michalski watches over his crew while working the phones. He places a call to his counterpart at Northern Command, just twenty minutes down the road at Peterson Air Force Base, and answers a call from his subordinate at Fort Greely in Alaska, 2,400 miles away, where forty of the brigade's interceptor missiles wait in silos. There is a five-man battalion crew at Greely that reports to Michalski's brigade crew. The soldiers at Greely watch over the missile field and will launch interceptors on Michalski's order—or they can launch on their own if something goes horribly wrong in the node at Schriever.

Michalski has two officers at his left, who are already on the phone with radar stations in the Pacific Ocean. To his right sit his deputy and his future-operations officer, who are analyzing time lines for engaging and destroying the incoming warhead with several interceptors. "Two minutes to engagement," Michalski tells the missile defense officer on the phone at Northern Command. In two minutes, he'll know if the North Korean warhead will come within range, if it can be intercepted.

An overhead US Air Force satellite had detected the enemy launch, an ICBM from North Korea. The satellite automatically sounded the Quick Alert. It also cued army radar stations on Japan and Guam, and navy Aegis-equipped destroyers fitted with radars in the Sea of Japan. These sentries found the inbound missile and identified it as a possible threat to the United States, then passed the target to Charlie crew's "primary eye."

"Thirty seconds to engagement," Michalski says. He's

speaking to the missile defense officer at Northern Command, but everyone is listening on the communications Ops Loop that can be heard at brigade headquarters and up at Greely too.

The primary eye is the massive Sea-based X-band Radar that floats more than nine-stories high and displaces more than fifty thousand tons atop a repurposed oil rig in the Pacific. Radar tracking data streams in through Charlie crew's current-operations officer. He's on the phone with the radar operators, making sure they're seeing what he's seeing. As more data comes in, the red threat fan grows. It's now pointing toward Alaska. "The missile is engageable," Michalski tells Northern Command. The missile defense officer relays Michalski's message.

At the back of the operations center sits Lori Robinson, the four-star general in charge of defending North America. She can see the same threat fan on the big overhead TVs in her headquarters. "Weapons release authority granted," she says. Her missile defense officer then tells Michalski, "You have weapons release authority." Charlie crew must destroy the warhead.

Michalski hardly moves throughout the exchange, and calmly tells his crew, "Go weapons free."

The radar tracking data is feeding into software, and the software is mapping the missile's path with such precision that the crew can launch its own missile to destroy the warhead in space. On Michalski's "go weapons free" order, the weapons operator on crew at Greely directs the system, known as the Ground-based Midcourse Defense, to allocate four interceptors to destroy the incoming ICBM. The system's fire control algorithms then compute the exact point in outer space where the interceptors will strike the nuclear warhead.

At Greely, four missile silo doors fling open. The system has calculated its shot and sent the information to fifty-five-foot-tall interceptors in the ground at the remote army post. Seconds later, the first interceptor's three-stage rocket booster blasts it out of the silo, up through the Alaskan sky, and into space to find the incoming warhead. Three more blast off in succession. "Four GBIs launched," Michalski reports, and the Ground-based Interceptors race to their target. The threat fan on the screen has grown into a full ellipse—North Korea's target is Fort Greely itself. They're trying to take out the army's interceptor missile field there.

Once in space, the interceptors drop the final booster rockets and release a kill vehicle. The 120-pound kill vehicles, now the only objects between an enemy warhead and the United States, move rapidly through the vacuum of space toward their target. But a nuclear warhead does not travel alone. Aside from a cloud of debris generated by its own launch, the incoming ICBM is fitted with decoys to confuse the kill vehicles and radars. The Sea-based X-band Radar has been providing updates to the interceptor about the warhead's path and its decoys, but after the interceptor acquires its target, it will no longer receive updates from the ground.

The kill vehicle is propelled through space by momentum from the launch, and continually directs and redirects itself into the warhead's path with four small rocket thrusters. While hurtling through space, the vehicle must determine which entity is the warhead and then use the thrusters to ensure a direct collision. The interceptor communicates its status back to Michalski's soldiers in Colorado, but after the launch all the crew can do is wait—and monitor for more missiles. The incoming nuclear warhead is now well over the Pacific Ocean, about 745 miles above Earth, traveling nearly fifteen thousand miles per hour. "Two minutes to intercept," Michalski reports.

Data streams into Charlie crew's monitors as the interceptor closes in on the warhead. Michalski and his officers watch.

Of the 1.3 million active-duty servicemen and women, more than 800,000 National Guardsmen and Reservists, and over 764,000 civilians working across the world for the Pentagon, only the five-person missile crews at Schriever and at Greely have the skill and equipment to *try* to shoot down an ICBM. And intercepting targets in space at the speed of an ICBM is extraordinarily hard. The technology is generally limited to addressing smaller numbers of missiles that do not carry advanced countermeasures. Russia's thousands of nuclear weapons and China's hundreds of nuclear weapons are thought to include countermeasures, such as decoys, and those larger arsenals would overwhelm the US fleet of interceptors.

Of the brigade's five missile crews, Charlie crew is by far the most subdued on intercept missions. That's the approach Michalski prefers. He's tall, athletic, and serene. He likes the node to be calm and quiet for missions. Mark Kiraly's Alpha crew is in the middle of the spectrum: they aren't quiet but aren't loud either. Mike Strawbridge's Delta crew is the loudest. Strawbridge's style is to stimulate the crew and get their adrenaline running, so they're almost yelling updates to one another or to their counterparts at Greely. Michalski wants the node like a library so he can meticulously think through scenarios.

And so Charlie crew is sitting there, calmly checking their monitors. "One minute to intercept," Michalski says on the Ops Loop. They wait.

The intercept is a success and the warhead is destroyed.

This was, of course, a training run. The scenario was relatively simple. The crews train for far more complex missions with many more warheads, or "fail-overs" in which the Colorado crew might need to work without the Alaska crew, or vice versa. Michalski walks through the scenario with his soldiers, finding small things they could improve, tasks that could've been done quicker, anything to boost their odds of a successful intercept. Millions of lives might depend on it.

Michalski has run thousands of training scenarios in the many years he's been a homeland missile defender, but circumstances are always changing: as the brigade's weapon systems advance, so do North Korea's missiles. The laconic crew director is one of the original members of the 100th Missile Defense Brigade. He was on crew when the system was first turned on, and he's a veritable maestro at destroying enemy warheads in space.

Michalski watched his brigade's interceptor system advance from distressing early engineering problems to become an avant-garde weapon, and he's seen North Korea evolve into a real nuclear power that can credibly threaten the country he's sworn to defend. Indeed, the brigade and its interceptor weapon have come a long way from inauspicious beginnings.

2

WEEKEND WARRIORS

LIEUTENANT COLONEL GREG BOWEN drove his pickup truck from Colorado to Alaska in five days, traveling fifteen hours a day. Bowen had been assigned as commander of the soon-to-be 49th Missile Defense Battalion, based at Fort Greely, about one hundred miles southeast of Fairbanks. He first reported to an Army National Guard facility in Anchorage, because Greely had been turned into a ghost town. There was no place for him to stay at the dismantled Greely, so the administrative work of creating the new battalion had to be done in Anchorage at first. The housing for families was in Anchorage, reliable internet was in Anchorage, food was in Anchorage. When Bowen first arrived at Greely in July 2003, it was more of a construction site than a US Army post.

A 1995 Base Realignment and Closure Commission recommended shuttering thirty-two US military facilities including Greely, which had been an Alaskan cold-weather testing station. The fort was closed in 1999. But as concern about North Korea grew, and the goal of shooting down intercontinental ballistic missiles gained favor, Greely was back on the Defense Department's map. An ICBM launched from North

Korea at San Diego or Los Angeles would fly about fifteen hundred miles west of Greely. One launched at New York or Washington would fly about one thousand miles north of Greely. The trajectories were ideal.

In late 2001, the eight hundred or so residents of Delta Junction, the nearby town that had been economically devastated by Greely's closure, were told the fort would be reopened. So now the Pentagon was trying to bring tiny Greely back as the cornerstone homeland missile defense site, where most of the interceptors would wait in silos.

Greely's barren commissary was still open to serve a handful of retirees in the area, but the post had no other amenities. What little it once offered had been closed. There was no chapel, no child development center, no doctor. There were a few small low-rise administrative buildings and some 1960s-era prefabricated housing. Bowen asked about using the gym. He was told the weights were rusty but he could use it whenever he wanted, as long as he could find the local fireman who kept the key.

Seven years earlier, Bowen was an air defense artillery training officer in North Dakota, where the Nixon-era Safeguard homeland missile defense site had been briefly activated. Under the 1972 Anti-Ballistic Missile Treaty, the United States was allowed to have one missile defense site in North Dakota and the Soviet Union was allowed to have one near Moscow. Given its history, North Dakota seemed a natural place to recruit officers to help work on the Pentagon's newest missile defense development effort in the mid-1990s. Bowen and a team of army air defenders were sent to Colorado Springs for a few weeks each quarter to serve as US Army Space and Missile Defense Command's "crash test dummies." The idea was to ask a group of Regular Joes to operate the newfangled strategic defense system, so the engineers could get some idea of how soldiers might react to seeing huge streams of data pouring onto small computer monitors.

Bowen discovered that engineers love tabular data, vast fields of rows and columns and numbers. This wouldn't work so well for soldiers trying to make quick decisions, so Bowen and the crash test dummies worked with the developers to get a better display, one that would show maps and trajectories and countdowns. By 1999 it appeared that the system might actually advance from development to production, and Army Space and Missile Defense Command hired Bowen full-time to work on the project at its headquarters across the road from the Colorado Springs airport. In January 2000, Bowen joined a team writing the "concept of operations" for what would become the Ground-based Midcourse Defense (GMD) system. Halfway through his tour, on December 13, 2001, George W. Bush announced that his administration would abrogate the Anti-Ballistic Missile Treaty and would deploy a homeland missile defense system. On June 13, 2002, the United States officially withdrew from the ABM Treaty, and two days later the Missile Defense Agency (MDA) held a ground-breaking ceremony at Fort Greely for six underground silos.

Bowen worked on planning for the new system in Colorado until 2003, when he was selected to build the unit that would launch the system's interceptors. The army major was promoted to lieutenant colonel, packed up his wife and one-year-old daughter, and shipped up to Alaska to establish the 49th Missile Defense Battalion.

Just a handful of soldiers had been assigned to the new unit. Like Bowen, they all sent their families to live at Fort Richardson in Anchorage—a six-hour, 330-mile drive away—because there was no place for families to live at Greely. Most of the soldiers slept and kept their gear in what the army called "temporary housing units." These were trailers. There wasn't much time for anything but working and sleeping anyway. The fort's handful of small, boxy concrete buildings were beginning to hum with life again.

A few hundred yards outside the fort's aging epicenter, the new missile defense complex for Bowen's battalion was just a series of holes and trenches. Bechtel, one of the United States' largest construction companies, with a specialization in megaprojects, was working twenty-four hours a day in three shifts to get a year's worth of work done in a summer, before the Alaskan tundra would refreeze. At all hours, workers were digging out silos for Missile Field One using huge tracked augers to bore out the holes, seventy-five feet deep and fifteen feet in diameter. The prefabricated silo shells weighed 130,000 pounds. They had to be lowered into the holes with two cranes, which would lift a silo up horizontally and then slowly raise the top end before the structure could be maneuvered into the ground. Other contractors were digging long trenches, called utilidors, to carry all the utility pipes and data feeds between the interceptor missile silos and the Readiness and Control Building where Bowen's soldiers would work.

The Missile Field One site was just south of the garrison perimeter, and presented serious construction challenges. Digging in a glacial basin is unpredictable, and some holes were packed with massive boulders. But Greely was an old army training and testing site too, so on top of dealing with rugged terrain, Bechtel also unearthed the occasional unmarked fuel drum that would require an inspection process to ensure it wasn't filled with anthrax or God knows what. Often, it was garbage. The army of the 1950s was content to drive a short distance from the garrison to bury trash.

For Bowen, the immediate deadline was October 2003. He had to get soldiers into the unit and get them trained and certified to stand watch 24/7 over the program's first piece of classified gear: an In-Flight Interceptor Communications System Data Terminal. The terminal, essentially a radio transmitter and receiver enclosed in a radome atop an equipment shelter, would allow the missile crews to send targeting information to the interceptor as it flew through space toward an incoming warhead.

But the Alaska Army National Guard had bitten off more than it could chew. It simply did not have the resources to stand up a battalion from scratch. Just getting the military policemen, known as MPs, hired and certified for their mission proved a significant challenge. First, the army had not specialized in fixed-site defense for many years, so Bowen traveled to F.E. Warren Air Force Base in Wyoming to learn how the airmen there secured 150 Minuteman III nuclear missiles in silos. Some of the battalion's procedures were copied from F.E. Warren and some were made up by Bowen and his team. Second, the unit was only authorized forty-four

MPs. Bowen and the state authorities began racing to fill the empty MP spots, and the battalion couldn't afford to be picky about who filled those spots. It had to meet a presidential deadline for getting the fort and the missile defense complex up and running—the White House wanted everything operational by October 2004.

The first elements of the battalion's MP company were ready when Northrop Grumman installed the data terminals in October. The construction crews, however, were not ready to have young soldiers with guns ordering them around. There was immediate friction. The workers, mostly contracted locals, were used to having their run of the place, and Alaskans generally don't like to be told where they can and cannot go—that's often specifically why they live in a state with 663,268 square miles and fewer than 739,800 residents. Bowen was already working seven-day weeks to get his battalion ready, and now also had to play referee between the contractors and the soldiers. He was well cast for the role.

An imposing officer with a big square jaw, sharp squinting eyes, and closely cropped blond hair, Bowen could be alarmingly serious and disarmingly approachable. It was the tough-but-friendly style of a hardworking prior-enlisted soldier from Grand Forks, North Dakota. Bowen was meeting several times each day with the contractors and representatives from the Missile Defense Agency, keeping everyone as happy and focused as he could. For Bowen, it was fast becoming the hardest and most rewarding job he'd ever had.

Once a small perimeter was secured around the first building, Bowen realized the MP unit would need to grow at least threefold to guard the entire missile defense complex.

Yet Greely was still barely livable. Spouses still couldn't stay on post so the army was rotating the soldiers back to Anchorage to visit their families every week or two. The soldiers had to fly back and forth on a C-23 Sherpa, a small twin-engine utility aircraft that had to regularly battle fifty-mile-per-hour winds blowing across Greely's airfield. Though the job was rewarding for Bowen, those flights would rank among the scariest experiences of his army career.

On January 4, 2003, Marcus Kent arrived at Building 3 on Peterson Air Force Base in Colorado Springs, where his new unit was temporarily based. He was directed to a large classroom with desks for twelve soldiers, and so began his career with the 100th Missile Defense Brigade. He never left.

Kent had mobilized with his South Carolina Army National Guard unit shortly after the attacks of September 11, 2001. He was sent to Iraq to manage airspace for theater-level missile defense. A year later, home from Iraq, Kent was trying to build a life at a construction company when the company filed for bankruptcy and he lost his job and his civilian career. Kent had heard soldiers in his National Guard unit talking about a new brigade forming in Colorado that was accepting applications for full-time jobs. It was open to anyone who was officially an air defense artilleryman.

The job announcement for joining the unit did not fully explain what was going to occur. It left out the complexity and the gravity of the mission. At the time, the entire brigade was Kent and eleven other soldiers. They were mostly from the air defense artillery community, and most were from the South Carolina National Guard. Two soldiers from outside South Carolina stuck out: Dave Meakins, a tall and droll lieutenant colonel from Georgia by way of Chicago, and Bill Spriggs, a tough but sneaky-smart staff sergeant from Mississippi.

Meakins got to Colorado Springs in March 2003 and spent the first three months working out of Peterson Air Force Base trying to get the brigade's paperwork in order. On Monday, June 2, Meakins started the GMD Qualification Course, in which he learned how to operate this new missile defense equipment, but he still didn't fully grasp the scope of what they were doing or what the standards would be. Meakins just knew that his rank meant he could be the director of a five-soldier crew, but he also knew that he needed to get above 90 percent on all his tests. He worried that he'd get kicked out of the unit if he didn't make the grade, so he studied hard each night.

Spriggs was in the class too, at a plain civilian office building on Academy Boulevard in Colorado Springs, learning how to fight with the GMD system. It was all done by PowerPoint slides. Spriggs was the honor graduate and was reticent about the "honor" part. He was a modest noncommissioned officer and downplayed his intellect. He almost didn't get a job with the brigade in the first place.

Spriggs had been a paratrooper and a medic in the 82nd Airborne Division, but he left active duty and was working as a respiratory therapist in Colorado Springs while serving in the army as a weekend warrior. Spriggs's brother, a recruiter for the Mississippi Army National Guard, called to ask if he'd heard of a new missile defense unit being established nearby.

Spriggs hadn't heard a thing. A full-time National Guard job sounded good though. He applied and was promptly rejected. Several days later Spriggs got a phone call from the Alaska Army National Guard, offering him a job as the battalion medic at Fort Greely. Spriggs was intrigued.

"What would you think about moving to Fort Greely?" he asked his wife. "It's in Alaska."

"We'll miss you very much," she told him, which meant Spriggs was not allowed to take that job.

A few days later he got another call, this time from the Colorado Army National Guard. Now they were offering him the position they'd just rejected him for. "The guy that we picked instead of you, his wife won't let him move away from Kansas—so it's your spot if you want it." Spriggs wanted it.

Aside from being his GMD class's honor graduate, however, Spriggs was also officially a medic and not an air defense artilleryman, so the army made him go to another school to learn a job that would qualify him as a so-called 14-series soldier. The quickest way to join that group was to send Spriggs to 14J School to learn to operate and maintain the Sentinel radar system. He went to the school, passed, and then never again touched a Sentinel radar.

In 2003, homeland missile defense was becoming a hot topic. Bush was publicly discussing the deployment of a complex system to detect and destroy ballistic missiles. That April, North Korea had withdrawn from the Nuclear Non-Proliferation Treaty, and four months later negotiations to dismantle Pyongyang's nuclear programs fell apart. The Bush administration had been keen on missile defense anyway, but now it was all in.

Meakins, realizing how important this new brigade might be, and how rewarding a full-time National Guard job was, had sent word of the opportunity back to his old unit in Chicago: the Illinois National Guard's 2nd Battalion, 202nd Air Defense Artillery Regiment.

The homeland missile defense system was to be manned by full-time National Guardsmen. Weekend warriors reporting for duty once a month would be insufficient, and active-duty soldiers would be too troublesome. The active-duty army in general didn't want the homeland missile defense mission because leaders were worried about the costs. The Missile Defense Agency proposed that its civilian engineers be used as developer-operators who could execute intercepts but also work to improve the budding technology. Secretary of Defense Donald Rumsfeld nixed the civilian operator idea and demanded it be a military role, so MDA offered instead to handle the funding, and the army's air defense community grudgingly offered its soldiers. Air defenders, though, are a stubborn tribe with a set way of doing things. They would bring too many of their own traditions and own ways of doing business. The mission was instead given to the National Guard, viewed as a more tractable group of weekend warriors who could build the unit up from nothing.

Some of Meakins's colleagues in Illinois's 202nd Air Defense Artillery Regiment were skeptical. Was shooting down ICBMs even possible? What if they got sent to live in Alaska? Weren't the winters there terrible? Captain Richard Michalski didn't care where he got sent. He wanted in.

Michalski was born in Poland and immigrated to the United States with his family as a boy. He was an all-star tennis player in each of his four years at West Point. After graduating in 1997, he earned a spot in the Army World Class Athlete Program and vied for the US Olympic team. Michalski didn't make the team and filed paperwork to leave the army as soon as he possibly could. He hadn't found anything in the service to be passionate about; it offered nothing he really liked, except tennis. Two years later, he was enjoying life as a bond trader in Chicago when the September 11, 2001, attacks changed his mind about the army. Feeling he had to do something, Michalski joined the Illinois National Guard. Putting in time with the 202nd Air Defense Artillery Regiment was more like a hobby—one weekend a month, two weeks a year—and Michalski's indifference toward the army boiled up again. He was quickly getting a reputation as a junior officer with a bad attitude. This new unit Meakins was talking about, however, offered a somewhat loftier mission: defend the United States against nuclear attack.

Michalski was married in November 2003 and the next month was accepted into the 100th Missile Defense Brigade in Colorado Springs. He would have a shot at joining one of the five missile crews there at headquarters, or one of the five subordinate crews at the 49th Missile Defense Battalion in Alaska.

It was snowing on Michalski's first day in Colorado Springs, December 18, a Thursday. He drove to the address he'd been given, but had no idea what he was getting into. It was not on a military base and looked like any nondescript office building. Just a few weeks before, the brigade had moved its slowly growing headquarters out from Peterson Air Force Base to a building across the street from the Colorado Springs airport. The brigade had taken over offices formerly leased by Army Space and Missile Defense Command—the same building where Bowen had been a crash test dummy. Outside it could easily be mistaken for any other midrise office building, with beige tiles and dark glass. Inside was a plain lobby and a pair of elevators that led up to office space more stereotypical of a small or midsized corporation. There were cubicles, small offices, and water coolers.

An energetic first sergeant spotted the puzzled Michalski and assured him that, yes, he was actually in the right place, and handed over an office key. Michalski hung around the brigade's newly leased headquarters building for the next two weeks, waiting to begin the GMD Qualification Course.

The overall approach to operating the GMD system was that five-soldier crews in Colorado Springs would work with five-soldier crews at the interceptor missile field 2,400 miles away at Fort Greely, and get their orders from Northern Command, which was buried under Cheyenne Mountain fourteen miles southwest of Colorado Springs. Computer algorithms would do all the calculations based on radar and intelligence data. The crews would need to get Northern Command's orders, launch the interceptors, and manage any glitches. If everything went right, the job should be straightforward. If something went wrong, the job would require a deep understanding of the software and its underlying algorithms. The crews would have to learn it all.

The December 2003 GMD Qualification Course had thirty-six students, required a minimum 90 percent grade to pass, and was an exceptionally odd experience. The classrooms were still at the building on Academy Boulevard. At this office, for the next eight weeks, the trainees were to wear civilian clothes to keep a low profile. Thirty-six soldiers, each with a high-and-tight haircut but all in civilian clothes, filed into the building each morning—Captains Geneen Tobey, Susan Frobe, and Leticia Walpole were the only women and could, of course, have longer hair.

This was only the third class to go through the qualification course and was by far its largest, as it would be the main pool of soldiers from which the missile crews would be chosen. To keep things intimate, the class was divided into two sections. Most of the instructors' credentials were simply that they'd helped develop the software or had passed one of the first two classes. Nobody had ever used this GMD system. It didn't exist yet.

Instruction was done by PowerPoint slides because mock-ups of the computer terminals hadn't been completed. The class was told what clicking buttons on the computer would do, but they couldn't click for themselves. *Here's a picture of what the screen will look like. Here is a description of what will happen if you click this button.* The abstract, hands-off nature of the training and the lack of expertise caused the trainees to become rather blasé toward the whole endeavor. These sorts of army seminars are sometimes merely "gentleman's courses"—and this one was filled with young captains and noncommissioned officers, and most of them were National Guardsmen. Frobe, one of the few active-duty officers in the class, expected the mentality to be especially relaxed because, after all, this was just the National Guard.

The lieutenant colonels who would soon become missile crew directors, and who were trying to select and groom their crews, did not share the soldiers' casual approach. To get the group's attention, the colonels sprung a surprise exam at the end of the first week. Of the class's thirty-six trainees, twenty-four failed the exam.

The class was ordered together and the future crew directors—Meakins, Tim Rahn, and Greg Simpson—ripped into the soldiers for not taking their task seriously. The directors wanted the unit's reputation to be strong and serious, something more akin to acceptance in the NASA astronaut training program and less like signing up for weekends camping with the National Guard. The course had to be difficult and the crew members had to be smart and dedicated. As each of the colonels went on at length about the seriousness of North Korean threats, or preparing for difficult shift work, or the burden of defending millions of lives, Michalski sat in the back and nodded slowly in agreement. *Exactly,* he thought, *why aren't you guys taking this seriously?*

Michalski not only didn't fail that first test, but didn't miss a single question throughout the entire eight weeks. Just a few months earlier he was marked as a junior officer with a bad attitude. Now he and Geneen Tobey, who also didn't miss a single question, were the two distinguished honor graduates in his section of the class. Frobe and Sergeant First Class Russell Hamilton were the distinguished honor graduates in the class's other section.

Between lessons, the soldiers tried to piece together how this enterprise might unfold: who would be selected for which crew, what job would they get on crew, how many jobs were open to each rank, and where would the active-duty soldiers be placed?

There was then a sort of draft to fill the five brigade and five battalion crews. The directors looked at the strengths and weaknesses of each candidate to ensure no one crew was only all-stars. First, they had asked each student who among them wanted to go to Alaska. The battalion crews for Greely where chosen from that list and then they arranged the brigade crews, careful to keep the active-duty soldiers on separate crews. Frobe knew she'd get a job as a deputy director, based on her rank and active-duty status. She was assigned to Meakins's Alpha crew, along with Spriggs as the readiness officer and Kent as the future-operations officer. Michalski was assigned as a current-operations officer on Lieutenant Colonel Lawton Kitchin's Bravo crew.

Before the crews could be trusted to defend the United States, though, each had to undergo a group certification administered by Army Space and Missile Defense Command. These certifications were what the army calls a "tabletop" drill. There was no system available to certify on, so it was done at an actual table. A civilian representative from the command walked the soldiers through various scenarios, and the crew members then said what button they would theoretically press. By the time they were on crews, though, they had access to training terminals and began constant practice.

Six times the crews were each called in for "gray beard" conferences. The gray beards—retired general officers now in big-time government and industry jobs—filled a huge auditorium at Schriever Air Force Base, joined by leadership from Northern Command, MDA, Army Space and Missile Defense Command, and anyone else who was worried that the human operators might be the weakest link in the homeland missile defense program.

The crews were sent behind the auditorium to a little room with screens set up in a row to do a practice run: destroying warheads on mock-ups of the computer terminals. After the simulated mission, they were led to center stage so the distinguished audience could pick apart the crews' performance. The gray beards interrogated the crews on every move they had made. *What happened here? Why did you do this? Why did you think that?*

It was intense. The importance of the mission and the seriousness of their job had been coming into focus over the last few months, but the conferences made it perfectly clear. The crews were given tremendous responsibility and there could be no screwups. The gray beards were worried that some young soldier might cause an intercept to fail or might accidentally shoot down a space shuttle. The conferences, though nerve-wracking, were giving the crews significant credibility. The gray beards were impressed, and turned their concern to the equipment.

All the crews were next sent out to Huntsville, Alabama, where the army and Boeing were designing the system's software. The soldiers were to help finalize the software and the procedures that they'd soon be deploying in the real world. Meakins and Alpha crew arrived first and were asked to do practice-run missions, but they found the contractors had a totally different setup.

The horseshoe of consoles the crews had been sitting inside for months now was inverted—they had to sit on the outside and Meakins couldn't see the crewmates' screens. Then they tried their first run and found nothing worked properly. It turned out that each of the crew members was only authorized to do their specific task at their specific console, but they had trained with everyone authorized to do everything. They had made themselves a sort of collective intelligence, an efficient team that worked faster together. With the new design, each soldier only had the software permissions to work in their own lane, which was meant to keep the soldiers from screwing something up.

"How come all the permissions aren't there now? Why is that?" an agitated Meakins asked one of the software engineers.

"That's the way it is now," he was told.

"No, it's not," Meakins said. "This is what's going to happen— we're not going to do any more runs until we're given the permissions, until we're able to fight the way we're supposed to fight. Okay?"

The crews had their tactics, techniques, and procedures set up the way they wanted; they'd spent months practicing and had been cross-examined on their every move. Meakins and the other crew directors weren't about to change all that.

Boeing and MDA convened an emergency meeting in Huntsville to discuss Meakins's demand. Alpha crew waited around for four hours, as Meakins considered warning the other crews that there might not be any reason to come out to Huntsville after all. But the engineers emerged in agreement that everyone on crew should get all the permissions. The crews had built up enough cachet that their comments were becoming military requirements.

3

ISLAND OF MISFIT TOYS

THE DRIVE FROM FAIRBANKS down to Fort Greely is impressive. It could also be dangerous when ice and snow make the small road disappear. Twisting down Alaska Route 2, the hilly tree line to the road's east is thick with conifers nearer to Fairbanks, but begins to thin out as the road meanders south. To the west, more tributaries and runoffs branch out from the Tanana River as the trees further disperse. The landscape flattens and gives way to subarctic tundra. On a clear day, when the road gets closer to Delta Junction and Fort Greely and turns past one of the few remaining hills, the snowcapped mountains of the Alaska Range suddenly frame the view in the windshield. For many of the small handful of soldiers now slowly funneling into Bowen's unit, this drive was their first experience in Alaska.

As Greely's secured perimeter grew, it was clear that more than the allotted forty-four MPs would be needed to guard the expanding site. While he awaited more soldiers, Bowen formally requested a stopgap solution for defending the fort. The Alaska Army National Guard mobilized a company of infantrymen to help for one year. They were not typical army infantry. Soon Greely became like the Island of Misfit Toys.

Bowen knew something was off the first time he asked a lowly private to help him with a task, and the private shrugged and walked away. Bowen called one of his Alaska Guard friends to ask why some of the army's lowest-ranking soldiers were ignoring a lieutenant colonel, and how should he fix this.

"Oh, you just have to go see Staff Sergeant Brown," his friend said.

"Why? What does he have to do with it?" Bowen asked.

"Staff Sergeant Brown is the village elder in the village where these soldiers come from."

Staff Sergeant Brown quickly became Lieutenant Colonel Bowen's most important ally. About one hundred of the mobilized guardsmen came from a group known as Alaskan Scouts. They were mainly native Athabaskan Indians, who had lived for centuries in the Alaskan interior among the spruce, willow, and birch, the labyrinthine river systems, and the climate extremes. They had a tradition of service in the former Alaska Territorial Guard, and since maintained a rare and important ability to reach the state's most remote National Guard armories via dogsled or snowmobile, no matter the weather. Although they sometimes mustered in Fairbanks, most of the Athabaskan scouts lived in the wilderness. The relative civilization at Fort Greely and Delta Junction was a novelty. They'd pile into a big truck for a trip into Delta Junction or up to Fairbanks, and only later would anyone in the battalion realize that none of them had driver's licenses. They normally had no need for that sort of driving.

In general, the soldiers were the best Bowen had ever seen in the field, and the worst he had ever seen in garrison. They knew how to survive and thrive in Alaska's extreme environment, but many of them had little use for the army's ranks or regulations. It wasn't just the Alaskan Scouts; some of the regular Alaska guardsmen proved troublesome too. One private, nicknamed Brewski, stood out among his peers. Brewski, during a few days off from his MP duties, rented a bicycle from the fort's recreation office and rode it seventeen miles to the Clearwater Lodge, the battalion's favorite nightlife spot (and really its only nightlife spot). Brewski got drunk and got arrested by an Alaska state trooper. He had to go to court a few days later and the judge was relatively lenient. When Brewski got another few days off the next month, he did the exact same thing. He got arrested by the same Alaska state trooper and went to court in front of the same judge, but this time showed up to court drunk.

The mobilized guardsmen fell under Alaska's code of military justice, which strictly limited how Bowen could discipline troops. Private Brewski was ordered to stop drinking, had his weapon taken away, and had to march his guard post at the missile defense complex carrying only a stick.

July 2, 2004, was a particularly hot and humid day in Washington, DC. Lieutenant General Ron Kadish, Major General Trey Obering, and Secretary of Defense Donald Rumsfeld stood together on a breezeless stage at the Defense Department's Navy Annex. They were on a small hill below the southern tip of Arlington National Cemetery, just above the Pentagon, but could barely see the building through the haze. Obering was about to take the reins of the Missile Defense Agency from Kadish, a close friend and fellow airman who was finally retiring.

Kadish, a stately air force senior pilot, took over the Pentagon's Ballistic Missile Defense Organization in June 1999. He'd become a career program manager and led the F-15 and F-16 fighter projects, and turned around the once-troubled C-17 cargo aircraft's development. Kadish didn't know much about missile defense at first, and was surprised how much he had to moderate policy arguments over whether missile defense was good or bad. There was an outside constituency that loved it, and another constituency in the arms control community and academia that hated it. Kadish—a dour Philadelphia native—felt like an arbitrator, explaining to advocates that the technology was harder to develop than they realized, and explaining to critics that intercepting enemy missiles was at least possible. He called himself a "hard-nosed realist" about the difficulties presented by homeland missile defense, and considered it a challenge as significant as the Manhattan Project or developing the Minuteman ICBM.

In late 2000, Rumsfeld had asked Kadish to stay in his job once George W. Bush took office. Kadish agreed, but with some conditions. He didn't want to develop missile defense systems while constrained by the 1972 Anti-Ballistic Missile Treaty, which banned US and Russian strategic missile defenses outside of the deactivated site in North Dakota and Russia's site near Moscow. He also didn't want his office to be just a funding mechanism anymore, handing cash over to military branches that were mostly uninterested in missile defense. He wanted an agency that had real authority and its own programs.

Rumsfeld was working to scrap the treaty anyway, and gave Kadish everything else he wanted too. In December 2001, the

White House announced it was withdrawing from the treaty, and a year later Kadish's organization was renamed the Missile Defense Agency and given leeway to bypass the strict acquisition and testing rules that other Pentagon departments had to follow—the agency's director was given executive power to act as he saw fit.

Rumsfeld had long been a vocal advocate for missile defense. He led a commission that raised eyebrows in July 1998 by prophetically reporting that Washington would have "little or no warning" before facing ICBM threats from North Korea and Iran. The next month, North Korea stunned Washington by launching into space a Taepodong-1 missile, a precursor to an offensive nuclear missile. By February 1999, CIA director George Tenet was warning the Senate that North Korea might soon be able to use the Taepodong-1 to strike Alaska and Hawaii, and in September a US National Intelligence Estimate added to the alarm by reporting that North Korea was "most likely" to develop an ICBM capable of attacking the continental United States by 2015.

So, leading the Pentagon for a second time (he first held the job in Gerald Ford's administration), Rumsfeld made deploying a homeland missile defense system one of his top priorities. He had been pleased with the efforts of Kadish, a Clinton holdover, and kept him in that role for five years. The sort of lieutenant general billet that Kadish had is typically only a two- or three-year job. For three straight years Kadish offered Rumsfeld his resignation, because that was the custom, and three times Rumsfeld sent it back. By 2004, though, both decided it was time for a change.

The answer was to tap Trey Obering, Kadish's comrade

and deputy, to lead the Missile Defense Agency. Obering would take over at a pivotal time too. The first operational interceptors were about to be deployed, the GMD system was about to be officially turned on, and major tests were on the horizon. When the pageantry of the agency handover at the Navy Annex was done, Rumsfeld pulled Obering aside. "Don't fuck it up," he said.

4

THE OLD FORT

IT WAS CHILLY AND rainy, around 6:00 P.M., when Captain Mark Kiraly pulled up to the Canadian border crossing near Lethbridge in Alberta, Canada. He was driving from Chicago to Fort Greely, with everything he could fit in his car, as fast as possible, eager to start his new assignment with the 49th Missile Defense Battalion. But the two young Canadian border guards were in no hurry. Kiraly had shown them his US Army orders but they were unmoved. His fully packed car was singled out for a search, and they routed him over to a sally port to open all his gear bags and rummage through his stuff. The big army captain was a prior-enlisted soldier, so he'd put in his time getting pushed around by some kid in a position of authority and was only mildly perturbed by the inspection, but his broad and friendly face turned into a scowl when the border guards opened his humidor.

"Oh my, these are nice. Is that a $10 cigar?" one guard asked the other.

"Oh yeah it is. These US officers must get paid a lot of money, huh?"

The first guard turned to Kiraly. "Some of these are from Cuba, ay? You know, you can't take these back into Alaska from Canada. I guess that could be smuggling," the guard said. "You'll have to smoke them all here in Canada. That'll be tough, all by yourself."

Kiraly, a gregarious Midwesterner, tried to keep in good humor. They were asking for his Cuban cigars as a bribe.

"I guess that's my problem," Kiraly said with a smile. "So don't you worry, I'll enjoy smoking each one." The guards let him keep the cigars and he drove off into a miserable, rainy evening.

In Chicago, Kiraly's wife, Ruby, was doing what most military spouses do when their partner gets a new assignment. She was putting the house up for sale, getting their young son ready for the move, and googling everything on her new home. There was, it turned out, quite a bit to learn about Fort Greely.

The remote, windswept, high-plains desert is an entirely different microclimate. Situated between mountain ranges, the temperature averages about minus 20°F all winter but can reach 80°F in the summer. It snows there, but not as much as the surrounding mountain areas. From the 1940s through the 1960s Greely was a cold-weather testing station for the army. This is all okay for the curious spouse; even the rustic, remote, no-doctor-on-post stuff has a certain charm. But then they start seeing stories about chemical weapons testing and decommissioned nuclear reactors, about radiation leaking into the Delta River that winds through the base, about caribou dying en masse just a few miles from the fort. They learn about nearby Blueberry Lake, where allegedly a pallet of artillery shells, loaded with VX gas and sitting on the ice one winter waiting for a test, was forgotten for months and fell through the ice during the spring thaw. The soldiers settling in at Greely tell their spouses not to worry, these are nothing more than silly rumors. Except the Blueberry Lake story wasn't a rumor. The lake had been drained to prove it once and for all, and sure enough the army found a pallet of artillery shells loaded with VX gas. For a city-dwelling engineer like Ruby Kiraly, it was a lot to take in.

Mark Kiraly had grown up in suburban Chicago and enlisted in the army in 1983 as an air defender. He was serving with Lieutenant Colonel Dave Meakins and Captain Richard Michalski in the Illinois National Guard's 2nd Battalion, 202nd Air Defense Artillery Regiment and, like Michalski and a handful of others, Kiraly had jumped at Meakins's idea of joining the new missile defense program as a full-time soldier, with an important strategic national defense mission. The paperwork took a bit longer, but he was accepted and told to report to Greely. He'd been assigned as the battalion's assistant operations officer to help Bowen set up security there and train the fledgling military police unit, Alpha Company.

Major General John Holly, the Missile Defense Agency's deputy director and its lead for the homeland missile defense project, had ordered a red digital countdown clock be placed at the agency's office on Greely. The clock was a brightly visible countdown to September 30, 2004, the deadline set by the Bush administration to declare the missile defense system officially "operational," even if in a strictly limited capacity.

The first interceptor was shipped into the Alaskan port of Valdez, where it was off-loaded onto a large tractor trailer and then driven 268 miles north to Greely. For this, MDA required shutting down much of Alaska Route 4, an important stretch of road for anyone who wants to drive anywhere in the state southwest of Denali. Alaskans weren't pleased, and Governor Frank Murkowski forbade the road to be shut down again, so the interceptors had to be flown into Greely instead.

The airstrip was difficult to keep clear though. Moose would wander onto it and were a danger to the aircraft. Since they couldn't have soldiers stalking around the runway shooting rifles at anything that moved, bowhunting was authorized as a relatively safe means of keeping the moose away, but this was soon canceled because its only result was that the moose walking around the airstrip had a few arrows in their sides—they were literally unmoved by the bow hunters.

Bechtel was still digging and Boeing, as the government's lead contractor for GMD, was managing all the work. On July 22, 2004, the first operational interceptor had been placed into a silo at Fort Greely. The interceptor stood about five stories tall. It was powered by a three-stage Orbital Sciences rocket booster that carried the 120-pound kill vehicle into space. That kill vehicle, packed with delicate optics, sensors, and navigation software, would use four small thrusters to steer through the vacuum of space toward its target. The weapon, with its delicate technology, was carefully driven out to the silo on a flatbed truck and then lifted by a crane with special guide rails up into the air, then gently lowered into its silo. Once the interceptor was wired into the brigade's command network, the silo's clamshell doors were closed and sealed. The backhoes and bucket loaders were working overtime to install four more interceptors before the countdown clock expired.

In September 2004, the contractors, the MDA, and the newly formed 49th Missile Defense Battalion were up against the White House's big deadline. But the battalion's Fire Direction Center, where the crews would sit to launch interceptors, still didn't have a classified communications network, known as the SIPRNet, installed. Without the network, they couldn't declare even a limited capability.

On Friday, September 10, Bowen ran into a friend who oversaw MDA's network communications. They began commiserating, and he told Bowen that the agency just didn't have the manpower necessary to get all the cabling strung underneath the flooring to set up the classified network on time. "Well, I'm here," Bowen said. "So I'll come and help." He spent the weekend crawling around underneath the Fire Direction Center's floor and pulling cable with the MDA guys.

Kiraly had just arrived, with his cigars, from his six-day drive across western Canada and the Alaskan interior, and went to meet his new boss. He found Bowen in dusty civilian clothes, stretched out on the floor in the Fire Direction Center, helping several contractors wire the facility. It's not normal for a lieutenant colonel—a battalion commander no less—to be doing that sort of work. Kiraly was impressed. This was clearly not like any army unit he'd served in before. The sense of urgency was unmistakable. Everyone, up to and including the commander, was doing whatever it took to get the system running.

In their scarce spare time, Kiraly and the battalion's other soldiers were scrambling to find off-base housing and establish some sort of life. Off-base housing was crucial: partly because nobody wanted to get hassled by their boss on a rare day off, but mostly because it was required to get Alaskan subsistence hunting tags to hunt for caribou and moose and fish for Arctic grayling. For most of the incoming soldiers, Alaskan hunting and fishing was an important reason for joining the unit, but nearly all the soldiers had to pay extra for their hunting tags. The precious few houses in Delta Junction had all been occupied by the Bechtel, Boeing, and MDA workers who got there first.

MDA had around a thousand people on Greely in 2003 and they had taken all the good stuff before the battalion began its formation. The agency got the nice warm storage areas for its vehicles; the battalion got some sheds by a sewer lagoon. Boeing had been given some of the nicer buildings as part of its MDA contract; the battalion was left with the crumbling Building 609. Fixing old facilities or erecting new ones wasn't as easy as it might be at almost any other army post. Everything cost three times what it would in the Lower 48, even the staff. The fort's dining facility was the only place to eat but nobody wanted to work there, so contractors were paid extravagantly—the dishwasher was making $20 an hour.

Many of the locals lived in converted buses, trailers, or modest cabins. There were no resident contractors to build new houses in town for any soldiers willing to buy them, so additional modular housing from the 1960s was delivered to the fort and the soldiers could at least now bring their families.

The housing for officers wasn't great, and the housing for

enlisted troops was terrible. The houses had red lights in the window that would turn on if the inside temperature dropped too low. That way, security on the post would know if a heater or power system had failed and the occupants were in danger of dying in their sleep from the extreme cold. Kiraly was especially handy, able to fix a leaking sink and familiar with the baseboard-heating systems that were used in the houses and regularly failed. Everyone called him to help fix their run-down homes. As the older, prior-enlisted officer, Kiraly quickly became a sort of big brother figure in the battalion.

Every army unit has a specific branch that it belongs to—Infantry, Aviation, Special Forces, and so on. But shooting at nuclear warheads in space is rather unique. Bowen, who hailed from the army's only even remotely close analog, the Air Defense Artillery branch, looked at GMD as "a surface-to-air missile on steroids." Military police were chosen to form Alpha Company, which would pull security around the fort and its missile fields, but the missile crews and battalion staff were nearly all recruited from Air Defense Artillery units. The battalion was soon a rare army marriage between air defenders and MPs, and it started off poorly.

The battalion missile crews had been training in Colorado Springs with the brigade crews, but by the summer of 2004 the first interceptors were in silos and Missile Field One was nearly complete. The MPs had been toiling outside at all hours in the harsh Alaskan interior for a year, while the missile crews had studied in relative comfort. There was an immediate schism between the two groups.

The MPs were still patrolling outside, while the crews merely had to drive down the road toward their seats inside the heated Fire Direction Center. At every chance they got, for every infraction they could find, every unbuckled seat belt, the MPs hassled the crews. To the MPs, the crews were just goldbricking button-pushers. To the crews, the MPs were just glorified hall monitors. Bowen was trying to de-escalate a small civil war, and was soon saved. A perimeter fence around the missile defense complex was complete, so the MPs had an enjoyable diversion with mock battles in which an assaulting force tried to break into the fort. Most important, though, the battalion soon rallied together in collective antipathy for sudden hordes of distinguished visitors—generals, congressional delegates, and defense industry executives who conspicuously only visited in the summertime, spent more days out fishing or hunting than learning about the battalion, and broke all their promises to send more resources to the austere post.

Specialist Jeanette Padgett and Specialist Mark Scott weren't as bothered by the distinguished visitor tourism. They were both born and raised in Alaska, and were used to tourists passing through and commenting on the quaintness and then never returning. Scott was from Wasilla and Padgett from Delta Junction, just down the road from Greely. She was what the soldiers and townspeople alike called a Deltoid, a true local.

Padgett even had a small role in saving Greely from a wildfire in June 1999, when she worked on a Helitack team for the Alaska Forestry Department between semesters at college. A training area south of the fort caught fire, and winds pushed the flames toward Greely. Her team joined smoke jumpers from Fort Wainwright to help fight the fire and evacuate Greely. As Padgett and the team worked, the fire consumed black spruce, birch, and cottonwood trees around the fort, and then it set off a random series of small explosions—the fire was igniting ordnance that had been buried or misplaced during Cold War–era training around Greely.

Padgett returned to Delta Junction after college, joined the National Guard part-time, and worked in a gym. Like her neighbors, she was aghast that Greely was being closed by Congress. The fort meant steady jobs for the Deltoids, and it often hosted Special Forces from all branches of the US and allied armed forces for training drills, which meant big money spent in town after the drills. The closing hurt the town badly and some residents moved away. The rumor, which was mostly welcomed because it meant jobs, was that Greely would be turned into a prison. After the 49th Missile Defense Battalion was established there instead, the town got a breath of life and Padgett got a full-time job. She joined the battalion in June 2004 as an IT administrator and would soon enjoy a steady rise toward becoming an officer.

Scott joined the battalion that October but would have a much rougher go of it. He was marked from the beginning as an outsider. A year earlier, Scott was a corporal in an elite US Marine Corps unit specializing in recovering downed aviators, and took part in the initial assault into Iraq. After his tour, he had returned to Alaska to a girlfriend, a new baby daughter, and a construction job that wasn't making ends meet, so he enlisted in the Alaska Army National Guard for some extra money, and learned of the rare full-time jobs being offered at Greely. Scott arrived on October 1, but the army would not let his girlfriend live with him because they weren't married—they fixed that quickly and Scott, his wife, and one-year-old daughter moved onto the fort.

For Scott, it was total cultural shock. He was used to the weather, the darkness, the remoteness, and the random dangers of Alaska. He was not used to the Army National Guard. Scott's USMC world was one of strict order and no questions. To him, soldiers at Greely seemed disorderly and questioned too much, and Scott couldn't keep quiet about it so he made few friends. He didn't even look like an army soldier—he only had his USMC uniforms, and Greely's Post Exchange only had three aisles of sparse shelves. He couldn't buy the correct clothing. The supply personnel told him, "You've been in before, just wear your old uniform." So Scott wore his old Battle Dress Uniform from Iraq. He took all the removable USMC stuff off and strapped on army tabs, but the Corps' distinctive eagle-globe-and-anchor insignia was sewn in.

Lieutenant General Larry Dodgen, head of Army Space and Missile Defense Command and one of Greely's more frequent distinguished visitors, was getting food at the chow hall when he noticed Scott's eagle-globe-and-anchor.

"Specialist Scott, come over here please."

"Yes, sir?"

"Why do you have the eagle-globe-and-anchor on your left pocket? Is that some kind of joke?"

"No sir. I was in the Corps in '03, in a TRAP unit in Iraq, sir. They just didn't have any uniforms for me when I arrived here."

"If that's the case, why aren't you wearing a combat patch?"

"I can't, sir. I was in combat with the Corps, not the army. Under army regulation I think I'd need some special sign-offs. It'd be out of regs, sir." This seemed okay to Dodgen. Wearing a marine uniform in the army was wholly "out of regs," but at least Scott was trying to comply.

"Ok, go ahead and do it," Dodgen said, and walked away.

The supply guys didn't know when they could get in an order for more uniforms. Padgett heard about the incident and offered to loan a few of her extra uniforms to Scott so he wouldn't get in any more trouble. He was happy to accept her offer. Two weeks later, a big box arrived at Scott's door, packed full of army uniforms. Inside was a note:

SPC Scott: Thanks for your service.
—LTG Dodgen

Back in Colorado Springs, the missile crews at the 100th Missile Defense Brigade headquarters had completed their training courses and their interrogations by the gray beards, and had been sitting for practice run after practice run on computer mock-ups. Finally, Meakins and Lawton Kitchin, two of the crew directors, took the graduates for their first tour of the new operating node at Schriever Air Force Base. Schriever felt legitimate. Security there was always tight; they protected a range of secretive US Air Force space missions conducted there, and now also the crew's node.

Meakins led the soldiers to the third floor of the MDA's Joint National Integration Center at Schriever. Their job was turning out to be quite complicated, and to add another layer of complication, they had to walk through the bureaucracy of being army soldiers in an MDA facility on an air force base. Obtaining security badges for new personnel was a nightmare.

Once inside, the brigade's area included a control node with a glass-walled conference room and a small admin area behind it. The node had five consoles in a horseshoe, each console with a small screen built into a low wall in front. It looked like a 1980s video game. When the screens were turned on, they had three colors: black, gray, and a different gray.

The soldiers following Meakins and Kitchin around Schriever knew what the mission was, and the qualification course had given them an idea about which buttons did what and why, but little else had been figured out yet. Kitchin tried to simplify it for the soldiers. "This is where we're going to work, we're going to be defending America against ICBM attacks," he said.

Right, Michalski thought, *with just five interceptors.*

5

GOING LIVE

LIEUTENANT GENERAL RON KADISH, when he was head of the Missile Defense Agency, had ordered GMD team leader Major General John Holly to get five interceptors in silos by the end of 2004. Holly chose to interpret that as "the end of fiscal year 2004," which gave him a three-month cushion in case things slipped until the end of the calendar year. Holly walked in on a meeting between Obering and Kadish and, as he had done at Greely, plopped another digital clock with the same September countdown on Kadish's desk.

On September 30, 2004, Holly's digital countdown clocks ticked toward zero at Greely and at MDA headquarters. Obering, now a three-star general leading the agency after Kadish's retirement, held a meeting at the headquarters near the Pentagon that day. All the stakeholders were there, including Larry Dodgen, head of Army Space and Missile Defense Command, and representatives from Northern Command. Obering had long checklists for technical reviews and for operational reviews. They had to decide if the Ground-based Midcourse Defense system was even remotely capable of intercepting an attacking nuclear warhead. They had to tell the White House if a "limited deployment" could be declared for the GMD. It was still only a prototype, but Obering argued that fielding the system was, quite simply, "obeying the law." That law was the one-page National Missile Defense Act of 1999. It stated:

> It is the policy of the United States to deploy as soon as is technologically possible an effective National Missile Defense system capable of defending the territory of the United States against limited ballistic missile attack (whether accidental, unauthorized, or deliberate) . . .

The GMD development program was on a relatively successful run of testing—five intercepts in eight tries—but these were of early prototype systems. The testing was done under the sort of controlled conditions that would not qualify as "real world" scenarios (launching a ballistic missile thousands of miles for an intercept test is an exceptionally tricky and expensive endeavor). Obering admitted it wasn't a fully tested and approved technology, "but what else do we have out there?" he asked. "If we have nothing, then anything that's of military utility would be of use." Obering's argument was that something was better than nothing, and even if each interceptor only had a 50 percent chance of success, they could improve their odds by launching multiple interceptors at each single warhead. It had the MDA director's endorsement, and he was a significant force.

Obering, a brash Alabaman, grew up wanting to be an astronaut and came closer than most who'd ever shared that dream, but NASA medical staff found a disqualifying problem during his physical. Still, on the path there he had graduated with honors from Notre Dame with an aerospace engineering degree, was commissioned in the air force, flew operational missions as an F-4E Phantom fighter pilot, and added a master's degree in astronautical engineering from Stanford. Obering couldn't be an astronaut, but he still got to work on several NASA assignments. He had worked at MDA developing a communications network for the 100th Missile Defense Brigade, and since 2003 had been the agency's deputy director. He knew missile defense history well.

The GMD system had succeeded in a 1999 trial but then failed in two key intercept tests the next year. For the first, on January 19, 2000, the target launched, the interceptor launched, and the kill vehicle separated from the booster and raced toward the target. But the vehicle's infrared sensor, which is designed to peer far out into space to track even the faintest heat emission, was severely nearsighted. It missed its target by seventy meters. A lengthy investigation found the sensor had not cooled to the minus 334°F that it required to properly see heat in space. Krypton gas was used for this cooling, and something obstructed its flow through the kill vehicle's intricate plumbing. Many of the kill vehicle's systems were redundant, meaning if one fails there are others as a fallback. It had two infrared sensors, for example. But the vehicle had only one plumbing system and adding a second was unfeasible, so the plumbing was completely revamped.

For the second test, six months later, on July 8, the interceptor failed not because of an issue with the new and highly advanced kill vehicle, but rather because of a problem in the

Minuteman booster's avionics processer. It malfunctioned and the kill vehicle never received its order to separate. CBS News' Dan Rather was there with a cameraman to film the entire failure.

During a test on July 14, 2001, however, the booster worked fine, the kill vehicle separated and recognized its position, then homed in on and destroyed a mock warhead in space. This opened a successful testing run that included three more hits in a row: December 3, 2001; March 15, 2002; and October 14, 2002.

Then, on December 11, 2002—just one week before Bush and Rumsfeld were planning a major missile defense policy announcement—the GMD program suffered an embarrassing and preventable failure. The kill vehicle didn't separate from its booster because a small pin had broken. The pin connected a computer chip to a circuit that was supposed to activate a small laser. The laser was supposed to separate the booster's restraining bolts, but a subcontractor had removed a tiny piece of insulation meant to protect the pin from vibrations, so it snapped and thwarted the entire homeland missile defense system. Raytheon, Boeing, and MDA were unaware the subcontractor had made the change.

Still, MDA viewed this as a management and quality control issue, not an indictment of the technology's effectiveness. After two years shaping its policy, the Bush administration on December 17, 2002, announced the president's decision to field the homeland missile defense system beginning in 2004 with an initial ten interceptors in Alaska and California, to be followed the next year with ten more in Alaska. Bush and Rumsfeld wanted to keep that promise. They wanted the system up and running, even if in the most limited capacity, and they wanted that done before the next year.

On Thursday, September 30, 2004, Obering asked everyone at his stakeholders' meeting if they were ready. All went through their checklists and all agreed: enough of the system was functioning that, in case of an emergency, the five interceptors could be used for combat. Four were ready at Greely and one at a test site on Vandenberg Air Force Base in California. They could try to shoot down one or two warheads.

The Bush administration declared the GMD system had achieved a "limited deployment option" capability. For the MDA and the 100th, there was little celebration, no champagne, only work to be done. It was more of a beginning than an end, and it was a controversial beginning.

The bar set by the National Missile Defense Act of 1999 was for intercontinental ballistic missile defense to be technologically possible, and for the GMD system to be "effective" against incoming missiles. Suffice to say, Phil Coyle felt the term "effective" did not apply to the new homeland missile defense system.

Coyle, an engineer by training, had been director of the Pentagon's equipment testing office from 1994 to 2001. He was deeply skeptical about GMD. Coyle believed the system's tests were done in unrealistically favorable conditions and ignored countermeasures such as decoys or other techniques that North Korea would use to fool defenses.

In a speech to the Carnegie Endowment for International Peace the week before Obering announced the system's limited deployment, Coyle argued that GMD should not yet be considered "effective" because it did not yet have a constellation of satellites to detect launches, did not yet have a high-powered X-band radar for tracking objects in space, and did not yet have an adequately performing kill vehicle.

Coyle was critical that building the site at Greely had taken priority over testing the developmental technology. "As soon as President Bush announced his decision to deploy the system, the priority went to construction and deployment, and the bottom fell out of the test schedule. There hasn't been a flight intercept test since December 2002, now twenty-one months ago, one week before the president announced his decision to deploy."

Coyle also believed that the tests were developmental in nature, and not indicative of how the system might perform in combat. "In these tests, the target launch time and location, the flight trajectory, the point of impact, what the target looks like, and the make-up of other objects in the target cluster have all been known in advance to plot the intercept. No enemy would cooperate by providing all that information in advance."

With the limited deployment publicly declared, the soldiers of the 100th Missile Defense Brigade and 49th Missile Defense Battalion were to begin manning the system. 24/7/365. Lieutenant Colonel Greg Simpson's Charlie crew had been in one of the nodes at Schriever the night before, running system checks, but the official first shift would begin at 6:00 A.M. on October 1, 2004, with Alpha crew: Lieutenant Colonel Dave Meakins's crew for the brigade in Colorado, and Major Joe Miley's crew for the battalion in Alaska. The soldiers were excited, and went into the shift ready to do *something* if they needed to.

Meakins was a sharp, easygoing officer, liked by everyone. Alpha crew enjoyed working together and had fun on the job. Still, they took the mission seriously and that inaugural shift was exhilarating for what it meant—the first soldiers that could, potentially, destroy a nuclear warhead and save millions of lives. Sergeant First Class Marcus Kent was the crew's future-operations officer, Staff Sergeant Bill Spriggs was the readiness officer, Captain John Edwards was the current-operations officer, and Captain Susan Frobe was the deputy director.

Thirty minutes before the shift, Meakins's Alpha crew went down into a secure room at Schriever Air Force Base for an intelligence briefing on everything that might be happening in the world during their watch. They then walked back up to the node, where Meakins signed on to the Ops Loop that connected the crews in Colorado and Alaska and Northern Command. He gave a briefing via the Ops Loop about the brigade's status—how many interceptors were ready to launch and what it was tracking. Then Alpha crew waited.

Meakins was ready to fight off a horde of missiles, but the shift was ultimately strange and dull. It went until 2:00 P.M., but only a few of the systems were powered up in front of the crew. Some of the screens weren't on yet and there was no attacking horde, so Meakins and the crew began developing procedures for emergencies. If there was a fire, who would lock up the classified materials, and so on. Like his soldiers, though, Meakins wasn't entirely sure what they could or could not do—so nobody left the node during the eight hours, not even to go to the bathroom.

For Spriggs, it was like the Pentagon had given them a never-before-used weapon system and told them to use it to defend the United States against nuclear attack. *Okay, but how do I do that?* The trainers at the GMD Qualification Course could teach soldiers how the system worked, but that was only part of it. It was still unclear how the soldiers would actually fight with it. They could communicate with Northern Command or Greely or radar sites in the Pacific, but what should they say?

At Greely, the declaration of a "limited deployment" meant the soldiers had to work harder to get the fort in better order. Kiraly was coaching young lieutenants and helping build up Echo Company, the military police unit charged with pulling security for the eight-hundred-plus acres of command centers and secretive missile fields. They had only just begun patrolling a perimeter fence. Every few days a moose or caribou breached the wire, causing an alarm and sending the new MPs to urgently reconnoiter the perimeter. Kiraly noticed the MPs were driving around to inspect the fences with .50-caliber machine guns mounted to their Humvees. For this sort of MP company, the big .50-caliber guns are standard for defending a base. On the small fort, however, the missile field was ominously close to the garrison and to base housing.

"Sir, we have TWIGs driving around with .50-cals," Kiraly warned the battalion's executive officer, Wayne Hunt. Teenagers with Guns—*TWIGs*. "A .50-cal will range into the garrison, right next to the missile field," Kiraly said. "What if there's something in the wire, and they shoot into the housing area? It's only a couple hundred meters."

The officers instead settled on using smaller 7.62 mm machine guns for mounted patrols, and Bowen and Hunt then had to start a lengthy requisition process to get more reasonable firepower. The army was trying to shoehorn existing concepts into the unique situation at Greely, like fitting a giant square peg into a small round hole. There was no normal equipment set, no playbook to go by.

Kiraly enjoyed the work of setting up the MP unit and training its young soldiers. They got to patrol the base in the sort of cold weather gear that normally only the exclusive Special Forces types used. They got to shoot hundreds of rounds at the range on a regular basis. Sometimes it was a combination of the two, with Kiraly ordering each soldier to dig themselves a narrow two-hundred-meter lane through snow drifts so they could see and shoot at targets while laying prone. This was unusual and exciting compared to most days in the army, and almost unheard of for the National Guard's weekend warriors. Kiraly loved it but made no secret of his ambitions. Shooting at targets in the snow was great fun, but he wanted to shoot at ICBMs. Kiraly wanted to sit at the top, become a crew director, and lead soldiers as they fired interceptors in defense of the nation.

The one-of-a-kind unit didn't have a deep bench. Once a soldier was trained and certified to operate the GMD system, they became one of about fifty people in the United States with the qualifications and the ability to destroy an incoming nuclear warhead. It was a small pool, so Kiraly figured he would get a chance at joining a missile crew, especially because he had experience as an air defender, but he knew there were limited spots open for his rank of captain.

Bowen had grown concerned that the missile crew members might, on the country's worst day, have its most important job—but they might also have dead-end careers. The army demands that its personnel experience multiple jobs and tick certain boxes to get promotions. The Alaska National Guard, however, didn't have any other air defense or military police units except Bowen's battalion. One of his solutions was to allow the smartest MPs to convert their military specialty to air defense. There was a career incentive to get promotions, but, more pragmatically, the soldiers were incentivized to get inside the heated Fire Direction Center and out of patrolling missile fields during minus 60°F winter nights.

Bowen felt it was important to have missile crews with an appreciation for the battalion's wider mission, and was pleased to have the MPs trying out to change roles. Likewise, young officers on the missile crews could move to Alpha Company to lead an MP platoon, if they needed leadership experience. Alpha Company didn't have the same prestige as the missile crews, but the security details, though typically peaceful, were no small matter. A ground attack on Greely would presumably be intended to take out the homeland defense system and therefore be a prelude to a nuclear strike. The MPs were to protect the missile fields at all costs. There was no backup at Greely. They were asked to be alone and unafraid on subarctic patrols.

The soldiers would have to volunteer to transfer in either direction, but moving to become an air defender and joining the missile crews was undoubtedly more academically difficult. Bowen's staff and the brigade staff had to first determine how many open slots there were and who was up to the challenge of the GMD Qualification Course. For most testing, the army typically benchmarks a passing grade as 70 percent or higher. Soldiers call it the "seven-o and go." That seemed low for guarding the United States against nuclear strikes, so the army determined that all prospective GMD operators would have to score higher than 90 percent on the tests.

"You'll have to get an A on every test essentially, or you will not pass the course," Bowen told his volunteers. "I don't want an average GMD operator protecting three hundred million Americans. I need a GMD operator that has mastered the weapon system and knows exactly how it works and what to do in any situation."

At Schriever Air Force Base, the brigade missile crews were settling into their nodes. Simpson and Meakins would bicker for years about who had led the actual first shift. After that shift, though, they all set about figuring out how they might use this new weapon. Each crew had passed their first Table 8 certification, meaning they were certified as a battle-ready crew and were cleared to pull shifts. But they had done those certifications on paper at another building. Sitting on their consoles was now at once empowering and bewildering.

The system was "capable" of launching interceptor missiles into space to destroy nuclear warheads, but it wasn't fully switched on yet and the crews didn't fully know how to operate it. It was apparent that the breakdown of tasks and the procedures would have to be created by the crews themselves, not the army or MDA or Northern Command or a defense contractor.

The brigade was proving peculiar. Spriggs and Kent had come from the active-duty army, where structure was important and clear. They had each been part of a platoon, which was part of a company, which was part of a battalion, which was part of a brigade, which was part of a division—they knew it and had the patches on their shoulders to prove it. Their ultimate master was Big Army. That all changed in the 100th Missile Defense Brigade. Suddenly they had to deal with the MDA, Northern Command, Strategic Command, the Army National Guard, and a parade of contractors. Their bosses changed depending on what they were doing on any given day.

The crews were odd too. A staff sergeant like Spriggs was a long way down from a lieutenant colonel like Meakins, and soldiers of those ranks would not normally sit down and chat about life for eight straight hours—but the crews had to work closely and the noncommissioned officers had to give quick, honest input to the higher-ranking officers. Frobe, the active-duty soldier on Meakins's crew, was still getting used to being a captain and sitting next to a lieutenant colonel.

It was a very different structure than the rest of the army, closer to the Special Forces community where ranks mattered, but so did experience. To foster that atmosphere, Meakins established a three-second rule—anybody could poke fun at anybody else for anything and they had three seconds to make a comeback or they couldn't respond, no matter their rank. Meakins brought a small bell into the node that he'd ring when the three seconds were up. They also began a tradition of "crew Fridays," which weren't necessarily on Fridays but on whichever day of the week was the crew's last before a few days off. It was a more relaxed shift with a sort of potluck dinner, everyone bringing in some dish or dessert. Frobe was in the midst of planning her wedding during the first few months of shifts, and realized she would be spending far more time with Meakins, Edwards, Kent, and Spriggs than with her fiancé, or with anyone else.

For Michalski, moving on from tabletop drills to sitting at his console in the node, the atmosphere and the mission finally felt genuine. It also felt cold. The temperature within the room was kept at a constant chill. Several Walmarts' worth of air-conditioning was needed to keep all the technology from overheating. Pulling his first shifts as the Delta crew's current-operations officer, Michalski began to think seriously about what all this equipment might mean. Until now, he thought, all we could do is say that something was going to hit us and brace for it; there was no defense. Even if it was limited, and even if all the screens weren't yet turned on, there was now at least some capability to provide some level of defense.

Michalski was a captain and there were two soldiers ahead of him in the chain of command—the crew director, Lieutenant Colonel Lawton Kitchin, and the deputy director, Major

Mike Tobey—so he wasn't the decision maker, but he was the button-pusher that could launch the interceptors. They had at their disposal an expanse of equipment from Japan to the central Pacific Ocean, to California, Alaska, Greenland, the United Kingdom, and beyond the atmosphere—all designed to find and destroy missiles traveling through space. That reality hit home.

The feeling was positive too, quite different from the tough philosophical position of the air force's nuclear missileers. The airmen must do their job knowing that, if they were successful, they would likely have killed millions of people. If the soldiers of the 100th Missile Defense Brigade were successful, they would have protected millions of people.

There were four interceptors in silos at Greely and one at Vandenberg in California, and the crews could, if called upon, launch them in defense of the nation. It was no longer just PowerPoint slides or learning algorithms or practicing "buttonology" in a small room. In October 2004, the crews finally felt they wielded a capability to destroy enemy ICBMs. The moment was sixty years in the making.

6

ORIGIN STORY

ON SEPTEMBER 8, 1944, the missile age began. A German V-2 guided ballistic missile was launched from Nazi-occupied Holland and about five minutes later, at 6:43 P.M., exploded in west London's Chiswick district. It left a thirty-two-foot crater on Staveley Road, killed three people, and injured twenty-two more. Chiswick's terrified residents thought they'd heard a second explosion, but the single missile moved faster than the speed of sound, so its approach wasn't heard until after it blew up on the street. More than a thousand V-2s were launched at the United Kingdom in the coming year, hundreds specifically targeting London, and hundreds more targeting cities in Belgium and France. Thousands died.

Ideas for defending against these *Vergeltungswaffen,* or "vengeance weapons," began emerging shortly after evidence of the first developmental V-2s was brought to British military officials in July 1944. In response, the British evolved radar teams to spot incoming missiles and were able to approximate where the weapon might strike. General Frederick Alfred Pile, commander of the British Army's Anti-Aircraft Command, argued the radar data could be used to direct antiaircraft guns to shoot missiles down with a massive barrage of exploding artillery shells. It was quickly determined, though, that firing a shield of aerial shrapnel over London was unfeasible, and would potentially kill more civilians than it would save. In this case, the Allied powers believed the best defense was a good offense, and they focused instead on bombing V-2 production or launch facilities.

Pile pressed on for a defensive solution. He developed a scheme to divide London into defended grid squares, and to use better radar data to more precisely target incoming missiles. But the general never got to test his idea. "Monty beat us to it," he wrote. Field Marshal Bernard Montgomery had liberated German-controlled missile launching areas in Holland, and the attacks ceased.

After the war, US military officials began to worry about missile threats, prompted by concern that Germany had been developing ICBMs to negate the United States' natural geographic advantage, and so might others, namely the Soviet Union. Washington was now working with Wernher von Braun, a German aerospace engineer who had developed the V-2 for Adolf Hitler, but Moscow controlled the original V-2 factory and test facilities. The United States and Soviet Union were in a desperate competition to harness the deadly technology and significantly boost its range. With this in mind, a number of US government studies in the late 1940s began exploring the feasibility of antiballistic missile defenses. These early efforts made little headway, with the army simply offering to modify its Nike air defense system that was designed to shoot down enemy bombers.

In 1955, the United States began to fear the Soviets might indeed soon field long-range ballistic missiles, so the Pentagon contracted Bell Telephone Laboratories to identify potential solutions. Bell reported that destroying a ballistic missile was possible, but powerful long-range radar needed to be developed for the job. That wasn't all. The military would also need communication networks, radars woven together to detect and track incoming missiles, data processing centers, more powerful computers, and advanced command-and-control systems. All this new technology would have to work together quickly and flawlessly. At the business end would be an interceptor missile, known as Zeus. In early 1957 the army began work on what it called the Nike Zeus "antimissile missile system." Nike Zeus seemed all the more meaningful when, in August 1957, the Soviet Union announced it had successfully tested its SS-16 ICBM. Two months later the Soviets launched Sputnik, Earth's first artificial satellite.

The army hoped to field Nike Zeus sometime in the early 1960s, but questions quickly arose about technical feasibility and high costs. The system's basic concept was captured well by the Atari *Missile Command* video game: the player identifies an incoming nuclear warhead and then launches his own nuclear-armed missile to detonate as close as possible to it, thereby destroying the ascending warhead (but hopefully not destroying his own radar, communications, and command-and-control systems).

Among other criticisms, a group of Pentagon engineers in mid-1958 reported that Nike Zeus could possibly work against one incoming warhead, but it would be overwhelmed and defeated if the Soviets developed a missile that carried multiple warheads. It could also be overwhelmed by decoys such as metal chaff and Mylar balloons, or simply rendered useless if its radar sites were destroyed first. The army ran a series of relatively successful simulated intercepts, with Nike Zeus interceptors flying close enough to the enemy warhead to theoretically destroy it by detonating its own nuclear device, but no live fire tests were done. The project had opponents in John F. Kennedy's White House and Pentagon, in Congress, and in the rival air force. It was relegated to a testing and development phase until 1963.

The missile defense program then progressed into the Nike-X program. Nike-X increased the interceptor's range from 250 to 450 nautical miles and renamed it Spartan, added a short-range interceptor known as Sprint, and introduced a far more advanced phased array radar. The army–air force rivalry had cooled as the ground service was officially assigned the new antiballistic missile role, or ABM. President Kennedy warmed to the idea of ballistic missile defense.

In 1963, the president was not yet willing to deploy it, however, and felt the system needed more development. Kennedy was surprised that scientists disagreed so strongly about the concept's feasibility, which he assumed was a technical issue on which engineers should find consensus. But they did not agree, and quarrels in the scientific community regarding missile defense persisted for another six decades. Kennedy would not weigh in on the debate further—he was assassinated that

November. His secretary of defense, however, would forever shape how the country discussed and viewed nuclear weapons and missile defenses.

Robert McNamara didn't fit in well at the Pentagon. He'd spent World War II in the Pacific, crunching numbers for the US Army Air Forces as a sort of operational accountant. He wore wire-frame glasses and slicked-back hair with a distinctive part in the middle. McNamara and the "Whiz Kids," a group of statisticians he'd worked with during the war, had helped turn around a badly managed Ford Motor Company, and the forty-four-year-old McNamara rose to become the company's president. Only weeks after this appointment, Kennedy asked him to run the Defense Department instead. McNamara called the Pentagon a "jungle" but was confident, bordering on arrogant, about his ability to tame it.

General Earle "Bus" Wheeler was the type of officer McNamara wanted as the chairman of the Joint Chiefs of Staff—the president's top military adviser. Wheeler was intelligent and politically savvy, and he and McNamara would get along personally, but almost constantly disagree professionally. Wheeler never led a unit in battle, but beginning in 1964 he led the Joint Chiefs to unify against McNamara, a rare feat given the officers' own significant disputes and rivalries. Wheeler and the Joint Chiefs were appalled by the intrusiveness of McNamara's Whiz Kids. Young systems analysts were telling military brass what to do, so the Joint Chiefs banded together behind Bus Wheeler.

During Wheeler's first year as chairman, calls to field missile defenses grew stronger when it emerged that the Soviet Union planned to deploy its "Galosh" missile defense system near Moscow. Wheeler, the Joint Chiefs, and many in Congress now began to support Nike-X. Still, the scientific community could not agree about the technology's prospects. President Lyndon Johnson and McNamara decided not to field it, but to maintain it as a well-funded research effort.

The decision was influenced by McNamara's evolved thinking about "assured destruction." He came to believe the United States could not launch a decisive first strike to defang the Soviet Union. The Soviets had too many nuclear weapons and would be able to shoot back with a so-called second strike. This concept suggested that neither could attack the other because they would both be destroyed, and led to arguments that defenses against ballistic missiles would tip that delicate balance by emboldening one side or frightening the other. McNamara therefore prioritized building a nuclear force robust and large enough to guarantee the ability to retaliate. Instead of an ABM system, he favored a national fallout shelter program.

In October 1964 the calculations for missile defense changed as China detonated its own nuclear device and demonstrated a successful ICBM two years later. Nike-X suddenly had to deter the Chinese threat too. McNamara ordered studies to determine how Nike-X might survive a first strike from China.

Wheeler and the Joint Chiefs in March 1965 began pushing strongly to deploy Nike-X, but McNamara stalled while awaiting assessments of the army's deployment plan. It was a surprisingly ambitious plan. Army officials wanted an initial phase that would cost $9.5 billion to defend sixteen cities by 1973; a second phase would cost $3.5 billion more to protect another nine cities by 1975, and two more phases for another $13.5 billion would have fifty-one cities protected from a more sophisticated missile attack by 1982. Wheeler rallied the Joint Chiefs to back at least the first two phases. Even the skeptical air force lent its support. However, the President's Science Advisory Committee reported that the system could be too easily overwhelmed, and McNamara agreed with the committee.

The following year, 1966, the debate intensified and Wheeler and McNamara reached an unbridgeable gap. The dispute boiled over during Johnson's budget planning session on December 6. Wheeler insisted that a "heavy" defense was needed to protect against large-scale Soviet attacks, or at least to deter the Soviets by creating doubt that their first strike could succeed. McNamara again argued that such a scheme would merely cause Moscow to build more offensive weapons, and that at best a "thin" defense could be built to shield against Chinese nukes or an accidental launch. Like Kennedy before him, Johnson was surprised at the gulf between missile defense's supporters and opponents. He asked his two top Pentagon officials why they had such different opinions. McNamara said it "lay less in rational calculation than in the inherently emotional nature of the issue."

Still, the Senate was pushing for an ABM deployment and Republicans planned to make it a campaign issue to portray Johnson as weak on defense for the 1968 presidential election. They had plenty of ammunition too: in 1966 alone

China had detonated what appeared to be a thermonuclear weapon, tested an armed missile, and then exploded another nuke. Congress even appropriated the first preproduction funding for missile defenses, daring the White House not to deploy it.

With Johnson now interested in deployment for domestic political reasons, McNamara estimated that allowing a minimalist program to address China was his best chance of limiting ABM to a "thin" system. On January 4, 1967, McNamara called Johnson to settle the issue. "So . . . if you were in my position, you'd do nothing?" Johnson asked, referring to a deployment. McNamara knew the political climate meant some sort of missile defense system would need to be built. He replied, "I'd go down fighting, and I'm damn sure I'd go down."

The "thin" approach sought to minimize concern from McNamara's camp that defenses would be upsetting for the Soviet Union and therefore destabilizing. It also conveniently served as a warning shot that the secretary hoped could be used to push Moscow toward negotiating an arms control deal.

Prior to making a Nike-X deployment decision, Johnson and McNamara's final hope was that Russia might negotiate a missile defense treaty so neither side had to spend its way to an offensive or defensive advantage. They met Soviet prime minister Alexei Kosygin on June 23 in the sleepy town of Glassboro, New Jersey, just south of Philadelphia.

In the heart of the Cold War, as fears of nuclear annihilation gripped the country, the summit's overall tone was remarkably friendly. Nonetheless, during the first morning meetings, the Russians made clear they did not share American concern about missile defense. Johnson tried again during lunch, with McNamara and a handful of other US and Russian officials at the table, but he became frustrated as Kosygin showed no interest in pursuing talks for limiting defenses. The president looked at McNamara. "Bob, you tell the prime minister what the problem is."

In his last-ditch effort to scuttle an American ABM deployment, McNamara told Kosygin the two should ban defenses because, otherwise, the United States would simply build more and more nuclear-armed missiles in order to overcome the Soviets' Galosh defense. Kosygin grew red in the face. He pounded a fist on the table and snapped, "Defense is moral, offensive is immoral!" His worry was solely offensive missiles. The United States at that time had a better than three-to-one advantage over the Soviet arsenal.

In a strikingly conflicted September 1967 speech in San Francisco, McNamara first railed against missile defense systems as futile for the United States, then announced the deployment of a missile defense system. The Soviets would not negotiate and Congress would not relent, so the White House determined a limited defense was the best option. McNamara revealed it would be a version of Nike-X. He halfheartedly argued the system could better protect the US offensive nuclear force and guard population centers against a Chinese nuclear capability that was expected to emerge in the next several years. "It would be insane and suicidal for her to do so, but one can conceive conditions under which China might miscalculate. We wish to reduce such possibilities to a minimum," McNamara said. This same reasoning would be applied thirty-five years later, by second-time Secretary of Defense Donald Rumsfeld, to deploy missile defenses against an emerging North Korean threat.

Interestingly, after announcing the ABM system would begin production by year's end, McNamara then warned against the dynamisms that drove the US government to this decision: "There is a kind of mad momentum intrinsic to the development of all new nuclear weaponry. If a weapon system works—and works well—there is strong pressure from many directions to procure and deploy the weapon out of all proportion to the prudent level required."

At the time, he expressed trepidation with the idea of fielding missile defense. He was afraid that defensive capabilities might creep beyond the limited or "thin" remit, and soon seek defense against the Soviets. He believed this would make nuclear Armageddon even more likely.

Later, when compiling a book of his own major speeches, McNamara would literally cut out the part of the San Francisco speech announcing the deployment, and hide those comments in an appendix. McNamara and Johnson had a falling out over how to handle the Vietnam War and the original Whiz Kid left the Pentagon soon after the San Francisco speech, but McNamara's position on missile defense was championed by Democrats and moderate Republicans that formed a growing opposition to it.

In 1968 domestic politics lumbered into the ABM debate with a strong case of not-in-my-backyard syndrome. Residents of Seattle, Chicago, Detroit, and elsewhere were not keen to have nuclear-armed missiles sitting in their neighborhoods, drawing the attention of Soviet targeters. Moreover, disagreements within the scientific community became public as missile defense opponents began publishing critiques and testifying to Congress as outside experts. The Vietnam War also started to weigh heavily on the public's and military's desire for investing resources in grandiose defense equipment. Even the army, long ABM's most enthusiastic supporter, was losing interest in the nuclear deterrence role as it focused instead on guerrilla warfare in Vietnam.

Momentum for the limited ABM deployment was stalling as Richard Nixon entered office. Within a month of Nixon's inauguration, the White House halted the deployment plan and ordered a review—options ranged from expanding toward a nationwide system against Soviet missiles, to simply abandoning missile defense. During the review, National Security Adviser Henry Kissinger supported an ABM deployment because he wanted it as a bargaining chip for dealing with the Soviets, but he harbored serious doubts about the technology.

Nixon's National Security Council debated several options throughout the day on March 12, 1969, with the president ultimately deciding to build a version of the ABM system and rename it as "Safeguard." It would be built in phases at twelve sites, potentially including Washington, DC, but otherwise moving the systems away from defending cities to instead defending Strategic Air Command's nuclear forces against Chinese and Russian attacks. Two days later, Nixon announced that Safeguard would be deployed.

Even after moving it away from cities and changing the

rationale, serious political opposition remained. Members of
the House of Representatives mainly supported the plan, but
it was strongly opposed by a Senate coalition of liberal Democrats and moderate Republicans who largely based their position on Robert McNamara's arguments.

A bevy of hearings were held, competing reports commissioned, and results debated during the spring and summer of
1969. Those in favor of deployment felt Russia was moving toward a better first-strike capability so defenses were required,
and those opposed felt Safeguard would be ineffective and
fiscally wasteful at best, or destabilizing at worst. Congress
would have to approve funding for Safeguard's deployment,
but by June, John Stennis, a Mississippi Democrat and chairman of the Senate Armed Services Committee, counted fifty
yeas and fifty nays for Safeguard. Stennis, a legislative pow-
erhouse and leader on national security issues, supported the
system but struggled to muster more than a tie vote.

By July Democrats coalesced against Safeguard. Leading
the opposition was the Senate majority whip, Ted Kennedy. But
on July 18, 1969, Kennedy drove his Oldsmobile off a bridge
on Chappaquiddick Island, killing his passenger, twenty-eight-
year-old Mary Jo Kopechne. The Chappaquiddick scandal
shattered his presidential aspirations, and ended his efforts to
whip up Democratic opposition to Safeguard. Kennedy would
remain a significant voice in the Senate against ABM for the
next forty years, but the scandal largely sidelined him for the
remainder of the first deployment debate.

Arguments came to a head on August 6. Despite more
than four months of intense quarreling and several changed

minds, the vote was still fifty yeas and fifty nays for Safeguard. Vice President Spiro Agnew cast the deciding fifty-
first vote in favor of Safeguard, pushing the first American
missile defense system from concept into reality.

Over the next two years, Safeguard marched toward deployments to protect ICBM missile fields at Grand Forks Air
Force Base in North Dakota and Malmstrom Air Force Base
in Montana, but the project was on technologically shaky
ground. Bell Telephone Laboratories, the lead contractor for
Safeguard, began to quietly express concern about the program. In April 1970 the company told the National Security
Council that the system might meet its technical specifica-
tions but could nonetheless be defeated by just a few missiles
attacking the radars or by simple countermeasures. Nixon
and Kissinger believed the real issue was Bell's reticence to
be a "defense contractor" and to expose itself to bad publicity,
so they were more troubled with the idea that Bell was being
critical than with the criticism itself.

The White House nonetheless conceded to Congress that
year that the system could be overwhelmed if the Soviet
Union built a larger nuclear force, and the following year
administration officials shifted to supporting it mainly as
a bargaining chip for arms control negotiations with Moscow. The bargaining chip premise meant the United States
needed its own missile defenses if it was to get Moscow to
give up its Galosh missile defenses.

Indeed, Strategic Arms Limitation Treaty talks in Helsinki

ultimately resulted in both offensive and defensive missile treaties, but Safeguard and its uncertain future proved a troublesome bargaining chip for the Nixon administration. The Soviets were at first unsure if Congress might halt Safeguard's deployment anyway. Ironing out wrinkles in the treaty took more than two years, but in May 1972 the United States and Soviet Union signed the SALT I agreement and Anti-Ballistic Missile Treaty. For offensive nuclear weapons, each side was somewhat limited in how many missiles it could field but each retained colossal destructive power. For defense, each was allowed a missile defense site with up to one hundred interceptors. The Soviet Union chose to continue defending Moscow and the United States chose to continue building Safeguard at the Grand Forks missile field. The treaty was to be reviewed every five years.

In less than that time Safeguard would meet a particularly inglorious end. The system began operations at Grand Forks on October 2, 1975, and one day later members in the House of Representatives voted to close the facility. They believed the radars were too vulnerable and Soviet missiles could easily overwhelm a paltry one hundred interceptors. Just six years after the tense 1969 Senate vote to approve the program, Congress pulled the plug. All told, building the Grand Forks Safeguard site cost about $5.7 billion; the army's related ABM efforts from 1954 through 1974 cost about $10 billion.

In short, the ABM Treaty left each country with impotent defenses. This cemented what became known as mutual assured destruction: neither state could really defend itself but either could retaliate, ensuring nobody would survive a nuclear war. It also set the stage for negotiations to limit or reduce nuclear weapons since neither side would need to build more to overcome defensive measures. US homeland missile defense was mostly shelved until President Ronald Reagan unexpectedly dusted it off eleven years later, and made it a major defense policy again.

"We're engaged right now in several negotiations with the Soviet Union to bring about a mutual reduction of weapons," Reagan said during a prime-time address on March 23, 1983. "Nevertheless, it will still be necessary to rely on the specter of retaliation, on mutual threat—and that's a sad commentary on the human condition. Wouldn't it be better to save lives than to avenge them?" Reagan then announced the start of an immense effort to "intercept and destroy strategic ballistic missiles before they reached our own soil or that of our allies." He directed a long-term research and development program with the lofty goal of "eliminating the threat posed by strategic nuclear missiles."

It was an ambitious program. Reagan's Strategic Defense Initiative sought nuclear-powered X-ray lasers to blast rockets from the sky, space-based particle beams to destroy ascending warheads, an electromagnetic railgun, missiles that deploy nets to catch warheads, and, as a last-ditch defense, an electron accelerator that essentially shot a bolt of lightning at the warhead. It would need space systems capable of always seeing Russian missile paths, radars and sensors to track missiles, a command network to tie it all together, and a brilliant computer system for exacting calculations—and everything would have to work flawlessly for the one and only time it would be used. It would also somehow have to skirt the ABM Treaty, which was still in effect.

The army was assigned an element of the program known as the Homing Overlay Experiment. It would become the first-ever system to prove it could destroy a missile by physically impacting it—a concept known as "hit-to-kill." The original weapon made its first intercept in June 1984. It was, however, a massive and expensive system that used a Minuteman rocket to blast a kill vehicle into space. The vehicle then expanded like the skeleton of an umbrella, with a thirteen-foot diameter web to destroy warheads.

Though it bore some fruit, eventually, Reagan's Strategic Defense Initiative was costly and met even stronger opposition than its predecessors. Senator Ted Kennedy mocked the program as "Star Wars." Kennedy and other opponents revived their enduring doubts from Safeguard in the 1960s and 1970s: Could this system survive enemy attacks and countermeasures? Was it too expensive?

By the late 1980s many of the projects were struggling to show theoretical progress, and Congress grew weary of the mounting costs. Then the Soviet Union collapsed. Missile threats no longer seemed so urgent and George H. W. Bush significantly scaled back Reagan's wholesale program. Several years later, Bill Clinton slashed even more funding for the Strategic Defense Initiative, relegating it to a small research effort. Some of the technology gleaned through Star Wars led to a slew of missile defense research projects in the 1990s, including a hit-to-kill system that would seek to destroy warheads in space by colliding with them at tremendous speeds.

Under political pressure from Republicans, the Clinton administration in 1996 settled on a plan to field missile defenses within seven years, and to outsource the system's management and development to a defense contractor. The fear was no longer an enormous Soviet barrage of nukes, but rather a "rogue" state such as North Korea or Iran launching a limited nuclear strike. This seemed an easier threat to defend against.

Boeing was the underdog in a competition for the lucrative project, but in April 1998 it beat a rival bid from a consortium of Raytheon, TRW, and Lockheed Martin—all of which already worked on national missile defense projects. Boeing's hardest initial task was selecting a builder for the system's kill vehicle.

Hughes and Rockwell had been working on competing designs, but the defense industry had just undergone a wave of consolidations. Raytheon now owned Hughes and Boeing now owned Rockwell. So Boeing, as the lead contractor, was choosing between itself and Raytheon. Both kill vehicles used infrared sensors to hunt targets. Boeing's sensor could see farther but needed more cooling power; Raytheon's was the opposite. Boeing used traditional statistical analysis for its sensor's algorithms, Raytheon sought a new analytical approach. Kadish, the Missile Defense Agency director at the time, thought, *Boeing's looked like a mean-machine; Raytheon's looked like a telescope.*

The agency appeared to be leaning toward Boeing. Then, in a bizarre and clumsy move, Boeing disqualified itself because members of its development team gained access to and exploited a confidential Raytheon design document. The government had sunk hundreds of millions of dollars into maintaining a competition, but, abruptly, the competition was over. Raytheon won by default. Raytheon and Boeing, now with a badly damaged relationship, awkwardly negotiated a subcontract throughout 1999.

The kill vehicle technology proved especially difficult to develop and suffered from early setbacks. There were a few successful proof-of-concept tests, but a slew of failures did not impress the already skeptical Clinton, who worried about encroaching upon the 1972 ABM Treaty. On September 1, 2000, Clinton announced that he would not field the system.

George W. Bush, however, went all out. He abrogated the ABM Treaty and ordered the rapid deployment of homeland missile defenses to guard against possible threats from Iran and North Korea. The United States was reeling from the 9/11 terrorist attacks, and Congress was in no mood to oppose any defensive measures Bush wanted to take.

7

FAIL

IN THE EARLY HOURS of December 15, 2004, Lieutenant General Trey Obering was at MDA headquarters at the Navy Annex, a small military complex atop a hill wedged between Arlington National Cemetery and Interstate 395, a few hundred yards from the Pentagon. Like many other buildings (and agencies and people) in Washington, the Navy Annex was supposed to have been temporary. The one-million-square-foot eyesore was built in 1941 as a provisional warehouse but was repurposed into needed office space during World War II. In 2001 the rapidly expanding Missile Defense Agency was sent there.

In previous jobs Obering had sat through intercept tests with contractors at Vandenberg in California or at Kwajalein Atoll in the Pacific Ocean, but for his first test as agency director, he wanted to sit at headquarters where he could absorb all the updates and telemetry data that streamed in on six overhead screens. Obering was a manager and delegated authority, but he was no novice at launching big rockets. He had worked on the space shuttle program and participated in fifteen launches as a NASA orbiter project engineer.

MDA had set up a command room at the headquarters

with real-time video feeds from the target launch site and the interceptor launch site, and had software that took real-time data to create telemetry-generated animation—a sort of technical cartoon that would show how the target and the interceptor were performing in space. Obering stood watching the screens as engineers at MDA and soldiers at the 100th Missile Defense Brigade prepared for the system's first test since it was declared operational, and the first since Obering became the director. It was the ninth test overall, and five of the previous eight were successful, but the program had been criticized for putting its tests on a back burner while focusing instead on getting Fort Greely and the missile crews up and running. It had been two years since the last intercept try, and this test was to be the most difficult yet.

The test had been delayed for nine months as MDA worked to fix wiring problems and other issues discovered during ground checks. The agency then had to reconfigure the test interceptor to more closely match the configuration of the eight operational interceptors now deployed in silos at Greely and Vandenberg.

Obering called the test a "zero-offset flyby." Intercepting and destroying the mock warhead was not necessarily a required objective, but they would still try to do it. The plan was to also use US Navy destroyers equipped with the Aegis fire control radar to see if the ships could provide data good enough to help guide the interceptor to its target. But, by the time the test was finally going ahead, the winter weather was so bad that rough seas in the Pacific exceeded "peacetime safety limits," so navy commanders withdrew the ships.

Still, it was to use a new Orbital Sciences booster for the

first time, add simulated input from the massive Cobra Dane sensor in the Aleutian Islands for the first time, and launch the interceptor from Kwajalein Atoll in the Pacific Ocean to strike a target traveling from Kodiak, Alaska, for the first time. Launching the target out of Kodiak meant Obering could test new angles for intercepting the mock warhead.

From his headquarters, Obering watched the video feed of the mock target missile as it blasted off from Kodiak. The sensors and radar then began their tracking. A simulated weapons release authority was granted by Northern Command and Meakins's Alpha crew was ordered to "go weapons free" and launch one interceptor. The crew moved through their procedures, preparing the system to launch one interceptor at one incoming target. It was a simple mission compared to the complex scenarios they trained on.

There were MDA and Boeing people watching over their shoulders in the node, and Alpha crew didn't want to be the reason a test failed, but otherwise the mission didn't cause them much strain. Spriggs's role as the future-operations officer was particularly simple during the test, and he passed much of the time beforehand playing solitaire. When the order came, he keyed in his launch commands.

Obering, listening on the Ops Loop, heard Alpha crew's countdown from the node at Schriever Air Force Base. It got to zero but the interceptor did not launch. Its booster rocket did nothing. The equipment failed. MDA headquarters at the Navy Annex was nearly silent, filled with shock and disappointment, as the mock warhead flew its trajectory unbothered, and splashed down in the Pacific.

For the crews, the test was strange. Even if the real interceptor had worked properly, they would not have seen it. They would have just seen icons on their screens telling them it had launched. Many of the soldiers had a background in air defense artillery, so not being able to see or feel a launch was anticlimactic. There also was no trigger to pull or firing lanyard to yank. Spriggs's job was to command the system to launch, but it was done with keystrokes and mouse clicks; there was no dramatic action involved. One of the distinguished visitors in the node had seen Spriggs playing solitaire before the test, but was even more incensed when he had not seen Spriggs make any discernible movement to launch the interceptor after he was ordered to "go weapons free."

"Why haven't you fired yet?!" the VIP demanded. Spriggs had fired, but it was just simple clicks of his mouse to tell the system's software to choose the exact right time to launch. The crews didn't need to know the complicated ins and outs of how the system worked for a basic launch. When something goes wrong, that was when their technical expertise and their thousands of hours of training mattered. Spriggs's nonchalant use of the computer terminals for the test was confusing to an outsider.

The next week, Alpha crew was on shift again on Christmas Day. Meakins bought a large red "easy" button from Staples and brought it into the node as a gag so Spriggs could jump up and make a show of pounding his fist on it after keying in the launch order.

Susan Frobe-Recella had found the test launch somewhat more nerve-wracking. The tests were important for advancing the space interceptor technology, and she knew they were expensive events—between $200 and $300 million. Nobody wanted to screw up the test. By the Christmas Day shift, though, Frobe-Recella's thoughts had turned to missing her eight-month-old son.

She had sat on the first shift, and had also given birth to the crew's first baby. Walking down Schriever's drawn-out corridor to the node, and eight months pregnant, Frobe-Recella realized the slog was getting too long. She warned Meakins that they really needed to get her temporary replacement in soon. The unit had been training one of Northern Command's missile defense officers for the job and put him on Alpha crew shortly thereafter, so when Frobe-Recella's kid was born, there would be no gap in coverage while she took two months of maternity leave.

Aside from the test launch and Alpha crew's first baby, the initial few months of operational shifts were quiet. The crews trained all the time. Whenever Meakins had to brief a distinguished visitor, he made sure to tell them, "I train more than any lieutenant colonel in the United States Army, and our crews train more than probably any other squad, section, or platoon in the army. We train every day, three to four hours a day." Still, they could not fully train during shifts because the software could not yet support training programs while also monitoring the real world, so somebody had to be left behind to keep watch while the other four went to a node down the hall.

The crews were also learning new lingo. When they spoke on the Ops Loop or to navy ships or air force radar outposts, they needed a common language. The airmen would respond to a radio call by saying "copy," but the soldiers would never say that on the radio, they were used to hearing "roger." And many of the soldiers were artillerymen for whom hearing "repeat" would mean they should fire again—and that could lead to quite a mistake with a $75 million interceptor and incoming nuclear warheads. Lexicon meetings were held to decide how they should talk.

Meanwhile, at Fort Greely's Missile Defense Complex, questions had arisen during winter about how effective the new defensive perimeter really was. The security system was designed by engineers in Huntsville who, living in northern Alabama's Appalachian region, perhaps lacked an appreciation for the environment in the Alaskan interior. The MPs had warned Bowen that the system might not be working right—they were getting too many false alarms.

On a stormy Saturday night, Bowen was sitting around considering the issue, and figured he better just test it himself. His plan was to break in to the In-Flight Interceptor Communications System Data Terminal, the first piece of highly classified equipment that the battalion was charged with guarding. He drove his pickup truck through the blizzard, onto the Missile Defense Complex, and easily broke in to the data terminal. Wind blew the snow horizontally, and Bowen stood out there in the cold, undetected, for about thirty minutes, waving his arms underneath the security cameras.

There had been freezing rain before the snow, and it loaded down the sensors on the perimeter fences and iced over the cameras. The MPs at first missed the real alarm because they had about 180 false alarms around the same time. Eventually,

Bowen was noticed and a response force raced out to the data terminal to confront the intruder. The first on the ground to spot Bowen was Specialist Shane Moore, known as "the Highlander" because he was by far the battalion's oldest soldier. Moore had his M9 pistol leveled at Bowen, a little shaky and loaded with real bullets. Bowen suddenly regretted his plan. But Moore did everything exactly right and got the intruder's face into the snow, handcuffed him, and took him into custody before realizing who it was.

The security system would have to be improved, and Bowen added that to his mounting list of challenges. Strangely, scheduling fun social activities to maintain morale was high on that list. In December, the sun at Greely was a faint orange ball that peeked above the horizon for just a few hours around lunchtime. Spring, summer, and fall could be beautiful at Greely, but were typically short. The long winters could be brutal.

To keep things cheerful, Christmas lights typically were hung up right after Halloween. By February, with the holidays over and the sun long gone, cabin fever set in—marital problems would emerge, colleagues stopped getting along, and the soldiers got grumpy. Bowen and the junior officers had to stay on top of everybody to ensure they were getting along okay, or even that they were just mentally okay.

In the battalion's earliest days, the families had been sent to live in Anchorage where the army could provide them with the sort of basic amenities they were used to, but in 2004 the families moved out to Greely and it had not gone well. There was nothing for them to do. The housing was mostly substandard. There was no movie theater. There was no child care. There was no medical facility. It was a treacherous two-hour drive to Fairbanks if they needed to see a doctor or wanted to go to Walmart or take care of errands. There was no internet in the family housing.

Making things worse for Bowen and his officers, the parade of senior VIPs that had been visiting throughout the summer—coincidentally when the weather was nice—had been meeting with the spouses and making lots of promises about amenities for the fort. Inevitably, they underdelivered on those promises. The families' outrage fixated on Bowen and Lieutenant Colonel Rob Cornelius, a Special Forces officer serving as Greely's garrison commander. The two colonels mostly just let them vent. There wasn't much else they could do.

After arriving at Greely, Bowen learned about 30 percent of people at that latitude suffer from seasonal affective disorder, or SAD, a type of depression linked to the sun's disappearance for almost the entire winter season. It can cause unhappiness, sap energy, create sleep problems, or even spur violent behavior. Bowen's wife suffered from it. The best treatment she found was a simple light box, a so-called SAD lamp, that mimics outdoor light. She stood in front of it for fifteen or twenty minutes each morning, soaking in some light, and felt much better. Soon, most of the fort had bought SAD lamps.

The grumbling and complaining began to spill over into a battalion staff meeting. Bowen spent a few minutes listening to the normal gripes about personnel and facilities, then set a SAD lamp at the end of the conference table and turned it on. "When that lamp is on, I don't want to hear any bitching, complaining, or anything. When that lamp is off, you can air your grievances." Bowen ran through his meeting, and then allowed the soldiers to speak their minds. "Sergeant Major, flip the switch. You can all air your grievances now."

There's no medical care on site, what happens if my kid gets hurt?

The admin staff needs to grow; we're processing twice as many soldiers.

My buddy in Afghanistan has a Green Beans Coffee shop on his base—we've got nothing.

And so on until Bowen had enough. "Sergeant Major, switch the light on."

At MDA's headquarters at the Navy Annex, Obering had his hands full too. Aside from the test failure, he was dealing with production delays. Boeing managed the project, Raytheon built the kill vehicle, and Orbital built the booster. The contractors' holdups would keep the 100th and 49th from getting a total of ten interceptors in the ground by year's end, a requirement based on intelligence estimates about North Korea's possible long-range missile capabilities.

Meanwhile, a Failure Review Board was investigating December's abortive launch and discovered a problem with a line of software code in the booster, the sort of software that a car uses to determine if the CHECK ENGINE light should be on. The software had run unnecessarily precise checks on systems in the booster and found one timing issue that was slightly outside its strict parameters, so it automatically aborted the launch. It was a relatively simple, fixable problem, but Obering was not pleased. He ordered another test in two months.

December's failed test was to be repeated on Valentine's

Day 2005. Again, Obering was watching at the Navy Annex, and again the target was launched and all the testing and instrumentation systems worked as planned, but again the interceptor did not launch. *What now?!* Obering thought.

Again, a Failure Review Board reported another unexpected oversight. One of the three support arms had rusted in the silo on Kwajalein. The three arms are supposed to fall away from the interceptor during the launch, but this one was corroded and didn't safely clear out of the way, triggering an automatic abort. Salt water from the Pacific had gotten into the silo during routine maintenance, and the salt air interacted with the glue in a hinge, which swelled and prevented the arm from clearing away during launch. The silo on Kwajalein was not representative of the real GMD system, so the test technicians had not made it a priority and the silo was not checked properly. It was another waste of time and resources caused by a small oversight, because nobody noticed a rusty silo arm. Obering was livid but saw no point in browbeating the MDA or industry teams. They poured heart and soul into those tests and were equally distraught by the failures.

Obering ordered the effort to stand down. He stopped production and directed what he called "a heritage review" of the entire program. Designs, manufacturing techniques, and processes for all elements of national missile defense were to be rechecked over the next six months. There was an interceptor on Kwajalein being prepared for a forthcoming test, and that too was ordered to come back so it could be rechecked at Raytheon's more sanitary Space Factory lab in Arizona.

The stand-down and review came at a tough time. In February, North Korea withdrew from disarmament talks. By April the North Koreans began threatening to test a nuclear weapon for the first time.

It was around twenty below zero when the party kicked off at Fort Greely. About two hundred people, from all corners of the post and Delta Junction, all wearing tank tops, Hawaiian shirts, shorts, and flip-flops under their huge down parkas, strode into the fort's big airplane hangar. Some set up beach chairs. Most went directly to the tiki bar.

There's only so much to do when it's always dark and so cold outside that skin cannot be exposed without risk of frostbite. The soldiers and their families were only willing to attend a limited number of square dances in the gym, and the nightlife options in Delta Junction didn't extend much beyond the Clearwater Lodge. The restlessness and depression and second-guessing career choices had become a real concern for Bowen by the end of February. Everyone desperately needed something more. Rob Cornelius, the Special Forces officer serving as Greely's garrison commander, decided the solution was to throw a party.

Cornelius ordered several dump trucks full of sand to be deposited into the hangar. He set up volleyball nets and a big tiki bar. Perhaps most miraculous, as only a resourceful Special Forces soldier could, Cornelius tracked down the only steel drum band in the polar region, and hired them to play for his big beach party in the middle of the Alaskan winter. Bowen was reverential. Cornelius's party was a huge hit and, importantly, it gave everyone something to talk about and to fondly remember for weeks.

Better still, Greely was about to join the twenty-first century. Larry Dodgen, the three-star general leading Army Space and Missile Defense Command, had become a frequent visitor at the fort and had been getting an earful from the spouses on each of his visits. He ordered money to be found in the command's budget to outfit the family housing area with high-speed internet, and by March 2005 the housing authority began offering a connection to the World Wide Web. On the first day, 150 people signed up. The first email that left Fort Greely's housing was from Bowen's wife, thanking Dodgen for getting them connected to the internet. In a matter of days, a FedEx truck became a familiar sight, rumbling into the garrison housing area almost daily. The soldiers and families still didn't have much they could do during the winter, but at least they could now shop online.

8

ANOMALY

ON MARCH 31, 2005, Obering was briefed on the unhappy findings of his heritage review. Following the homeland missile defense system's two failed tests, he had asked Paul Hoff, MDA's technical director; Bill Nance, a former GMD program director; Rear Admiral Kate Paige, director of the Aegis ship-based missile defense program; and several outside experts to study the overall effort—and its successes and failures—from top to bottom. The briefing warned of future interceptor failures and recommended, among a long list of changes, making quality control more important than schedules, getting independent "readiness" assessments before flight tests, and conducting more ground tests. As part of the review, they gave Obering a prioritized list of recommendations to fix the GMD equipment itself, which still was an operational prototype.

The fixes would require time and money, but the system had just consecutively failed two big tests, so Congress cut its budget from $3.3 billion the previous year to $2.5 billion in 2006. To Obering, it was the opposite of what systems engineering should be: just when they had found problems to fix, they would get a 25 percent budget cut.

The review had netted a variety of "punch list items" that weren't major changes but, together, could improve the project's workmanship and the system's reliability. Some were funded, some were not. The review also raised concerns about a phenomenon that had been noticed in previous intercept tests. This phenomenon hadn't caused any failures yet, but it worried the engineers.

As the interceptor's kill vehicle flies toward its target, it gets in-flight updates from the ground to help it find the enemy warhead in space. All the radar tracking data is sent up to the kill vehicle by the In-flight Data Terminal that Bowen's soldiers were guarding. Once the kill vehicle gets close enough, however, it tries to pick out the warhead from the debris and decoys, and begins tracking everything on its own. Poring over data, the review team saw that, during several tests in the early 2000s, the kill vehicle's sensors would unexpectedly drop their target and then reacquire it. It was as if the device were blinking its eye and having to refocus. The problem never interfered with an intercept, but the engineers didn't understand what was causing it. They called it the Track Gate Anomaly.

Specialist Jarrod Cuthbertson had enjoyed a few beers. He was walking back at night from a friend's house, concentrating on just getting one foot in front of the other and moving himself across the small campus at Fort Greely and toward his bed at the barracks. Suddenly he stopped. It was late, but the Alaskan midsummer night had only reached a faint dusk. In the slight glow Cuthbertson realized he'd walked right up to a large moose. He could have reached out to touch it, but he took a step back, spun round, and began walking away. Cuthbertson could hear the moose breathing heavy and could hear its footsteps slowly following him. He tried not to move abruptly, but walked faster. The moose walked faster too. Cuthbertson was sobering up fast and picked up his pace. Now he could hear the moose galloping behind him. Cuthbertson broke into a dead run toward the closest building: the Missile Defense Agency's Greely lodging quarters. He leapt up onto a picnic table and from there jumped over the lodging fence. The moose slammed into the picnic table, destroying it, as Cuthbertson scrambled into the building. He watched from a window as the moose stood around for a few minutes and then ambled away.

Cuthbertson's friend woke up the next morning and saw a missed call and voicemail. It was Cuthbertson, hyperventilating and frantic, calling from inside the Missile Defense Agency lodging and yelling about the moose that had tried to kill him.

In the clarifying light of day, Cuthbertson felt as though he'd overreacted. Maybe it had just been drunken excitement about an otherwise normal situation—after all, moose were all around Alaska and bears were what really worried him. He told the story that afternoon to a bearded, rough-looking old Deltoid out in town. "Son, moose are the most dangerous thing you can come in contact with up here," the man told him. "They'll stomp you into the ground until you're pulp in the grass." Cuthbertson had never seen a moose before in his life, and had only been in Alaska a few months.

Cuthbertson's Illinois National Guard MP unit had been activated and deployed to Iraq in 2003 for a twelve-month tour, but it was extended to fifteen months as the war there worsened. He returned to Illinois the next year, and during a weekend drill a recruiter from Washington told him of the full-time jobs available with a new battalion forming in Alaska. Cuthbertson had turned nineteen and then twenty years old while serving as an MP in Iraq, and wasn't heading to college as he had planned. A three-year tour in Alaska sounded interesting enough.

In March 2005 Cuthbertson and Specialist Jeremy Christensen, a buddy from his Iraq tour, loaded up their trucks and drove in a mini-convoy through Canada and into the Alaskan interior. They moved into the barracks at Greely and began working eight-hour shifts guarding the Missile Defense Complex's big stretch of tundra with Alpha Company's 1st Platoon.

After Iraq, life at Greely was paradise. In Iraq, Cuthbertson's and Christensen's days consisted of eight hours of patrol, eight hours of perimeter security, and eight hours of standby as a reaction force. They slept when they could, but that was tough without air-conditioning in the Mesopotamian heat. Getting sixteen hours off each day to sleep or relax or have fun in Alaska was freedom. They embraced it.

Sixteen hours was plenty of time to go four-wheeling or snow-machining (as Cuthbertson learned, the Alaskans go snow-machining, they do not go snowmobiling), and several days off in a row meant an overnight hunting trip or hanging out all night by a campfire.

Staff Sergeant John Robinson had arrived at Greely with his wife and daughters in pleasant weather, on May 1, 2005. He was assigned as platoon sergeant for Alpha Company's 1st

Platoon. The Alaskan Scouts were still a key part of the MP unit, but they were slowly transitioning out as more full-time guardsmen were hired. Getting the new soldiers formed into a working unit was a challenge, and Robinson loved it.

It was soon reported to Robinson that one of his soldiers, Cuthbertson, had been caught patrolling in his Humvee without wearing a seat belt. Robinson gave the young soldier a gentle talking to. In response, Cuthbertson swung the pendulum as far as he possibly could in the other direction: he began sneaking around Greely looking for anyone he could find without seat belts in their vehicles. Cuthbertson dubbed himself the Seat Belt Police, and was startlingly effective. He even managed to catch Robinson taking off his seat belt before fully stopping a Humvee.

The relationship between the MPs and the missile crews had improved and Cuthbertson and his friends weren't picking on them quite so much. The crews were mostly left alone for their solemn drive from the post's nucleus, where all the administrative buildings and housing were, out onto the eight-hundred-acre missile defense complex. Greely's "downtown" was austere, with just a handful buildings and some row houses, but the missile complex was especially vast and empty. From a roundabout near Greely's center, a road shoots diagonally out toward the Alaska Range, and stops at a garage that serves as a small "access control" security station.

The mountains loom in the background as the soldiers approach the complex's perimeter. There are large warning signs posted at the gate in Russian, Spanish, and English. After clearing security, the crews board a special van that drives them the rest of the way, about a half mile down a raised single-lane road, toward the mountains, to the Fire Direction Center where the crews work their shifts. To the right is nothing but open tundra and Greely's perimeter, and to the left are the missile fields. Near the fields are signs, in English only, explaining that a horn and flashing lights will signal the interceptors are changing status: green is all clear, yellow means there is a "period of interest" or some maintenance activity, and red means run away fast.

After clearing security, the vans drive the crew members past the In-flight Data Terminal—a small building with a radome on top. They then reach the Fire Direction Center, the size of a large house, where the van drops them off. Out past this structure is the fort's Defense Satellite Communication System terminal, with two big radomes on either side.

At the farthest end of the missile complex is the Interceptor Storage Facility, a sort of underground bunker that juts up on top of an entranceway. The MPs took great pride in driving things over it. Cuthbertson jumped it with a four-wheeler. Mark Scott was able to maneuver to the top of the bunker in a big SUSV, the boxy tracked vehicles meant to navigate the snowy arctic. It was good fun until Bowen noticed the tracks all around and all over the bunker.

Guarding the missile fields was tough. There was no system for the Missile Defense Agency workers or their contractors to badge in and out of the missile fields, so the MPs had to physically open the missile field gate and then park by and guard any open entrance in a Humvee or SUSV to let workers in or out. Beyond the missile fields was difficult terrain. A dense tree line came right up to the road that ringed the missile complex. The MPs patrolled with two soldiers per

Humvee so they weren't alone, but when it got dark, it got *really dark*—on some nights there was no ambient light whatsoever. Approaching that heavy tree line in total blackness was unsettling. The soldiers couldn't see beyond the road and it seemed anything might suddenly emerge from the woods. An attacking force. A bear. A moose.

As Cuthbertson had learned, moose came in and out of the complex regularly. Even after the perimeter fence was complete, there were still open gates and roads onto the fort. The MPs put down electrified pads at the gates, but the moose didn't seem to mind. Early in 2005, a bear came into the perimeter and attacked one of the moose. Robinson's soldiers, stunned, watched the attack through their FLIR thermal sights. They were not allowed to bother the bear and were ordered to keep everyone away from the area until the bear was done with its meal. It was an astonishing display of Alaska's raw nature for the soldiers.

Cuthbertson had already learned what the extreme weather could do. Some MPs had taken him up to Chicken, Alaska, for his first caribou hunt. The soldiers at Greely liked to note that somewhere below freezing, it won't really matter what the temperature is. It would feel the same whether it was minus 15 or minus 50. For Cuthbertson's hunting trip, it was minus 50. Taking his first shot, he got "scope bite" as the rifle scope recoiled back into his forehead. He felt it, but the impact had not hurt and he wasn't bleeding. Everything seemed okay until Cuthbertson got back into his truck and warmed up in the cab. His skin thawed out and blood began to stream down his face—the rifle scope had gashed open his forehead but the wound had frozen solid. The reason the temperature does not seem to matter after a certain point is that skin will go numb and then freeze, the early stages of frostbite. The colder it is, the faster skin goes numb.

At colder than minus 20, the schools in Delta Junction canceled recess. At minus 50, many of the services in town shut down. The MP's missions, however, never stopped. They had to be outside no matter what. The army's seven-layer Extended Cold Weather Clothing System, better known as the Michelin Man Suit, typically kept the soldiers quite warm, but keeping too warm could be a problem. The MPs were in and out of Humvees and had to be careful about temperature changes. If they sweated while inside the Humvee and then took a turn outside in the gunner's turret, or dismounted to open a gate or inspect a fence, the sweat could freeze and cause frostbite.

The soldiers had to consider more than just the temperature. Gale-force winds meant the Humvees had to be parked into the wind, because otherwise the door would whip around off the hinges and then the motor pool would be down a vehicle, and the maintenance team was woefully short on manpower as it hadn't yet grown with the battalion. The mechanics constantly had to deal with windshields pitted with cracks from small rocks flying around on freezing gusts of wind. The trucks were generally taking a beating and it was driving the former marine, Mark Scott, completely nuts.

Scott had moved to a job in the slowly expanding battalion maintenance shop. He was naturally handy and knew the right people in Anchorage, so he could always get parts sent out quickly. As an Alaskan, Scott also didn't mind the cold as much and was better suited for working on the battalion's handful of SUSVs, which were too big to fit in the maintenance bay so most of the work had to be done out in the cold. But he was still a marine in the Army National Guard.

Scott was appalled with how poorly the soldiers kept their equipment. He had calmed a bit since first joining the unit, but grew increasingly furious at the MPs for mistreating the vehicles and not being held accountable. He was blowing up at everyone, from the MPs abusing the equipment to the maintenance guys who weren't fixing it properly. All the screaming and yelling was how Scott had been taught, but it reinforced his "disgruntled marine" stigma and didn't endear him to many soldiers.

Jeanette Padgett, the other Alaskan and a born Deltoid, was getting along better and had been selected to attend the rigorous GMD Qualification Course. She left her role managing IT and network security for the battalion and that summer was sent to Colorado Springs to train for becoming an alternate crew member. Padgett hated Colorado. It was far too hot and stifling and she felt like she could never get enough oxygen. She was also surprised at how difficult the training course was—they were actually demanding she learn the algorithms that the computers used to calculate missile intercepts in space. It was the hardest course she'd ever taken, but she graduated and would get a chance to sit as an alternate crew member on the GMD homeland defense system.

Padgett and Scott and the other soldiers of the 49th Missile Defense Battalion had been wearing Army Space and Missile Defense Command patches and unit insignia—they did not have their own. Bowen and the officers simply hadn't had time to worry about such things. As the group was settling in, they felt the need to begin forming some history, some fellowship, some traditions exclusive to their unique unit. They wanted to foster a feeling of "us against the world," a sort of tight-knit family, to make it easier on the MPs and the crews when they pulled an eight-hour shift on Christmas Day. The soldiers set to work creating a patch, coin, and motto.

On August 17, 2005, the Army Institute of Heraldry granted the soldiers their own distinctive unit insignia: an eagle atop the globe, perched just north of Alaska, with the Polaris pole star over its head and a bolt of lightning on each side of the star, all set against the black backdrop of outer space. DEFENSIMUS PATRIAM, "defending the homeland," was an obvious choice for the motto underneath the patch. Getting the unit patch just required an assignment there. Getting the unit coin would require a bit more.

A new officer in the 49th had to earn their coin. The Cavalry would give its troopers the emblematic Stetson hat, but spurs had to be earned with a "spur ride." The 49th's version of initiation was somewhat different. They established the unofficial Diligent Sentry Officers Association, and any new member of the association had to first salvage their coin from the bottom of an arctic canteen cup filled with The Grog. The Grog was a mixture of various liquors, hot sauces, and water from the Delta River; and the arctic canteen cup was twice the size of the standard sixteen-ounce canteen cup. The newbie chugged the canteen and retrieved their coin in their teeth. Then they were in the club.

The Diligent Sentry Officers Association resolved to meet monthly in Fort Greely's Building 661, in a conference room adjacent to the new Sidelines Sports Bar. Sidelines wasn't particularly nice, but it was walking distance from anywhere on the small fort, so nobody had to drive home afterward. The association based its meeting upon *Robert's Rules of Order*—a guide to parliamentary procedure written by an army officer in the 1870s. There was a sergeant at arms, and nobody could speak without obtaining the floor and being recognized by the meeting's chair. Members had to pay a fine if they spoke out of turn or broke the rules (somebody would yell *"point of order!"* at the offender). Kiraly loved it. He thought the fledgling unit was beginning to develop a significant esprit de corps and sense of duty.

Wayne Hunt, the battalion's executive officer, asked Kiraly to put his handyman skill to use and design and build plaques for awards to be handed out at the meetings. One award recognized exceptional service, another recognized exceptional stupidity. The stupidity plaque was billed the nuclear detonation, or NUDET, award. Kiraly found an iconic picture of a NUDET over Bikini Atoll, with a big orange mushroom cloud, and got a beautiful two-foot-by-two-foot piece of spalted maple wood that he carved into a shield. Every month, somebody's name got engraved on the NUDET plaque. As the association of soldiers sat around their big mahogany table, telling stories from the month, they would eventually begin nominating each other for the NUDET award. Typically the nominee was a young lieutenant or somebody who did something dumb, but a nomination only required a shred of truth and most were wildly exaggerated.

For leaders at the Missile Defense Agency, the previous year's excitement at meeting the system's deployment deadline had given way to concern about the risks taken to meet that deadline. The White House required some capability to shoot down incoming missiles and MDA had raced to provide it, but that meant they had to advance the needed technologies while designing and testing and producing the system—all at the same time.

A stinging government audit of the program summed it up: MDA put some missile defense assets in the field faster than originally planned, but to do so it had strayed from a "knowledge-based approach that allows successful developers to deliver, within budget, a product whose performance has been demonstrated." Instead, the agency had "fielded assets before their capability was known." They had deployed a homeland missile defense system, but now they were underdelivering.

MDA had expected it would have twenty interceptors in the ground at Greely and Vandenberg by the end of 2005, but on New Year's Eve it had just ten. The number had steadily dropped throughout the year: an explosion at a subcontractor's facility meant there wouldn't be enough booster rockets, then two unsuccessful flight tests meant more interceptors had to be set aside for ground tests, and then production slowed further because technical issues and quality control problems were being uncovered left and right.

In its own investigation, MDA found a series of "quality control weaknesses" with Raytheon's kill vehicle and with Orbital's booster rocket, which were the two key parts of the interceptor. In some cases, the agency found that for the kill vehicle's subcomponents, the assembly plan was not always followed—different parts or different configurations were sometimes used and not properly documented—and the contractors were not requiring "space-qualified parts" capable of tolerating the severe conditions in outer space. In short, MDA's investigation found it could not accurately determine the kill vehicle's reliability or its life expectancy.

9

ICEFOG

ON JANUARY 24, 2006, Mark Kiraly pulled his car up to a red light just outside the main gate of Fort Wainwright in Fairbanks. It was a surreal predawn scene—the city was experiencing a phenomenon known as icefog. Ice crystals and car exhaust and whatever else get trapped in the frozen lower atmosphere and form a dense haze. Kiraly looked at the bank sign across the street, which said it was 4:00 A.M. and −46°F. Then he looked in the passenger seat at his very pregnant wife, Ruby, who was aghast.

"Why are you stopped?! There are no cars for miles! Keep driving!"

So Mark blew through the red light and toward the maternity ward at the Greater Fairbanks Community Hospital. The Kiralys' second son was born a few hours later. The army had a "Storknesting" program that allowed families to stay closer to civilization, at a hotel on Fort Wainwright, once a mother was ten days from her due date. The idea was to spare families from a one-hundred-mile mad dash to a hospital through the snow and ice and darkness. Instead, the Kiralys had a five-mile drive from Wainwright to the hospital. Still, nothing in Alaska was easy. The main doors at the emergency drop-off entrance were closed for the night, and Kiraly had to find an open entrance around the side.

The next month, he was sent down to Colorado Springs for the GMD Qualification Course—his chance at joining one of the battalion's missile crews. Ruby was not thrilled with the idea. Mark had coerced her into living in a big cabin about thirteen miles away from Greely, and now was proposing to leave her there for eight weeks with the newborn and an eight-year-old, but the course was a career step he needed to take.

He had been doing operations work, mainly trying to keep the MPs trained and certified, and had been in charge of the battalion marksmanship program, and coaching one of the MP softball teams. He enjoyed it, but Kiraly's goal was to lead soldiers in combat, and for him that meant becoming a crew director, to be the leader who got weapons release authorization and fired the interceptors. He felt like everything else was an ancillary task meant to help those crews be ready.

The best-performing MPs could be selected to try the qualification course, but it was especially selective for junior-grade officers like Kiraly. He'd had to watch as the best MPs were selected and sent to the course in Colorado Springs, and then came back to join the missile crews instead of standing out in the freezing cold guarding the wire. He'd had to wait two years for his turn to try out.

Not every soldier who was offered a spot in the eight-week qualification course took it. The curriculum was hard, the never-ending review boards that followed it would be demanding, and the long shift work could take a serious toll.

But the crews had the most competitive billets, so that's what Kiraly wanted.

The GMD Qualification Course had evolved since Michalski's and Frobe-Recella's big class. It was somewhat more structured, and now the students had regular access to computer terminals that simulated the real job. There was a spotlight on Kiraly's class because the incoming brigade and battalion commanders—Colonel Michael Yowell and Lieutenant Colonel Ed Hildreth—were both in it. Specialist Anthony Ray Montoya was in it too. He was shocked to find his low-ranking self attending the same course as noncommissioned officers, junior-grade officers, and the colonels who would be unit commanders.

Montoya had been serving as a short-range air defender, guarding the sky over Washington, when a recruiter for the 100th Missile Defense Brigade stopped by to give a presentation on the larger homeland missile defense mission and to find soldiers they could send up to Greely. The presentation piqued his interest, and he raised his hand and said he'd like to go. Everyone else in his platoon thought Montoya was crazy for wanting the job. They warned him, "It's cold, it's miserable, it's dark—don't do it."

Montoya was ordered to first report to Colorado Springs to take the GMD Qualification Course. He had no idea what that was. He was given the address of a building near downtown on Academy Boulevard, and told to wear civilian clothes so he wouldn't be recognized as military. The students had to size one another up and determine who was who since they weren't wearing uniforms with names or ranks or insignias. Some, Montoya found, weren't even in the army.

"What unit are you guys coming from?" he asked one group.

"Oh, none. We work up at Northcom."

"Where's that?" Montoya asked.

"The Mountain."

"The Mountain?"

The men explained that they worked at the combined command center for Northern Command and the North American Aerospace Defense Command (better known as NORAD), buried inside Cheyenne Mountain in Colorado Springs. They were attending the course so they could better understand what the missile crews did, since ultimately the order to launch interceptors would come from Northern Command. Montoya had never heard of any of this. They told him that the battalion in Alaska feeds up to the brigade in Colorado Springs, which then feeds up to Northern Command in Cheyenne Mountain.

Northern Command, as the higher headquarters getting orders directly from the secretary of defense, can direct the crews in the overall battle and order them to deviate from the plan. If missiles are heading toward Washington, Northern Command might direct the crews to use more firepower defending the capital, and less defending someplace else.

"Two ICBMs incoming toward Los Angeles. Two ICBMs incoming toward Washington. Engaging each target with four GBIs," a crew director might tell Northern Command.

"Deviate. Defend Washington with all interceptors," the command might say.

"Roger that," the crew director must reply.

Montoya, Kiraly, the incoming commanders, the Northern

Command guys, and everyone else found themselves studying almost every day after the course—it was not a typical army experience. They spent lots of time in classrooms looking at PowerPoint slides, lots of time on different mock-ups of their computer terminals, and then lots of time studying. For the most part, though, they enjoyed it. Kiraly was relishing an early spring in Colorado instead of a long winter in Alaska. And halfway through the course the Northern Command guys got them a tour inside Cheyenne Mountain.

The Command Center was hidden deep inside Cheyenne Mountain's tunnels, with all the dark wood paneling and navy-grade steel one might expect from a Cold War–era facility built in 1961. Cheyenne Mountain was home to several organizations within a sort of office complex of fifteen two- and three-story buildings. The offices were about a mile into the mountain and about two thousand feet under its summit, so the personnel took small buses from the entrance. The Command Center itself was in a large room with a high ceiling. At the front were huge screens displaying data and imagery of all kinds, faced by several groups of workstations each with a bank of its own screens; several phones; and massive, well-organized books of checklists outlining procedures for an array of emergencies. At the back, atop a low mezzanine, was a workspace for the Command Center's director, and additional space for when operations were dire enough to be led by the head of Northern Command—the four-star officer in charge of defending all of North America. The complex was protected by the mountain's solid granite and two twenty-three-ton blast doors, and the buildings sat on fifteen hundred three-inch-think springs so they could survive the shock from a direct hit with a nuclear weapon. Specialist Montoya was impressed.

On April 11, fourteen students passed the qualification course. Captain Chris Berisford was the honor graduate with an overall grade of 99.9 percent, and Hildreth, the new battalion commander in line to replace Greg Bowen, was named a "distinguished graduate" for earning 99.3 percent in the course. He would not actually sit on a crew, but as the unit's leader he needed to understand its unique weapon system. The other graduates were assigned to crew positions—Kiraly would be slated as a deputy director and Montoya would be a communications operator—and they had to begin a new round of training on the specifics of their new posts.

Kiraly found that learning how to *fight* with the system was actually more like learning how to *constrain* the system. The software was designed to see threats, calculate intercepts, and then launch interceptor after interceptor until there were no more. If not constrained, the system would automatically take an aggressive approach and not necessarily the approach Northern Command or the White House wanted to take. The crews learned how to control the system and launch a certain number of interceptors, at a certain cadence, against each incoming warhead. They also learned and practiced to fight in any conceivable scenario: communications failure, Greely goes off-line, fire in the control node, Schriever goes off-line, crew director passes out, Northern Command goes off-line, one missile incoming from North Korea, five missiles incoming from North Korea, and on and on.

Montoya would be Bravo crew's communications operator. If a radar site or communications link broke down, it would be his job to notice and find out what's happening. Montoya was also charged with ensuring the missile fields were clear and the MPs were ready if interceptors needed to be launched. Kiraly had no job. There were no spots open for his rank of captain, which normally serves as a crew's deputy director or director. He was instead working on the battalion's staff, again biding his time before a spot opened, and watching as the unit prepared for a change of command.

It was Monday May 8, 2006, and Bowen was handing over leadership of the 49th Missile Defense Battalion to Lieutenant Colonel Ed Hildreth, an air defense artillery officer with combat experience during Operations Desert Shield and Desert Storm. A strong wind steadily raked across the dry, yellow grass on Greely's parade field, keeping all the heraldry flags full throughout the ceremony. After three years spent turning Greely from an abandoned cold-weather testing station into a launch facility for homeland missile defense interceptors; hiring and training soldiers for a site-security MP company; and staffing the world's longest-range air defense crews, Bowen was moving on. His next job would be working missile defense for US Strategic Command.

Kiraly was already established at Greely. Montoya had to drop his car off in Los Angeles to get it shipped up to Alaska, and then catch a flight to Fairbanks. He got to his barracks room at Greely around 3:00 A.M. and went to sleep. At 10:00 A.M. another soldier in the battalion, Specialist Roy Tomasch, knocked on Montoya's door, waking him up and offering to show him around the small post.

"But first, we're going to see this guy—he just got attacked by a bear," Tomasch told him. Montoya was taken to Captain Dale Titus's house, where a group from Greely had assembled to stare at and discuss the injuries. Titus had his shirt off to display deep scratches across his back, the parting gift of a bear that was now hanging from his porch.

Titus had been out with his rifle and his black Lab, scouting hunting spots for when the season opened. He'd seen a moose carcass just off the road and was building a small rock tower so he could find the spot again later. He heard something behind him, looked back, and saw a black bear take two strides before it jumped at him. Titus fell partly under the bear but had managed to pump a round into the rifle and shoot the bear as it lunged. He drove back to his house with the dead bear and some nasty gouges along his back. He called the Department of Natural Resources to report the incident, and then invited his friends over to watch him skin the bear. This was Montoya's first morning in Alaska.

In Colorado, Alpha crew, the first crew at brigade to pull a real shift on the homeland missile defense system, had been at work for almost two years and it was time for a break.

The soldiers had put in considerable time together. Spriggs and Edwards had spent the better part of two midnight shifts embroiled in a ludicrous debate about the difference between magma and lava—and everyone took sides. As the shifts started to seem longer, Meakins had pulled rank and demanded control over the television remote; it would be nothing but college basketball throughout the early spring (he had played college ball for Georgia Southern). He was one of the few soldiers in the unit that wasn't an avid hunter and couldn't take the nonstop hunting stories, so he banned those on midnight shifts. Meakins also wasn't a J. R. R. Tolkien fan, and banned all screenings of the popular *Lord of the Rings* trilogy in the node.

Still, Alpha crew loved the work. It was two morning shifts, two afternoon shifts, two midnight shifts, and then four days off. Frobe-Recella hardly saw her husband and missed her baby's first Christmas, but her unusual schedule meant her toddler was often with one of his parents and rarely in day care. For a year and a half, it had all worked, but as an active-duty officer she would be required to move on, and ended her tour with the unit in January 2006. It was the best assignment she'd ever had and the minute she left, she wished she could go back. Spriggs was happy to keep working shifts, and was moved over to Echo crew.

Meakins and Kent were sent to be the brigade's representatives at Vandenberg Air Force Base for a few months. It was meant to be a relaxed assignment for them to get some needed rest. They ended up stuck at Vandenberg for five months, the last four weeks of which they had to pull watch 24/7 between the two of them, as the threat of North Korean missiles began to feel authentic.

US intelligence analysts had been monitoring satellite feeds of the Tonghae test facility near East Korea Bay, watching what appeared to be the North Koreans assembling a Taepodong-2 rocket, ostensibly a satellite launch vehicle. North Korea had been under a voluntary long-range missile testing moratorium since 1999, but tensions between Pyongyang and Washington had grown significantly.

In 2002 President George W. Bush labeled North Korea as part of an "axis of evil" that included Iraq and Iran. Later that year, arms control agreements between the United States and North Korea collapsed amid allegations of cheating from both sides—the United States was not providing the energy aid it had promised and North Korea was enriching uranium. In 2003 North Korea withdrew from the Nuclear Non-Proliferation Treaty. To salvage the situation, Bush then repeatedly sent veteran diplomat Chris Hill, a member of the negotiating team that helped end the Bosnian War, to Beijing for six-party talks to peacefully address North Korea's nuclear program. The talks went nowhere. The poor results and constantly moving goalposts ultimately led the US government to lose faith in North Korea's promises. Diplomacy suffered badly. The Bush administration opted to sideline Pyongyang as best it could through isolating sanctions, but the regime's efforts toward nuclear weapons and ICBMs persisted anyway.

Intelligence reports differed on the Taepodong-2's range, but most agreed it represented an ICBM that could possibly reach the United States.

10

TAEPODONG-2

IN JUNE 2006, FORT Greely was on edge. Hildreth, the new battalion commander, had ordered the fort to Alert Status. Work on the missile fields and silos stopped in order to clear the area in case interceptors needed to be launched at a moment's notice to shoot down North Korea's Taepodong-2.

John Robinson, platoon sergeant for Alpha Company's 1st Platoon, was dealing with some very concerned soldiers and families. *Would North Korea really attack? Would their warheads come toward Greely? Would we launch interceptors? What would it mean for my house if ten interceptors blast off across the street? What if my kids breathe in the rocket fumes?!* Robinson did his best to keep everyone calm. It wasn't easy. He lived in the same housing area, a few hundred yards from Greely's missile fields, and had the same concerns for his wife and daughters. The closest NASA lets civilians get to rocket launches is in a media viewing area two miles away from the launchpad.

The missile crews at Greely and in Colorado Springs, and the watch crews at Northern Command in Cheyenne

Mountain, knew a major North Korean missile launch was coming, and they might be called upon to intercept it. The Taepodong-2 was not mobile, but rather a one-hundred-foot-tall three-stage rocket that was taking weeks to set up on a fixed launchpad. The crews were waiting for what the intelligence analysts believed would be the North Korean launch window, likely in early July.

The crews ran constant drills. Before they could begin a shift, the operators would come in early and get an intelligence update about what had happened in the last twenty-four or forty-eight hours, then they would do a couple of practice runs for whichever scenario the intel team thought was most likely that day, and then they would take over as the crew on shift. Again and again, crews at Schriever talked to crews at Greely and to the Northern Command watch teams at Cheyenne Mountain over a communications Ops Loop, rehearsing intercept missions. The most likely scenario was that the North Koreans would launch the Taepodong-2 as a test, and not as an attack, but the crews had to prepare for worst-case scenarios.

Kiraly was sitting in an office in Building 609 at Greely, doing battalion staff work and eating his lunch. He was still waiting for a crew spot. Wayne Hunt, the battalion's executive officer, burst into the room.

"Get your ass out to the missile field right now," Hunt said. "You're taking over Echo crew." Kiraly was stunned. Hunt could not give him an explanation. "Go, now," was all the XO said.

Kiraly ran to his car, raced out to the missile field, parked, and took a lonely shuttle ride out to the Fire Direction Center. As he walked into the small building, the Echo crew director was walking out. "Hey, what's happening?" Kiraly asked.

"Sorry Mark, I can't tell you," he said, and left.

Kiraly opened the door to the node. "Okay, I'm your new director. Let's get to work."

After their shift, Echo crew told Kiraly what had happened. The crew director and a missile defense officer at Northern Command got into a squabble over the finer points of intercepting a North Korean missile. Words were exchanged, and some of the language used was indelicate. That might have been okay, but the argument was hardly private. The profanity-laced quarrel took place on the open Ops Loop that could be heard by all the crews, everyone at Northern Command, and all the relevant commanders.

The crew directors would be the ones in the fight, so they did not like being told how to do their job—and certainly not by an officer buried safely under Cheyenne Mountain. The feeling was especially strong at Greely, where the battalion sat across a small road from the interceptor fields. If there was a front line in nuclear war, Greely would be it. The battalion's soldiers lived on the frontier, guarding and launching interceptors near the top of the world. But they had to be professional. Kiraly was brought in to replace the crew director.

Now Captain Mark Kiraly was not only on crew, but he was a battalion crew director, waiting along with the other directors for a chance to engage North Korea's Taepodong-2. By the end of June, the North Koreans disavowed their long-range missile test moratorium and had finished fueling the missile. A launch was expected soon.

Meakins was at the wheel of a Hertz rental car, driving slowly across Vandenberg Air Force Base with the car's emergency flashers on. Following him was a fifty-five-foot-long, fifty-thousand-pound interceptor on the flatbed of a semitruck. Behind the semi was Kent, bringing up the rear of the convoy in another Hertz car, also with his flashers on.

There were only two interceptors in silos at Vandenberg, and a failure had been detected in one of them. There had also been some rare and significant rain at Vandenberg that flooded the silo with the single functioning interceptor. This left Meakins and Kent with a malfunctioning interceptor in a good silo, and a good interceptor in a malfunctioning silo. It was a manageable problem, but with North Korea now building what could be an ICBM on a launchpad, it was a problem that had to be solved immediately.

The malfunctioning interceptor was to be removed from the good silo and put into storage, then replaced with the good interceptor. Meakins could not believe the scene that was unfolding, that he and Kent were escorting a $75 million space interceptor weapon in two rented sedans, but they had to get it moved.

Once the brigade and battalion had gone on alert, Meakins and Kent had been ordered to stay at Vandenberg. One of them would have to enable the interceptor there for launch if the order was given to destroy North Korea's Taepodong-2 missile. Meakins bought a sleeping bag and cot that he set up in the fifteen-by-fifteen-foot windowless Command Launch Equipment shelter at Vandenberg. The launch area at the base was cleared out and fenced off and guarded by MPs— only Meakins, Kent, and an air force operator from the base were allowed in. Meakins set up a watch schedule, rented hundreds of DVDs, and bought cases of Rockstar energy drinks. For nearly a month, the two soldiers traded shifts. When one's watch was over, he'd take a few hours to get some food or more energy drinks and wash clothes or whatever else had to be done, then come back to the little Command Launch Equipment shelter for some sleep and the next watch.

Meakins was asked to brief Colonel Jack Weinstein, the air force wing commander at Vandenberg, on what would happen if interceptors were ordered to be launched. He explained that since nearly all the interceptors were in silos in Alaska, the procedures would have the soldiers launch from Greely and keep the one interceptor at Vandenberg as a backup. Weinstein was satisfied that it was unlikely the soldiers would be launching from his base. Weinstein's 30th Space Wing was the main tenant at Vandenberg, and they were accustomed to meticulously planned and executed military space launches, not just shooting off a missile at any time.

The next day, after Meakins had finished a full night on watch in their fetid equipment shelter, he was told that Rumsfeld had just changed the interceptor launch procedure. Meakins and Doug Boothe, MDA's representative at Vandenberg, went to update Weinstein on the change.

Meakins had not showered or shaved in a day, and was strung out on Rockstar. He was grateful to have Boothe there helping to brief the busy wing commander. Boothe, a civilian in a suit and tie, put a better face on the troubling news. They told Weinstein that Rumsfeld had changed the plan: now, if the crews were ordered to engage the Taepodong-2, the very first interceptor launched would blast off from Vandenberg. The colonel was not pleased, but offered to help however he could.

Meanwhile, Major Ron Hoard had taken over as director of Echo crew at the brigade in Colorado, and Hoard was constantly butting heads with Bill Spriggs, who was now working as the crew's future-operations officer. Within a few weeks, the relationship between the two was badly fraught. Maintenance contractors were in the node for work during one of the shifts, and one was not wearing his security badge inside the secured room. Hoard asked him to display the badge, and the contractor got snippy and started making fun of the crew director. Spriggs, a big former paratrooper and drill sergeant from Mississippi, stood up.

"Yo buddy, I'm the only one in here that gets to irritate Major Hoard," Spriggs warned. "Keep talking your trash and I'll whup your ass."

The contractor did keep talking, and Spriggs leapt over the console for a fight. Hoard and the others jumped in to separate Spriggs and the contractor. After that, Hoard and Spriggs were okay. Hoard might have been finicky and Spriggs might have been a smart-ass, but they were crewmates—and they were scheduled for a shift on the afternoon of July 4, 2006.

The intel community was reporting that the North Koreans were likely to launch the Taepodong-2 shortly after Echo crew's shift began. The crew sitting shift before them gave the usual handover briefing, but then appeared to be stalling and none of them left at the normal time. The off-duty crew wanted to witness the North Korean launch. They were milling around, and Echo crew had just begun the unit's most important shift yet. This time, Hoard stood up.

"You all need to leave, right now," he said. "I've got the mission; you guys are going to be in our way if something happens. You need to leave."

As the last soldier walked out and the door to the node closed, the Quick Alert went off with its piercing *beep-beep-beep.* For a second, Spriggs froze in his seat. He soaked in the reality of an actual North Korean launch, no training run this time. Then he went into motion, using muscle memory built over thousands of training hours, and Spriggs and Hoard and Echo crew went about their business, tracking the launch and relaying every detail over the Ops Loop.

Kiraly's Echo crew was on shift at Greely, and his reaction was the same. The Quick Alert sent his heart into his throat, and he allowed himself a moment of shock, and then turned to his task like a robot.

Meakins had been hearing the intel briefings from the Command Launch Equipment shelter at Vandenberg. He had been told North Korea's Taepodong-2 launch was approaching, likely any hour. Weinstein was at Vandenberg's July Fourth Family Day celebration when Meakins reached him on a secure line. He warned the commander that the launch appeared imminent. Weinstein was surprised to be getting so much intel from Meakins—the unshaved army guy out in the Command Launch Equipment shelter—and not from his own people.

Meakins was surfing the internet and checking live footage of NASA's space shuttle *Discovery* launch to kill time before North Korea's launch. As the countdown to *Discovery*'s launch ticked toward liftoff, the phone rang in the shelter and Meakins was ordered to enable the interceptor. For a moment, he was confused. *Are we tracking the right launch? Would North Korea fire a missile at the same time as the Discovery shuttle launch? I guess so.* He armed the weapon, and then ran outside the shelter and jumped atop one of the MP's trucks so he could watch if the interceptor rocketed off from the California coast.

Secretary of Defense Donald Rumsfeld had been at his vacation home in St. Michaels, on the eastern shore of Maryland, but his motorcade was now racing back to the Pentagon after intel reports said the launch was coming. At 3:01 P.M. in Washington, the Taepodong-2 launched from the Tonghae test facility. Northern Command and the missile crews got the alert immediately and set to work, but Northern Command could not get Rumsfeld on the phone—Rumsfeld's motorcade was crossing the Chesapeake Bay and he could not be reached at the moment of the launch.

The drama was intense but short-lived.

The Taepodong-2 did not get far. It failed or was aborted before Hoard and Kiraly could even begin preparing calculations for an intercept. Crew members with the 100th Missile Defense Brigade and the 49th Missile Defense Battalion were, for the most part, disappointed. The feeling was particularly stark at Greely. Urgent projects there had been put on hold. A crew director had been relieved of his position. And in the end, the Taepodong-2 hadn't flown past its boost stage.

Nobody wanted to see a war break out, but they all wanted to put their skills to use, to take a shot at that missile. Instead, it disintegrated after forty-two seconds of flight. Hildreth, the battalion commander at Greely, described the whole episode as "a letdown." Meakins and Kent flew back to Colorado.

For Obering at MDA, the Taepodong-2 incident was sobering. Not because Rumsfeld was temporarily unreachable for the engagement order: they had launch authority already delegated to Northern Command for that very reason. Not because the missile might have been capable of reaching the United States: that was still unclear. Obering was concerned because North Korea had also launched five shorter-range missiles around the same time as the Taepodong-2—and the spy satellites had not seen those until they launched. They were easily hidden road-mobile missiles. He was worried that future defense against North Korea would only get harder, that the North Koreans might someday be able to conceal road-mobile ICBMs instead of building them on a launch pad throughout the summer for every satellite to see.

Two months later, Obering traveled with Rumsfeld to Alaska for a tour of the operation at Greely. The soldiers there were used to a throng of distinguished-visitor tours throughout the summer, but not from anyone as senior as Rumsfeld, whom many of them viewed as the reason their jobs existed in the first place. It was Rumsfeld who had pushed so strongly for this homeland missile defense system, and it was a big deal that he was coming to visit them, especially now. The war in

Iraq was going terribly, and the armed forces were stressed by the unrelenting tempo of deployments to Iraq and Afghanistan. Among all that, Rumsfeld's aggressive leadership style had won him few friends in the Pentagon, and he was now facing calls for his resignation—not just from politicians but from senior generals who felt he had mismanaged the invasion and occupation of Iraq.

The soldiers of the 49th Missile Defense Battalion, who were virtually unknown inside the army, let alone in the Pentagon, were nervous to get a visit from the big boss. Rumsfeld was a particularly intimidating figure too. The soldiers had seen him on TV doing press conferences in which the former college wrestler and longtime political operator seemed to be berating reporters from his raised dais. Hildreth asked the gregarious Kiraly and his Echo crew to brief Rumsfeld during the visit. The plan was to use Kiraly, one confident Chicagoan, to get on the good side of Rumsfeld, another confident Chicagoan.

Even before Rumsfeld arrived, his advance team was prowling around Greely making sure the airfield and missile field were secure. The battalion's soldiers were rehearsing what they would tell the secretary. Everyone was uptight and nobody wanted to look foolish.

On August 27 the secretary and his entourage came charging onto the base in a motorcade of black SUVs, and a huge gaggle of hangers-on walked with him directly into the building where Echo crew was waiting in one of the two control nodes. The room was packed. Base commanders from all over Alaska, the state's adjutant general, Senator Ted Stevens, and every defense contractor who could finagle some face time with the secretary of defense was squeezed into the node, along with some anxious soldiers. After all the hype, Kiraly was surprised at how slight Rumsfeld appeared, like a friendly grandfather, and he looked even smaller because it was cold in the node and somebody had lent him an army BDU jacket that was two sizes too big. A small grandfather swimming in digital camouflage.

Kiraly figured he should break the ice.

"I'm Major Kiraly, sir, from Chicago, Illinois," he said with a big Midwestern grin.

"Where are you from in Chicago?" Rumsfeld asked.

"Palatine, sir."

"North Side!" Rumsfeld said. "You must be a Cubs fan?"

"Absolutely, sir."

"Outstanding!"

Rumsfeld and Kiraly kicked off the briefing by talking Cubs baseball, and Echo crew and all the hangers-on sighed in relief. The secretary was a politician and long accustomed to these visits; he knew everyone was standing there shaking in their boots and was happy to put them at ease. He learned that Greely had become a bit less austere. It housed about seventeen hundred people—around two hundred soldiers, plus defense contractors and everyone's families. The base's Brownie troop now had sixteen girls. Its missile silos now had eleven interceptors.

After his briefing Rumsfeld told a handful of reporters, "The people here are very carefully selected; they are dedicated and they're doing a terrific job and we appreciate it, and I wanted to come up firsthand and tell them that."

Still, the testing failures loomed large and Rumsfeld made

clear he was not yet willing to say the homeland missile defense system was fully ready. "I want to see it happen," he said. "And I have a lot of confidence in these folks and have a lot of confidence in the work that's been done, and I particularly have a great deal of confidence in Trey Obering. But [I want to see] a full end-to-end process at some point, where we actually put all the pieces together—that just hasn't happened. We still have some more sensors that they're putting in place."

Rumsfeld, though arguably the program's most important supporter, was echoing some of the program's biggest critics, who argued that homeland missile defense had not been proven effective because there had not been an "end-to-end" demonstration that used all the satellites, radars, software, and hardware that would be used in combat. Much of the testing had been done with simulation or surrogate systems. Asked if he was frustrated with the program, Rumsfeld couched his cautious optimism for missile defense in its long history:

The word "frustrated" is not one that is appropriate for my personal approach to things. I don't get frustrated. I've lived through this entire process. I was there that night when President Reagan announced his vision, and I've been involved in it in one way or another over a good many years. I lived through the period where the arguments and hostilities and debates were hostile and heated and indeed theological at various points, and I've seen the thing calm down to the point where it's now national policy in law, that the United States develops a capability to defend itself against limited types of threats.

So we've seen the debate as to whether it should be space-based or sea-based or land-based. We've heard the arguments that nothing should be deployed until it's perfect and tested and end-to-end perfect, and I think that's just not a valid argument. I have always believed that the way you get from where you are to where you want to be is you start. And you put something in the ground and you work with it and evolve it and change it and fix it and improve it and let all the people and critics who stand around and say, "Oh, you missed," or "You didn't get it," or "You missed a deadline," or whatever they want to do—and you just keep your head down and you get the job done and you arrive in the year 2006. And we've got a leader of this program who says we now have a capability, a limited capability, to do just that. Not bad.

Kiraly escorted Rumsfeld back to his aircraft in Greely's hangar.

"Well, what are you gonna do next, sir?" Kiraly asked the secretary.

"You know, I've got a lot of notes. I think I'm going to write a book," Rumsfeld told him.

Three months later, Rumsfeld resigned. Five years later, Rumsfeld had just published his book and came to Fort Carson in Colorado Springs, where Kiraly showed up to get the former secretary to sign a picture from their briefing at Greely. Rumsfeld remembered Kiraly and autographed the photo with an inscription: "Go Cubs."

11

GLANCING BLOW

OBERING AND MDA HAD planned another intercept test for September 1, 2006. This test was to have an operational interceptor, with the same hardware and same angles of attack that a real combat scenario might have—just like Rumsfeld wanted.

MDA had been test-launching interceptors from the mock silos on Kwajalein Atoll in the Western Pacific. The target, a derivative of a Minuteman II missile, was launched out of Vandenberg Air Force Base. It was a decent setup for initial testing, but intercepts from those angles weren't representative of combat against North Korean missiles. To make it more realistic, Obering wanted to launch interceptors from the real site at Vandenberg and launch targets from Kodiak Island in Alaska, so the angles would be closer to shooting at North Korean warheads from Fort Greely. It also meant they could use a TPY-2 radar in Juneau, Alaska, as a stand-in for the TPY-2 radar in Japan, and they could use the Upgraded Early Warning Radar at Beale Air Force Base in Northern California as a surrogate for the big Cobra Dane radar at the end of the Aleutian Island chain.

Rear Admiral Kate Paige, who had helped with Obering's heritage review of the program, had become especially vocal about simplifying the tests. She did not think the GMD system should attempt another intercept test, so Obering called it a "zero offset flyby" instead. MDA would set its expectations low, and just demonstrate that the kill vehicle could see its target. Obering would try for an intercept anyway, but he would do it quietly. He feared that anything deemed "unsuccessful" would set Congress after his budget again.

The agency's budget was exactly the topic of an April 4, 2006, congressional hearing in Washington, when Senator Carl Levin dug in to Obering's testing plan. Levin, a Harvard-educated civil rights lawyer, was a member of the powerful Senate Armed Services Committee. He knew how the expectations game was played.

"As I understand it, you are going to try then to intercept the target. Is that correct?" Levin asked Obering, peering over his reading glasses.

"No, sir. If an intercept occurs, it will be a by-product of it. But it is the first time we're flying the interceptor out of Vandenberg," Obering said. "We have not flown this version of the kill vehicle against a target as it relates to the radar track information we get from the Beale radar. So that will be the primary objective."

"I know that's your primary objective, but is it not an objective to intercept a target?" Levin asked again.

"We're putting a target out there because we want to be able to do the tracking of the target across the radar, feeding that information into the fire control system, getting the interceptor into place, comparing that with the target characterization that is seen by the interceptor. And so, if an intercept could occur, yes, sir, but that is not the primary objective," Obering said.

"Is that a secondary objective?"

"Yes, sir, it would be."

"Okay," Levin said, "that, to me, is an objective. It may be secondary, but it nonetheless is an objective, and I think it is important that we know that."

The target missile blasted off from Alaska's Kodiak Island on Friday morning, September 1. Shortly after, at 10:39 A.M., an interceptor launched from a silo at Vandenberg Air Force Base. The interceptor released the kill vehicle into space, it detected the target, and then maneuvered toward it.

For tests, the kill vehicle is outfitted to send real-time test data back to the engineers at MDA. The agency also wraps the mock warhead in a fiber optic network—and as soon as the kill vehicle hits the target, it burst-transmits data to the ground that explains how the fiber optic network came apart. That data is then run through so-called hydrocode analysis that generates an animation of how the target was destroyed. Or not.

In the Navy Annex, Obering watched the live feed as the kill vehicle closed in. On the overhead screen, the infrared image showed the kill vehicle impact its target with a bright orange flash. *Success!*

But at MDA headquarters, the hydrocode analysis soon

showed that it was not a direct hit, and rather was what would become known as a "glancing blow." There was debate about whether it would have been a full intercept or not, and MDA's technical community was split. Some felt the hit was not decisive—a direct hit normally vaporized about 50 percent of the warhead and another 40 percent then burns up in the atmosphere. Others argued the kill vehicle's strike would have knocked off a real warhead's heat shield, meaning the warhead could not have survived reentry into Earth's atmosphere, and therefore it was a kill. Obering agreed that it was a kill.

As far as the general was concerned, this was a success. They hit a target traveling in space from three thousand kilometers away. The test would have met its primary objective as long as the kill vehicle flew and collected data—and it not only flew, but it struck its target.

About an hour and a half after the test, Obering walked into the Pentagon pressroom. "Well, good afternoon, I'm pleased to announce that the test that we executed today was a total success," he told reporters. "In fact, it exceeded even our primary objective on the test, and we also met all the secondary objectives of the test."

Whether that strike might have destroyed the physics package of a real nuclear weapon, however, continued to be a matter of quiet debate within the Defense Department. More than five years later, during another budget hearing, Dr. J. Michael Gilmore, director of the Pentagon's Operational Test and Evaluation Office, appeared to randomly reveal that he actually scored the test as "a hit, but not a kill."

He said ground testing using rocket-propelled sleds, along with computer modeling and simulation, demonstrated the kill vehicle could strike its target in a location that might not destroy the target, and that this was the case during the September 1, 2006 test. MDA disagreed and insisted it was a successful intercept.

A month after the "glancing blow" test, the North Koreans announced they would detonate their first atomic bomb. On October 3, 2006, they did exactly that.

The North Korean nuclear test set Dr. Jeffrey Lewis to work. Lewis was a vocal member of a budding open-source nuclear intelligence community and a scholar at the Middlebury Institute of International Studies at Monterey, about two hundred miles up the California coast from Vandenberg. Using public information from the Geophysical Survey of the Russian Academy of Sciences, and the US Geological Survey, along with the geology of the test site and some rough math, Lewis calculated that the bomb was a dud, with an explosive yield about one-twentieth of the weapon dropped on Nagasaki. "No one has ever dudded their first test of a simple fission device," he wrote. "North Korean nuclear scientists are now officially the worst ever."

Lewis argued the North Koreans' failure was likely due to a combination of shoddy engineering, a push to skip directly to an operational design, and fear of telling dictator Kim Jong-il there could be problems with skipping ahead. Still, Pyongyang had abandoned its missile testing moratorium and had tried to fly its failed Taepodong-2, it had successfully launched a series of short- and medium-range missiles, and now the North Koreans could claim to have a nuclear device too—albeit a dysfunctional one.

In March 2007 the Pentagon allowed Terry Moran, from ABC's *Nightline,* to bring the first television cameras into Greely's secretive missile fields, as long as he and his crew didn't mind a snowy, thirty-below-zero tour. They got lucky with the weather too; the week before was forty-four below. Moran was allowed to film a utilidor leading to a silo and film a live interceptor in the silo, armed for launch. He was allowed to speak with some of the first crew members. He was well aware, however, of *why* he was allowed to do it. "The Pentagon wanted us to see all of this—silos, command centers, test missiles—because they have a story they want to get out: It works, they claim," Moran told his viewers when the segment aired on April 25.

Colonel Thomas Besch, director of the Missile Defense Agency's Alaska programs, told the camera he was "absolutely confident" that the fourteen interceptors now in their silos at Greely would be successful if launched to destroy enemy warheads. Moran was then shown a simulated intercept of a North Korean attack against San Francisco, Seattle, and Chicago (the latter Moran's hometown).

"Weapons, engage threat to Chicago, one GBI out of Fort Greely," Major Roger Hoselton, the on-duty crew director, told his weapons operator.

"Threat to Chicago has been engaged with one GBI out of Fort Greely," the weapons operator responded.

"Weapons, engage threat to Seattle, two GBIs out of Fort Greely."

"Threat to Seattle has been engaged with two GBIs out of Fort Greely."

"Threat to Chicago has been destroyed." And so on.

After the simulation, Moran asked Ed Hildreth how sure he was that the system would work in the real world. The commander didn't hesitate. "I'd bet my family's life on it," he said. Hildreth even struck a sort of confident, John Wayne pose when he said it. The crew members, the soldiers who had to fight with this new weapon, were not as enthusiastic.

"The systems are all working in a way that will knock the missiles down, you think?" Moran asked Hoselton, the crew director who had just "shot down" the simulated attacks.

"Ummm . . ." Hoselton took a six-second pause.

"From where I'm sitting . . . ," and then another long pause before he shrugged and said, "*I* think so. I *think* so." The other soldiers in the room gasped.

Hoselton was not thinking of the programmed answer. He was thinking of his crew's reliance on a huge network of sensors, its reliance on Boeing's contract managers and Northrop Grumman's software designers and Raytheon's aerospace engineers—and he knew the Missile Defense Agency had only scored six successful intercept tests in eleven tries (and one of those six was the glancing blow). Hoselton's crew might execute a mission flawlessly and the system might indeed knock the missiles down, but it would have to depend on a complex web of equipment that they couldn't control and that had struggled in testing. He had reason to pause.

One of the top criticisms of the soldiers' weapon, of the overall GMD homeland missile defense system, was that the testing done so far showed the equipment to still be in a sort of developmental prototype phase (which it was), that these tests weren't entirely realistic (which they weren't), and that the system wasn't yet complete (which it wasn't). The target ranges and intercept speeds were different than real life, chaff or countermeasures meant to confuse the kill vehicle were sometimes lacking, and the system still hadn't been hooked up to its most powerful sensor: the Sea-based X-band Radar, or SBX.

It is difficult to shoot down a single target flying thousands of miles per hour in space, but it is extremely difficult to discriminate between what is the warhead and what is debris or chaff—also flying thousands of miles per hour in space. A potent radar is necessary for this, and it is generally agreed that radars would have the best chances of success in discrimination if they operate in the X-band of the electromagnetic spectrum, where short wavelengths can provide high-quality images. When Meakins's Alpha crew sat its first shift in October 2004, the system did not have much ability to discriminate between a warhead and chaff. It was reliant upon two early warning radars: the Cobra Dane radar on Shemya Island at the western end of the Aleutians, and another at Beale Air Force Base in California. These could guide interceptors to targets but neither was very good at recognizing the warhead from the chaff, which required an X-band radar.

Originally, MDA had wanted to build an X-band radar on Alaska's Shemya Island. In 2000, Lieutenant General Ron Kadish, then the agency's director, had gone a few times to visit possible sites on the island for the new radar. Fort Greely seemed isolated, but it was like Midtown Manhattan compared to Eareckson Air Station on Shemya Island. Shemya is just under six square miles, but strolling around the island can be unpleasant. Its temperatures normally range between the high twenties to high fifties, and there is almost constant cloud cover and a misty rain that blows in on thirty-mile-per-hour winds. It's home to a small group of airmen and contractors, a large runway, and sarcastic signs marking the SHEMYA FALLS (an old sewer runoff), the SHEMYA GRAND CANYON (a shallow gully), and MCDONALD'S JUST AHEAD (fifteen hundred miles away). The island is also home to the Cobra Dane radar and some significant seismic activity.

Kadish was convinced that building a new radar on Shemya Island was going to be expensive and hard to support because of earthquakes. In early 2001 he instead began leaning toward a scheme to put the X-band radar on a massive seagoing oil rig, and figured it was a better bet. In March Kadish was ready to brief the idea to Rumsfeld.

While preparing for an 11:00 A.M. meeting with the secretary of defense, Kadish opened *The Washington Post* and—of all things on all days—saw an image of a huge Petrobras oil rig, damaged by a series of explosions, on its side and sinking into the Atlantic Ocean off the coast of Brazil. When Kadish walked in, Rumsfeld had on his desk the same newspaper opened to the same picture. It didn't help Kadish's argument, but ultimately Rumsfeld approved the project.

In early 2003 MDA bought a semisubmersible, fifty-thousand-ton seagoing platform from Norway's Moss Maritime. The platform would need quarters and workspaces for its eighty-six officers and civilian personnel, a command bridge, control rooms, power generation, and a helipad. It would also need equipment to communicate with the homeland missile defense system and with the interceptors themselves. Most importantly, it would need a massive X-band radar: forty-five thousand transmit/receive modules to form a powerful and precise radar beam. This would be housed under a 103-foot-high, 120-foot-wide radome. It looked like the world's largest golf ball.

In July 2005 it was officially named SBX-1 during a ceremony at a shipyard in Ingleside, Texas. The rig was 240 feet wide, 390 feet long, and 280 feet high, and could travel at about eight knots. It was far too big to traverse the Panama Canal, so a Dutch heavy lift ship sailed it down the South Atlantic, through the Strait of Magellan, and by January 2006 it had reached Pearl Harbor in Hawaii.

The plan was for SBX to be mostly stationary, based in a cove near Adak, Alaska (west of Shemya in the Aleutians). The rig would be held in place against constant high winds and rough waters with eight seventy-five-ton anchors drilled into the seabed. It was originally supposed to be there by the end of 2005, but problems abounded. In March SBX was getting ready for the trip from Hawaii to Alaska when alarms in the rig's engine room detected a leaking valve letting in water. In June circuit breakers went haywire with an electrical fault.

The radar itself appeared to be working well, though, and MDA ordered it to collect data from North Korea's failed Taepodong-2 launch in July and from the agency's glancing blow intercept in September. By January 2007, the colossal golf ball on the gigantic oil rig was finally ready for its shake-down cruise around the Bering Sea.

About the time the SBX set out northward, Mark Scott was hunting by himself, walking across a large field out past Delta Junction, when he spotted a big canister that looked like an auxiliary fuel tank from a military aircraft, called a drop tank. This struck him as a fun project to fix up and turn into a lawn ornament. Scott tried lifting it onto his four-wheeler but the tank was too heavy and he couldn't get it completely on. He went back to the fort to get his MP buddy, Francisco Marrero. The technically savvy Marrero was pretty sure it was not a drop tank. He warned Scott to back away and snapped a picture of the tank's data plate. Back at Greely, they googled the numbers on the data plate and figured it was probably an Agent Orange canister, per-haps dropped there some years ago. Scott and Marrero called Greely's Range Control to send out an Explosive Ordnance Disposal team from Anchorage to recover the canister.

The EOD team was all too familiar with Greely, and some of the technicians recognized Marrero from the previ-ous year. The young soldier had booby-trapped his barracks room before he'd gone on leave so nobody would mess with his stuff. Somebody tried to get in the room anyway and got a face full of tear gas, which promptly led to a call for the

EOD team to come clear Marrero's room. They had a laugh about it while Scott and Marrero drove the team out to the canister in one of the big tracked SUSVs. The EOD guys stopped laughing once they got to the canister and looked up the numbers on the data plate. There were some frantic radio calls and Scott and Marrero were ordered to leave. They never found out why.

Soon afterward, while the MPs were clearing the woods away from the perimeter to build a new headquarters facility, they stumbled upon a buried batch of old Chinese mortars. And after that, contractors were digging new telephone lines near the fort's chapel, and about five feet down they unearthed a large sealed drum. Scott and his patrol were ordered to guard the drum until EOD arrived the next day. He never found out what was in it.

Despite its odd past, Fort Greely was becoming somewhat more comfortable. There was finally a commissary to buy reasonably priced food. No more $5 gallons of milk from the IGA Food Cache in Delta Junction. The Coffee Shoppe opened next to the base's gas pumps, and it was a big deal. The crews at Greely had plenty of friends deployed to Iraq or Afghanistan, and in 2007 soldiers fighting either of those wars could still go to a Green Beans Coffee shop in almost any forward operating base. Now the battalion could buy coffee from a shop too.

Even more impactful was that Rob Cornelius, the garrison commander, had the gas station open a structure about the size of a small bathroom, inside which he hosted a make-your-own-hot-dog stand. It was a tremendous hit. The hot dog stand was so beloved that Cornelius had to hire somebody to run it full-time.

12

BAD VIBRATIONS

IN TUCSON, ARIZONA, A group of Raytheon engineers was working through the Track Gate Anomaly problem—the phenomenon seen occasionally in the interceptor's kill vehicle. They had been studying reams of test data to understand what was causing their sensor's eye to open and close, but it was tough work.

Raytheon in 2002 had opened its Space Factory as a state-of-the-art facility for the kill vehicle design team to work in. Now, printed schematics and diagrams covered floor-to-ceiling magnetic walls, equations were written and rewritten across yards of whiteboards, and offices were littered with models of missiles, miniature kill vehicles, Marvel comics posters, and *Star Wars*–movie action figures. But more important, this engineer's paradise had facilities to keep three-dimensional objects clean from even microscopic obstructions. Stainless steel covered the Space Factory's myriad test chambers, many of them used to simulate the chill of space. Sensors constantly measured the facility's air pressure and humidity, and could detect dirt particles on a nanometer scale. Cleaning crews would continually scrub floors and surfaces, and pumps would replace the air in some labs every twenty-seven seconds. Still, replicating the environment of outer space and the behavior of advanced optical tracking sensors traveling at thousands of miles per hour is difficult on Earth, even at the Space Factory.

The engineers had a theory, though, and flew out to MDA headquarters to brief Obering on the Track Gate Anomaly. "We think it's electromagnetic interference that's caused by ionization of the plume of the kill vehicle's directional rocket thrusters," the lead engineer told Obering. The general's fighter pilot manner belied his technical knowledge, his Stanford astronautical engineering degree, and his NASA experience. He thought for a minute. "That is ab-so-lute bullshit," he said in an Alabama drawl. "That's so far-fetched, I'm sorry, but I can't believe it."

Obering thought the ionization theory was ridiculous and wanted more data. He directed resources to add instrumentation to the kill vehicle so they might better understand the problem. On May 25, 2007, they would try another intercept test. This time an intercept would be the goal, both publicly and privately, and the kill vehicle would be specifically instrumented to gather data on the anomaly.

The test was a dud.

A target missile was launched from Kodiak Island in Alaska, but the target malfunctioned before it came within range for the missile crews to even begin tracking it, let alone take a shot with an interceptor. Four months later, Obering, MDA, Raytheon, the other contractors, and all the other hangers-on were ready to test again.

Meakins had just seen the movie *300*, a historical fantasy based on the Battle of Thermopylae. Gerard Butler starred as King

Leonidas, who led three hundred Spartan soldiers against an invading Persian force of three hundred thousand. The Spartans defended—to their death—a narrow coastal passage at Thermopylae. Meakins made the connection immediately. The 100th Missile Defense Brigade and the 49th Missile Defense Battalion added up to about three hundred soldiers. The US population was about three hundred million.

He arrived at brigade headquarters the next day, and told everyone: "We're the 300, defending 300 million!" It was partly in jest. Somebody took to Adobe Photoshop with a poster for the movie and put Meakins's head on Gerard Butler's muscles. Instead of a Spartan sword, he held an interceptor missile. In the background, instead of the Greek-Persian battle, were sepia-toned images of the SBX radar barge, a Humvee patrolling at Greely, and a soldier at his console in the node. At the bottom, instead of production credits, it said:

> In a world plagued by death and mayhem one unit stands ready to defend against intercontinental ballistic missile (ICBM) attacks on the entire continent of North America. The 100th Missile Defense Brigade (GMD) and the 49th Missile Defense Battalion (GMD) contain only 300 soldiers, but defend over 300 million Americans 24/7/365 using Ground-Based Interceptors located at Fort Greely, Alaska, and Vandenberg AFB, California. We 300 will protect all Americans. "Guard, Engage, Destroy."

It was a gag, but half-serious. "Guard, Engage, Destroy" was the official slogan. Lieutenant Colonel Greg Simpson, the Charlie crew director, had written up a whole document that explained the reasoning and symbolism for the unit's patch and slogan, and it was voted on by the soldiers and then officially approved by the Army Institute of Heraldry. Nonetheless, the soldiers began using Meakins's "300 defending 300 million" whenever they could sneak it in.

Simpson still liked to tease Meakins that it was actually his Charlie crew that had pulled the first real shift on the GMD system. Meakins teased Simpson that this couldn't have been the case, because Alpha crew meant they were the best, like the alpha wolf in a pack, so obviously they were placed first. Both Meakins and Simpson were "plank holders"—a term borrowed from the navy for those who were the very first to serve on a ship or, in the army's case, a new unit—and both had helped form the brigade into what it now was. They knew well that no crew was meant to be entirely all-stars, that the Alpha, Beta, Charlie, Delta, and Echo monikers were just alphabetic. They needled each other to keep things light in a job that could simultaneously be boring and stressful. Simpson in particular took the job as a powerful responsibility: launching a weapon into space to stop an incoming nuclear attack. He and Meakins both liked to compare the unit to the NASA astronaut program.

So, on September 28, 2007, as Simpson and Charlie crew walked down the long hallway at Schriever Air Force Base to the node, and sat down at their consoles, with a large crowd gathered behind to watch them at their craft, Simpson really did feel like he was something akin to an astronaut—carefully selected and trained to operate a complex defensive weapon system. He had fired off plenty of larger rounds as an air defense artillery officer, and had been a crew director during a GMD interceptor flight test, but never for an actual intercept attempt against a target. It was an easy scenario compared to their daily training, but there was palpable tension surrounding this mission.

After the failure in May, MDA mounted a camera on the target looking aft so they could watch to ensure the thing would successfully fly away from its launchpad on Kodiak Island. This time, it did. The target missile traveled southeast for about seventeen minutes. The big Soviet-era warning radar at Beale Air Force Base, just above Sacramento, tracked the target and sent guidance information to the interceptor at Vandenberg. Simpson gave the order to "go weapons free" and launch the interceptor. The silo's clamshell doors swung open, and the interceptor boosted up into space. About seven minutes after that, the interceptor's kill vehicle was racing westward, toward the target, when its sensor picked up a group of objects where the radar had said they would be.

The target did not use countermeasures, but debris from the boosters and other rubbish was flying along with the mock warhead. The sensor cycled through each of the objects, looking for its target. As it cycled through the objects, its algorithms were voting on which were debris and which was the target. It found it. The kill vehicle's thrusters pushed it into the faux warhead's path. It collided with and destroyed the target. Simpson and Charlie crew were pleased.

Obering was thrilled. Not only did he have an unqualified success with an operational interceptor, but the captured video was especially encouraging. It showed the kill vehicle cycling through debris and finding the right target. "When people say we don't have any ability against countermeasures, it's bullshit," Obering said. Complex countermeasures would be harder—such as a balloon meant to mimic the shape of the warhead—but Obering believed North Korea would not have anything more complex than the system had just dealt with.

MDA and Raytheon also now had more data on the Track Gate Anomaly. The data showed sporadic, high-frequency vibrations had likely been causing the sensor to stop tracking properly. Still, they could not figure out where those vibrations were coming from.

The on-site Sidelines Sports Bar sufficed for meetings of Fort Greely's Diligent Sentry Officers Association. But the Clearwater Lodge, about a twenty-minute drive from the post, was *the* hangout for the 49th Missile Defense Battalion. Built in 1954, the lodge had long been a favorite headquarters for snowmobilers, fishermen chasing Arctic grayling, and anyone who wanted a decent meal near Greely or Delta Junction. The lodge was quintessentially Alaskan. It was nested in a coniferous forest about fifty yards behind one of the many winding bends on the Clearwater River. Inside smelled strongly of stale cigarettes and musty creosote-treated timbers, like smoked meat.

Every time one of the battalion missile crews passed their biannual certification, every time a family member visited, every time a crew member departed for a new assignment—they went out for "a beer and a shot" at the Clearwater Lodge. They ate burgers and halibut and they stepped out back for some fresh air or a few casts into the river. And Echo crew was there on a beautiful June night to say farewell to Captain Mark Kiraly.

When the Kiralys first moved to Alaska in 2004, Mark had told Ruby, "You don't have to do anything. You can open a coffee shop if you want. You can do whatever." Ruby had been an engineer in Chicago, and after about three months of staying at home, she got restless and went back to work. She took a job with Boeing doing quality control on the missile field and worked alongside Mark Scott's wife, who also couldn't stand being at home any longer. But four years later, both Mark and Ruby were looking for new challenges.

In June Kiraly was on shift and talking on the phone with Captain Reggie Hammond, a current-operations officer on one of the brigade crews in Colorado Springs.

"Yeah, mama's getting tired of this up here," Kiraly told Hammond. "We'd like to come down to the Springs."

"Really? I'd actually like to get back up there," Hammond said. He'd served at Greely before and missed the environment there, the vast openness of Alaska and the tightly knit community at Greely. Since they were both captains, it could be an easy swap. They agreed right then to try.

Colonel Michael Yowell, the 100th's commander, was visiting Greely that day, and came into the node to say hello. Kiraly pulled him aside.

"Sir, you got any heartburn if me and Captain Hammond, we just do a one-for-one swap? He's wanting to come back to Fort Greely and I want to get out of Greely, and he said he'd do it and I said I'd do it." Yowell agreed. Within the hour Kiraly and Hammond each filled out Department of the Army Form 4187, and within the week their transfer was approved. The Kiralys sold their big cabin outside Delta Junction to the Scotts, and left.

By July 2008, Kiraly was settling into staff work at the brigade in Colorado Springs. The staff work was a relief. He was working for Meakins again, whom he'd worked for in the Illinois National Guard and who had recruited him into the homeland missile defense unit in the first place. It was mostly Monday through Friday, 8:00 A.M. to 5:00 P.M. If his kids got sick at school, he could leave to pick them up, and didn't have to worry about dressing them for recess at minus 20°F.

Kiraly pulled an occasional crew shift as an alternate current-operations officer to stay sharp. When he had been on crew at Greely, Kiraly and his soldiers did not like the brigade crews butting in, mucking around in their business, or even giving orders during an intercept mission. The battalion crews at Greely saw themselves as the primary warfighters— they would launch the interceptors, and were perhaps even a target themselves. The brigade crews in Colorado were one rank higher and were in charge of getting authorization to shoot, but if the battalion had a failure for whatever reason, the brigade could take over the fight, and vice versa.

From his seat at Greely, Kiraly had seen the brigade as a sort of annoying oversight, something that had to be dealt with, but that could be done without. In Colorado Springs, he was seething when he learned that most brigade crew members had a sort of derogatory, condescending view of the battalion crews at Greely. He thought, and said, that anyone who had not experienced the challenges at Greely should keep their mouth shut. He also thought, but did not say, that he was beginning to see how important the brigade crews were to the mission.

On January 11, 2007, Greg Simpson's Charlie crew had been on shift. The intelligence community was reporting that China might be soon testing a missile that could destroy satellites in space. Simpson and all the other crew directors were well aware of China's Xichang Space Launch Center, about forty miles northwest of Xichang in southern China and often used for a variety of peaceful satellite launches. But even publicly planned and announced space launches cued the unit's infrared satellite systems and set off the Quick Alerts. That Thursday, however, Simpson and Charlie crew watched a missile boost off from the launch center, travel 534 miles up, and destroy an inoperable Fengyun-1C weather satellite in low earth orbit.

About eleven months later, a week before Christmas, Obering received a call from Scott Large, the director of the National Reconnaissance Office. The NRO builds and operates American spy satellites, and Large wanted Obering to destroy a US satellite. Specifically, he wanted to destroy USA-193; it was meant to be a highly advanced spy satellite, but had proven a disastrous failure. USA-193 was launched in December 2006 and almost immediately lost contact. The satellite was having trouble staying in orbit and officials were, they said, concerned about its toxic hydrazine fuel tank. They took great care not to mention they were also concerned that China had successfully demonstrated an anti-satellite missile when it destroyed the Fengyun-1C weather satellite—a significant new capability for the Chinese military.

The Pentagon branded its own anti-satellite mission as humanitarian in nature, intended to protect civilians from the hydrazine fuel. It served two other important purposes. One was to destroy a secret spy satellite before it limped so close to Earth that any adversary with a decent telescope could get a good look at it. The second was to showcase that the United States could destroy satellites too. China could hit a satellite with a ground-launched missile. Fine. The United States would, in short order, modify a sea-launched missile to do the same.

Officially it would be a US Strategic Command mission because it was "offensive," but the Missile Defense Agency would do all the work with its contracted teams from Raytheon and Lockheed Martin. The agency chose to modify an SM-3 interceptor and launch it from USS *Lake Erie,* a Ticonderoga-class guided missile ship. The interceptor and the ship were both specifically chosen because of their test record. The SM-3 was a smaller but newer "hit-to-kill" interceptor in the same vein as the GMD homeland defense system. It was also created by Raytheon and relied on similar design concepts. But, unlike the long-range GMD, the shorter-range SM-3 and its Aegis software were not burdened by demands for rapid development and deployment. The engineering process unfolded more methodically, and it boasted a strong test record, scoring thirteen intercepts in fifteen tries. *Lake Erie,* meanwhile, had been involved in more interceptor tests than any other ship.

In January 2008, Bush approved the mission: Operation

Burnt Frost. On Valentine's Day, Vice Chairman of the Joint Chiefs of Staff General James Cartwright announced that the Pentagon would try to destroy the errant satellite. Six days later, just after lunch, Defense Secretary Robert Gates checked in with the White House and then approved the mission to go ahead.

Once again, Simpson's Charlie crew was on shift in the node at Schriever Air Force Base. They had been on shift and got the Quick Alert when the Chinese launched their anti-satellite interceptor the year before. Now, at 8:26 P.M., they got another Quick Alert when sailors aboard *Lake Erie* fired off their own interceptor from the Pacific Ocean. Charlie crew's running joke that day was: *If the navy misses, can we try?* A few minutes later, the navy's weapon collided with and destroyed the USA-193 satellite.

The other running joke was that Michalski was about to be sent back to Poland. It was half-serious. MDA had been working to implement a White House plan to get ten interceptors deployed in Poland—to mirror the setup in the Pacific but on the other side of the globe to address a possible Iranian missile threat. The Bush administration had been quietly working this idea since 2002, and Obering had been involved nearly as long. Throughout 2007 and 2008 he had been flying in and out of Brussels, briefing NATO leaders constantly, but they were not particularly excited about the Bush administration's plan.

Then Russian tanks rolled into Georgia and annexed its South Ossetia region. Other Eastern European countries were alarmed, and Polish leaders suddenly liked the idea of having US Army soldiers and weapons based permanently in their country.

By August 2008 a deal was reached and the Polish government agreed to have the interceptors there. A gigantic SBX radar would be shipped to Europe and placed in a heavily forested military training area in the Czech Republic, which the previous year had agreed to host it. Another TPY-2 radar could be sent someplace else in Europe, and the system could use an existing ballistic missile warning radar at RAF Fylingdales, a British air station in northern England. All this was projected to cost about $3.9 billion and be ready by 2012.

The soldiers at the brigade expected Michalski to be running the operation in Poland—he was born there and Polish was still the primary language spoken in his parents' home. Northern Command and the brigade had even trotted Michalski out once during an official visit from the Polish prime minister. Michalski gave the "change-over" briefing in Polish, updating the incoming Northern Command watch director of the crews' status, how many interceptors were available for launch, and so on. He found the experience oddly funny.

Michalski had lived in Poland until he was six and spoke the language fluently, but his briefing was choppy at best. Words like "interceptor" didn't translate easily—nor did the many military acronyms and portmanteaus—and, although it was all for the benefit of the visiting minister, Michalski was briefing an American watch director who couldn't understand a single word. Still, he wanted to support the effort

Fort Greely, Alaska, circa 2003. *(US Army photo)*

Soldiers from one of the first Ground-based Midcourse Defense Qualification Courses. *(US Army photo)*

· Training inside an early version of the missile defense operations node. *(US Army photo)*

· Dan Austin, left, and Dave Meakins training. *(US Army photo)*

Marcus Kent, center, in a missile defense operations node. *(US Army photo)*

Utilidors being dug at Fort Greely. *(US Army photo)*

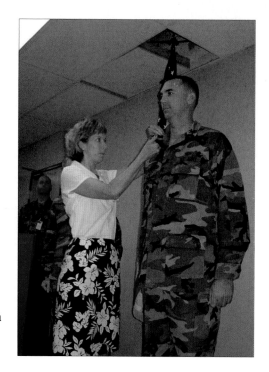

Dave Meakins during a
promotion ceremony.
(US Army photo)

From left, Marcus Kent sits beside Greg Bowen and Russell Hamilton, then brigade commander and command sergeant major, respectively, during Kent's promotion to Warrant Officer 1. *(US Army photo, Benjamin Crane)*

Greg Bowen during a ceremony at Fort Greely. *(US Army photo)*

Bowen hands the guidon to Captain Orlando Cobos, signifying Cobos's assumption of command and activation in 2011 of "Detachment One," the brigade's unit at Vandenberg. *(US Army photo, Benjamin Crane)*

The SBX traveled from Hawaii to Alaska's Aleutian Islands in early 2007. *(Missile Defense Agency photo)*

Military police with Alpha Company, 49th Missile Defense Battalion, patrol the Missile Defense Complex at Fort Greely. *(US Army photo, Jennifer Staton)*

Staff Sergeant Jamie Montes, an MP with Alpha Company, 49th Missile Defense Battalion, on patrol at Fort Greely. *(US Army photo, Zachary Sheely)*

Bill Spriggs, right, shakes hands with Greg Bowen, then brigade commander, during Spriggs's retirement. *(US Army photo, Benjamin Crane)*

Marcus Kent, left, and Richard Michalski on their consoles at Schriever Air Force Base, circa 2014. *(US Army photo)*

The Clearwater Lodge entrance. The lodge was rebuilt in 2016 after it was destroyed by a fire in 2014. *(courtesy of the author)*

The Clearwater Lodge's back deck, overlooking a bend in the Clearwater River. *(courtesy of the author)*

A guard post at Fort Greely. *(courtesy of the author)*

The 100th Missile Defense Brigade's Charlie crew, with Richard Michalski, far right, pose for a photo at Schriever Air Force Base in 2018. Michalski, in a real mission, would be unlikely to look away from his own console. *(US Army photo, Ronald Bailey)*

Ground-based Interceptors launched from Vandenberg Air Force Base on March 25, 2019, in the first salvo engagement test against an ICBM-range target. The two GBIs intercepted a target launched from Kwajalein Atoll. *(US Missile Defense Agency photo, Lisa Simunaci)*

to get the interceptors in Poland, and wanted to be sent there to lead the effort. GMD's European site was to be in Redzikowo, a lush area in northern Poland near the Baltic Sea. Michalski would happily move his family there if he could.

John Robinson was at his house on Fort Greely when Jarrod Cuthbertson stopped by. Robinson was the platoon sergeant, the noncommissioned officer leading Cuthbertson's platoon, so he figured the young soldier was looking for some advice. Cuthbertson was actually looking for Robinson's daughter, and figured this was as good a time as any to reveal that he had been dating the platoon sergeant's oldest child. It was a small town and an even smaller post, so Robinson couldn't fault them for finding each other. Not long after that they were married. In October 2008 they welcomed a baby boy. With a wife and newborn, Cuthbertson left the shift work of the MP unit and moved into an administrative role for the battalion. Things had slowed down somewhat for the jocular leader of the Seat Belt Police.

A month later, in Washington, things were about to significantly change for the Missile Defense Agency too. Since July 2003 Obering had been MDA's deputy director and then its director. He had lived and breathed missile defense for more than five years. Obering loved the people he worked with and was in awe of the technological capability his agency commanded. But it was time to get fresh eyes on the problem. On November 21, 2008, Obering handed MDA over to Army Lieutenant General Patrick O'Reilly.

Missile defense had been new to Obering at the start of

his tenure, and he approached it more as a top-level manager. O'Reilly was steeped in it. During his career, he had served in both command and staff officer positions, and as an army physics professor. He had tours as program manager for developmental laser weapons, Patriot air and missile defense systems, Terminal High Altitude Area Defense interceptors, the GMD itself, and more. He was a West Point graduate with master's degrees in physics, national security and strategic studies, and business. On paper, O'Reilly could hardly have been a better fit for the job.

Obering was happy to be leaving after a successful intercept test and a successful Operation Burnt Frost, but it was still a bittersweet moment. After the change-of-command ceremony was over, Obering pulled O'Reilly aside. "Don't fuck it up," he said.

13

THE CULLING

CAPTAIN RON "BEETLE" BAILEY walked from his house on Fort Greely to the Missile Defense Complex. It was December 5, 2008, and it was a relatively balmy 8°F. He was used to much worse and regularly made the walk at minus 40°F or colder, in a steady wind. Bailey did not want to be late, partly because he loved his job, partly because being late meant he would have to bring donuts for the entire crew, but mostly because this would be his and the battalion's first time launching an interceptor missile for a live test.

Bailey had been at Greely for more than three years and was immensely proud of his work. He'd gone there to see Alaska but found that the state's natural wonders were just a side benefit compared to the feeling of being on a battalion missile crew. Being on crew made him a part of history. It also made his family part of a larger surrogate family now fully formed by the soldiers at Greely. Bailey had grown up in a tiny farming community and was pleased that he and his wife could raise their two boys among a similarly cohesive group.

None of the soldiers on post—aside from true-local Jeanette Padgett—had any relatives within hundreds or thousands of miles, so the unit became everyone's extended family. Bailey liked that if somebody was making the trip up to Fairbanks, they'd ask around to see if anyone needed anything. He liked that the community cared for its own with things like a "winter tracker" hotline—and called the hotline to make sure they knew when he was driving up to civilization through bad weather. He once forgot to let the hotline operator know that he had arrived safely in Fairbanks, so they called to check in. When Bailey confirmed that he was okay, the operator asked if, since Bailey was okay and in Fairbanks, he could please help so-and-so haul a large treadmill back to Greely, and he gladly did.

Bailey was the deputy director for Charlie crew, and on that enjoyably mild December morning, Charlie crew was firing off an interceptor from Vandenberg against a target launching from Kodiak. They would be using targeting data from a TPY-2 radar in Juneau and the big Upgraded Early Warning Radar at Beale Air Force Base in California. It would also use an Aegis SPY-1 radar on guided-missile destroyer USS *Higgins* sailing near Alaska, and the massive SBX radar chugging along off the coast of Southern California. Most important, it would be the first time they tested an operational interceptor against a target with complex countermeasures. It was going to be a challenging day.

For Bailey and Charlie crew, the mission itself was less complex than their training. It was, however, equally as serious. The crew was eager to get the live data collected from their weapon in action; they were also a little more anxious given the added pressure of thirty extra people crammed into the node watching their every move. The audience was a constant reminder of how important, extensive, and expensive each of these tests was.

The December test alone would cost more than $210 million. Just preparing each handmade interceptor was a major undertaking. For this test, the kill vehicle was built at Raytheon's Space Factory in Tucson, Arizona, it was then attached to an avionics module in Huntsville, Alabama, before being shipped off to Vandenberg where the three-stage booster rocket was assembled, stacked, and armed with the kill vehicle.

The Missile Defense Agency planned to soon give the missile crews a new, second-generation interceptor—but before that, they wanted to gather data on how the first-generation weapon handled difficult countermeasures. MDA had planned to do two such tests to gather that data, but the first never happened. It had been scheduled for early 2007, but suffered four lengthy delays. By May 2008, Obering had decided to delay the test a fifth time after manufacturing defects were discovered in a telemetry device that was needed to transmit valuable flight test data from space. A week later, Obering canceled the test entirely, deciding that it wasn't worth holding up the rest of the program. Instead, the December 2008 test, now under O'Reilly's watch, would be the only opportunity to demonstrate the interceptor against a warhead carrying countermeasures, devices meant to distract or fool it into striking the wrong object.

The target launched from Kodiak, flew southeast, was tracked by the radar in Juneau, then by the radar on *Higgins*, and then by the big radar at Beale. With those radar reference points, Bailey and Charlie crew cued the SBX radar where to look in space so it too could track the target. The brigade crew gave the order to "go weapons free" and Charlie crew launched the interceptor. It hit and destroyed its target.

The target, however, had failed to release its countermeasures.

It was a successful intercept, but the test did not achieve its goal and MDA and the missiles crews did not get their data on how the system worked against complicated defenses.

MDA's plan had been to take one big step in each test. The first-generation interceptors had been proven against simple targets during the 2006 and 2007 tests, then they were supposed to be proven against a better defended target before the agency moved on to testing the newer second-generation interceptor. Because of the target failures and manufacturing issues, the first-generation weapons had now only been tested against simple targets without countermeasures. MDA pushed this requirement to its next test, which would now have to assess, for the first time, both a brand-new interceptor and a "complex target scene." Instead of healthy strides in each test, all the delays and cancelations meant the agency would have to strain for giant leaps.

The missile crews had twenty-four of the first-generation interceptors waiting in their silos. The second-generation interceptors had not yet been tested but were already being lowered into silos too. MDA was working to get a total of forty-four interceptors ready in the next two years.

On the evening of April 5, 2009, Mark Kiraly was in the basement of the brigade headquarters, pulling a Sunday shift as the battle captain in charge of the Brigade Operations

Center, or the BOC. The brigade was under a "period of interest" as intelligence reports suggested North Korea might soon attempt to launch a three-stage Unha-2 rocket from the Tonghae Satellite Launching Ground. It was ostensibly a satellite launch vehicle, but was based upon the Taepodong-2 and was by most accounts an intercontinental ballistic missile test.

Kiraly called upstairs to Colonel Mike Yowell, commander of the 100th Missile Defense Brigade, to tell him the intelligence reports were now suggesting the launch appeared imminent. Yowell made his way down to the BOC.

The brigade's crews might have the most consequential jobs in the United States if nuclear war ever morphed from nightmare to reality. The brigade's commander, however, had a largely managerial job. At the unit's headquarters by the Colorado Springs airport, the commander was, indeed, in command. But, once a crew walked into its secure operating node a few miles down the road at Schriever Air Force Base, they were no longer directly under his authority. The brigade itself was part of the Colorado National Guard and reported to the governor of Colorado, but once in the node the crews became part of the US national command structure and reported to the president of the United States.

The brigade commander was responsible for everything that happened outside the node but did not have an operational role and usually lacked the crew members' specific expertise anyway, and so he was not to interfere during a mission. He still needed to be aware of what was happening, and having him call in to the node would have been a needless distraction. So the BOC was established to give the brigade commander some idea of just what was going on during a real mission. It was a "sensitive compartmented information facility"—a room with secured communications gear—in the basement of brigade headquarters, intended to give the commander a place to soak in whatever information he might need.

The BOC, unlike the nodes, did not have the operating consoles or access to the global radar and satellite network or the communications Ops Loop. There was no alert system. It had access to intelligence reports through official army lines, and several televisions showing cable news. Yowell and Kiraly stood in the BOC, eagerly waiting for an update. *Had the North Koreans launched?*

The North Koreans had launched. Yowell and Kiraly learned this by looking up at the television tuned to CNN.

While the BOC was no better informed than anyone with cable TV, the brigade and battalion crews were, of course, tracking the entire event. The Unha-2 got farther than its predecessors. It was supposed to have put a small satellite into orbit, and Pyongyang claimed it succeeded, but the crews saw that the rocket's third booster stage appeared to have failed. The rocket's final stage, along with the satellite payload, lurched back toward earth and crashed into the Pacific Ocean, about two thousand miles from the launch site.

The day after the Unha-2 nose-dived into the Pacific, Secretary of Defense Robert Gates announced his recommendation that Congress cut the MDA's budget by $1.4 billion.

"We will not increase the number of current ground-based

interceptors in Alaska, as had been planned," he told reporters at the Pentagon. Funding would instead go toward improving GMD's ability against a limited long-range missile attack, "a threat North Korea's missile launch this past weekend reminds us is real."

Gates and the new Obama administration were plotting a strategic shift, away from a focus on conventional war against Russia or China, to also include the sort of unconventional conflicts that had been simmering since 2001. This meant a shift away from some costly weapons designed for high-end warfare, and toward adding soldiers and marines and buying the sort of intelligence gear and mine-resistant vehicles designed for counterinsurgency. The US economy was doing terribly, and the military campaigns in Iraq and Afghanistan were straining to maintain fragile gains. Regional missile defense would be a cheaper and easier mission, with an impact on conflicts in Iraq and Afghanistan.

A month later, on May 25, North Korea detonated what appeared to be a small nuclear weapon. This time, it was not an obvious dud. The test had an explosive yield of more than 2 kilotons. For good measure, North Korea also took the occasion to fire off two missiles that day and then three more the next. The nuke was still just a fraction of World War II–era yields and the missiles were short-range, but it was not an encouraging few days.

At MDA, things were even less encouraging. Aside from budget cuts to some of the agency's long-standing programs, O'Reilly was moving to revamp the agency, which he felt was bloated and inefficient. O'Reilly believed he had inherited a poorly functioning organization that was about to undergo unpopular cuts and unpopular office moves—a congressional Base Realignment and Closure Commission had ordered most of his staff to move to new offices (or resign) within two years. The headquarters was moving from the old Navy Annex near the Pentagon to Fort Belvoir in Virginia. The building would be new and facilities far more high-tech, and though it was only twenty miles south of Washington, it was typically a heavily congested hour-long drive. On top of that, O'Reilly was seeking to eliminate thirteen hundred contractor support positions, to hold new competitive bids for contracts, and to begin meticulous program reviews.

To run the agency, make executive decisions about major acquisitions, and supervise the forty-two program managers that reported directly to him, O'Reilly instituted execution reviews for all the projects and created new program executive positions, an executive management board, and an executive management council. Obering had held ongoing meetings with all the colonels (and civilian equivalents) or higher, but O'Reilly's interaction with the staff went far deeper.

Anonymous complaints about his hands-on leadership style began trickling into the Pentagon. Some of the complaints were dismissed as grumblings from contractors who were losing cushy jobs. To his bosses, O'Reilly appeared to be an outstanding director and a brilliant technical mind. Many MDA personnel did not believe he was an outstanding director, but nearly everyone agreed that O'Reilly was intellectually gifted and an extraordinarily hard worker. His technical brilliance meant that, in many cases, he understood the programs and their underlying technologies better than the experts running those programs.

O'Reilly had also called up a suddenly out-of-work Michael Griffin. When the Obama administration took office and began nominating its own personnel, Griffin found himself without a job. His unemployment did not last long.

Griffin had a bachelor's degree in physics from Johns Hopkins University, a master's degree in aerospace science from Catholic University, another master's degree in electrical engineering from the University of Southern California, an additional master's degree in applied physics from Johns Hopkins University, still another master's degree in civil engineering from George Washington University, and a master's degree in business administration from Loyola University. He also had a Ph.D. in aerospace engineering from the University of Maryland. Griffin had worked for years on missile defense and held positions at Johns Hopkins University's Applied Physics Laboratory, NASA's Jet Propulsion Laboratory, and as the deputy for technology on Reagan's Star Wars program—he called himself an "unreconstructed cold warrior."

He had been the NASA administrator during the second half of the Bush administration and was hoping Obama would keep him on, but on January 21, 2009, he was replaced. The next day, O'Reilly called and asked if he'd come to Huntsville to lead a "red team review" trying to solve the Track Gate Anomaly problem. Griffin was pleased to do so. He settled right into the Track Gate Anomaly team, and also took a position as the King-McDonald Eminent Scholar and professor of mechanical and aerospace engineering at the University of Alabama in Huntsville.

The original theory that the kill vehicle's tracking issues were caused by electromagnetic interference was proven to be, as Obering had put it, absolute bullshit. Sporadic, high-frequency vibrations that overloaded the tracking systems were determined to be the cause, but the origin of those vibrations was especially hard to find. A series of solutions to the problem were proposed and O'Reilly ordered the fixes to be implemented and tested the next year.

Meanwhile, Michalski's thoughts of possibly moving back to his brief childhood home to run the European GMD site were firmly done away with on September 17, 2009. The Obama administration had just finished a wide-ranging ballistic missile defense review, and decided the Polish site for strategic defense was no longer a good idea.

Gates instead that day revealed a new plan to send SM-3 interceptors—the same type Obering had used to destroy the errant spy satellite—into Europe on land and at sea to defend regional targets against Iran's growing stock of shorter-range missiles. Gates had recommended the European GMD site to the Bush White House in December 2006, when the intelligence community was reporting rapid progress in Iran's effort to build intercontinental ballistic missiles. Now, however, the intelligence community assessed that those efforts had slowed, and that Iran was progressing faster with short- and medium-range ballistic missiles.

In the Pentagon briefing room, the very first question reporters asked Gates: Was the Obama administration scrapping GMD in Europe as an overture to Russia? It was a good question; Obama was scheduled the next week to meet with Russian president Dmitry Medvedev, who adamantly opposed Bush's plan.

"The decisions on this were driven, I would say, almost exclusively by the changed intelligence assessment and the enhanced technology," Gates said. He noted that Russia would be displeased with any US missile defense efforts in Europe, but added that two key changes would "allay some of their, what we think, unfounded concerns."

One of Russia's concerns was that the big GMD interceptors in Poland could be fitted with nuclear warheads and become an offensive weapon. The other concern, which was perhaps more legitimate, was that the powerful 360-degree SBX radar in the Czech Republic would be able to see into Russian territory. The new plan used SM-3 interceptors that were too small to host a nuclear warhead, and a less powerful radar that could look in only one direction.

O'Reilly stepped in to defend the new plan too. He was quick to note that ten GMD interceptors in Europe to defend against the new projected threat—a bevy of smaller Iranian missiles—was not a good investment. The twenty-five-ton, $75 million interceptors would be wasted against the slower, shorter-range missiles. Instead, O'Reilly argued, it would be better to send up the two-ton, $10 million SM-3 interceptors.

The move was criticized by many Republicans but ultimately was not blocked. It was backed by Gates—a Republican and former CIA director for Ronald Reagan and George H. W.

Bush—but it also represented a sort of middle ground: Obama wasn't outright canceling the European interceptor program as some Democrats wanted, he was scaling it back from a strategic homeland defense effort to a more tactical regional defense effort, and was promising to get the equipment there seven years sooner.

The culture shock of coming to or leaving from Greely was, mostly, a novelty. For the soldiers who wanted to live life at a remote Alaskan post, the latest social trends in the Lower 48 were fascinating. They had friends and family in American towns who regularly used iPhones to hail a car or order food for delivery. Meanwhile, some of the soldiers living in Delta Junction kept cabins that could be reached only by boat or snowmobile, and instead of ordering whatever dinner they pleased on a nightly basis, many of them planned each season's storage of hunted fish and meat. Services like Uber or Grubhub were not available in the area, and sometimes timely emergency services weren't either.

John Robinson and his family, originally from Florida, had thrived in Alaska for four years, but the time had come for some changes. In December 2009 Robinson was assigned as a future-operations officer and joined Ron Hoard's Bravo crew at the brigade.

"Beetle" Bailey's walk, the previous December, to the Missile Defense Complex had been pleasant enough, but harsher weather had soon blown into Greely. It had been an unfortunately cold and miserable summer, and soldiers and their families had been hoping for a mild winter but didn't get it. The weather was bad enough that Robinson's wife was stricken with SAD. To maintain morale, Robinson held potlucks with his platoon's families in the chapel at Greely, just to get everyone together to see how they were doing.

Then Robinson's number had come up for a shot at the GMD Qualification Course, to leave the MP unit and become a crew member. If a spot opened, he could move to Colorado Springs. He took it. Robinson graduated from the course in April. There were no jobs for him at brigade yet, so he came back to the battalion in Alaska and managed Greely's antiterrorism / force protection program until he could transfer. The opportunity came in December, so Robinson packed up his house and wife and two daughters, said goodbye to the daughter now growing a family with Cuthbertson, and drove six hundred miles through Canada down to Haines, Alaska, took a ferry to Washington State, and then drove the remaining fifteen hundred miles to Colorado Springs. All in ten days, in winter.

14

MANAGEMENT BY
BLOWTORCH AND PLIERS

STAFF SERGEANT PATRICIA YOUNG had never heard of the 100th Missile Defense Brigade or its mission of guarding the United States against nuclear strikes. And that was odd, because she worked down the road in Colorado Springs at Army Space and Missile Defense Command, one of the unit's supervisory commands. None of her friends had heard about the brigade or its mission either. But the 100th was hiring and Young needed a new job. She was an active-duty soldier, pregnant with her first child, and was coming up on another permanent change of station. To keep the family in place, Young's husband got out of the army and she took the job at the mysterious unit.

With experience at Army Space and Missile Defense Command, she was a good candidate for the GMD Qualification Course. Young successfully completed the course while still pregnant, so they didn't put her on crew for a few months. She had her son in March 2009 and six weeks later was pulling shifts on Echo crew as the readiness officer. The shift schedules more or less worked out. Sometimes she could come home, hang out with her son, then go to sleep while he was off to day care. She could volunteer at the day care during her off days, and shopping in an empty supermarket on a Tuesday at 2:00 P.M. was great. She was also meeting an interesting flock of new soldiers.

One of those soldiers was Meakins, who was now off crew and running operations and training for the brigade. Another was Greg Bowen, who was back with the homeland missile defense mission, and now commanding the brigade as a full colonel. Leading the brigade in Colorado Springs was wholly different from building the battalion on the Alaskan frontier. Suffice to say, it was more bureaucratic. Meakins spent so much time in Bowen's office helping to navigate that bureaucracy that he printed himself a name tag and taped it to a chair. Only Meakins could sit there.

Bowen spent the majority of his time dealing with the unit's two bosses: Army Space and Missile Defense Command, and US Northern Command. He was shuttling between the two while trying to lead the brigade and expand it to California and Japan. A detachment was finally sent to Vandenberg to help run tests and oversee the handful of interceptors deployed at the missile field there. Another detachment would soon be sent to Shariki, Japan, to help run the TPY-2 radar there that monitored for North Korean missiles.

Bolstering the Shariki site was particularly difficult. It had been up and running since 2007 (October 2006, officially, but it was not fully set up until the next year). The radar's mission was supposed to be led by the army, but it was Missile Defense Agency equipment, operated by Raytheon employees, and guarded by Chenega Blackwater Solutions—a joint venture between Chenega Security and Blackwater. The entire US Army contingent at Shariki consisted of First Sergeant Ben Williams and Captain Will Hunter. Bowen was plotting to get them some backup.

MDA had been deploying the much-anticipated second-generation interceptors to Fort Greely. It had not been tested in an intercept yet, but Raytheon and agency officials hoped the newer equipment might move them past the manufacturing problems they had suffered through on the first generation, and move them past the Track Gate Anomaly. They also now had Raytheon's SBX radar barge in the Pacific to provide an especially high-resolution radar picture.

A January 31 test was planned to validate the new and improved system. The weapon had never flown before, but it would launch from Vandenberg, fly out over the Pacific Ocean, and intercept a target defended by simple countermeasures. The target would, for the first time, launch out of Kwajalein Atoll in the Marshall Islands. It was a longer and more difficult mission than intercepting targets flying out of Kodiak (the target doesn't fly the entire distance, but Kwajalein is about twice as far from Vandenberg so the target can achieve higher speeds). The SBX radar would track the target and help guide the interceptor.

At 4:40 P.M., in the node at Schriever Air Force Base, the Quick Alert announced the target missile had been launched from Kwajalein. It was flying east toward California. About six minutes later, one of the new second-generation interceptors was launched from Vandenberg. The interceptor flew toward its target.

Then it flew past its target.

At some point the gigantic SBX radar had stopped providing tracking data to the interceptor; it seemed to have shut itself down. O'Reilly, the MDA engineers, and Raytheon engineers at first thought the radar had caused the kill vehicle to miss its target. A closer investigation, however, uncovered the sort of workmanship issue that had dogged the program from the beginning. A manufacturing technician hadn't installed a small part, known as a lockwire, which caused the kill vehicle's thrusters to malfunction. It was a small error that ruined a $236 million test.

A few weeks after the failed test, O'Reilly and some MDA staff had flown out to Tucson for an executive steering committee and to meet with a Japanese delegation to discuss the agency's assets in Japan and their shared interest in defending against North Korean missiles.

O'Reilly's agency was strained. It was no longer operating as the sort of advanced technology research-and-development organization that had originally been envisioned. During Kadish's and Obering's times as director, the agency had the latitude to throw ideas against the wall, and see what stuck. Some of those ideas, like the GMD system, had since become established programs with budget lines and equipment and interested parties in Congress.

MDA had evolved from a development agency to a development, deployment, management, and sustainment agency—and after the 2008 financial crisis, it could not count on congressional largesse at budget time. Necessity had driven the agency to become more cautious. All this weighed on its brilliant, mercurial director.

It was around 2:00 A.M. when O'Reilly and his staff arrived at the JW Marriott Starr Pass Resort in Tucson. They had suffered through hours of flight delays and O'Reilly was exhausted. He was also angry to find his staff had booked such a fancy hotel. A resort! Secretary of Defense Robert Gates had told department leadership not to hold meetings at resorts, not while they were begging Congress for each dime in the Pentagon's $712 billion budget proposal. O'Reilly had told his own people not to stay in resorts, so why were they here now? He asked why, and did not get a satisfying answer. He checked in and got his room key from the front desk, then again demanded to know why they were staying at a resort, which he had expressly forbidden.

O'Reilly tracked down the MDA staffer who had arranged the trip, and cornered him in a hallway near the lobby elevators. O'Reilly again asked why they were at a "resort" but was still not satisfied with the answer. He lost it. Pointing a finger at the staffer and screaming at the top of his lungs, O'Reilly leaned in to a ten-minute verbal flogging in the public lobby hallway.

"I see no remorse on your face! You fucked up, you tell me you fucked up, you admit you fucked up! This is fucking unacceptable to me!" This went on at full volume. Other MDA personnel checking in at the front desk could hear, and after a few minutes began to worry that they would all be kicked out of the hotel—or resort.

The baleful staffer tried to explain that the JW Marriott Starr Pass Resort was chosen because the Japanese delegation wanted to share a hotel with the MDA delegation, and availability, location, and an on-site restaurant for a planned dinner were the key factors. Plus, the hotel, or resort, rates were within the per diem limit. But O'Reilly would not end the public lambasting unless the staffer admitted he fucked up. The staffer said he didn't use profanity. "I want you to tell me that you 'fucked up.'" Eventually, the staffer relented: "I fucked up."

Later that day, after the executive steering committee meeting had ended, O'Reilly thanked the staffer for arranging the trip, and gave him a commemorative MDA Director's coin.

O'Reilly raised even more eyebrows with his reaction, a few months later, to a test that had been successful, but for which his phone line at headquarters had not functioned as he'd requested. The agency was testing a prototype of a new interceptor concept: using a two-stage booster rocket instead of the three-stage booster.

The idea was that adding a two-stage interceptor would give the crews a wider window for intercepting warheads. The kill vehicle could not separate from the booster until after the rocket motors burned out, so having one less rocket stage meant the kill vehicle could begin hunting its target in space about seventy seconds earlier. All this meant was that intercepts could happen later in the battle, when the warheads were closer to earth. It meant more options.

The test, on Sunday, June 6, 2010, had gone well. Even the Pentagon's scrupulous testing directorate gave the event a thumbs-up, stating, with its typical nonchalance, that the "two-stage interceptor could prove a viable boost vehicle."

O'Reilly's staff were ready for a rare high-five moment. But everything wasn't perfect.

O'Reilly was dialed into the test via a video-teleconference from his headquarters, which was now up and running at Fort Belvoir in Virginia. The audio connection was not "open," however, as O'Reilly had wanted it to be. After the test, from an adjacent room, MDA personnel could hear O'Reilly tear into his executive officer and deputy director. What followed was mostly profane screaming about how they did not know what they were doing, they did not follow the plan, they were ill prepared, and on and on.

Everyone agreed O'Reilly was a missile defense virtuoso—a remarkable thinker who knew his subordinates' business better than they did. He was driven, dedicated, and armed with exacting technical knowledge. O'Reilly held daily meetings with his team, grilling and correcting them on the minutiae of their projects, but his temper was getting the best of him and O'Reilly was screaming at the managers when they fell short of his expectations. The staff began morbidly noting that O'Reilly's leadership approach was "management by blowtorch and pliers."

In June 2010, Kiraly was ready for some time off crew. He had been steadily doing shift work on missile crews since 2006. He'd been on crew about two years at the battalion at Greely, and then on and off crews or serving as an alternate crew member for another two years at the brigade in Colorado. Kiraly took a two-year billet as the administrative officer for the nearby Colorado Army National Guard Training Center.

His new job was to help mobilize guardsmen from Colorado that were deploying across the world. Kiraly planned to return to the brigade, and wanted to get on crew again, but first he wanted to enjoy a normal work schedule (and to perhaps sneak in a combat tour in Iraq or Afghanistan). The training center was more of a nine-to-five job with flexibility to spend time with his sons, coaching their baseball and Pop Warner football teams—the sort of parental commitments that were nearly impossible when on crew.

Michalski, on the other hand, had rarely left crew life. He was a tennis pro at a racquet club in Colorado Springs, but could coach on whatever schedule he pleased—including lessons for his young daughter. Michalski had served as a current-operations officer, then as a deputy director, then come off crew for most of 2008 to lead the brigade's operational readiness evaluation team, which ensured the crews' tactics were up-to-date and tested the crews for their certifications. He then went back on as a deputy director for about ten months before a director position on Charlie crew opened in October 2010. Michalski got it. He was leading a brigade crew. It would be his order to launch the interceptors, his responsibility to destroy enemy nuclear warheads. And two months later he would be leading Charlie crew on shift for the second GMD intercept test that year, a retry of the failed attempt from January.

On December 15, Michalski's soldiers began their shift at Schriever, knowing they would be participating in MDA's second-generation interceptor test. The new kill vehicles had been fitted on ten of the thirty interceptors now deployed with the unit, but they had not yet been proven.

The target launched as planned from Kwajalein in the Pacific, Michalski and his crew tracked it, and Michalski gave the order to "go weapons free." The interceptor's booster lifted it off from Vandenberg and up into space, as the SBX radar continued to send along tracking data. The kill vehicle separated from its booster and set off on its path toward the target, which it then flew blindly past. The intercept failed.

It was a depressing result, especially for the soldiers on Charlie crew. They had just done everything right. They knew their weapon was under scrutiny, and considered by many critics as an expensive boondoggle. Two big failures in one year would not help.

Michalski tried to perk up his crew: "How often do you send a soldier into battle with one round in his weapon?" Never, he told them. In testing, only one interceptor was launched, but in combat they would fire as many as five at each incoming warhead. They planned for misses because it's rare for every bullet to hit its target—especially a target moving through space at fifteen thousand miles per hour. Michalski wanted his crew to approach their jobs with this frame of mind, confident in their ability to use their weapon, and to overcome whatever defects it might have.

Michalski's pep talk would have been little consolation for the engineers at MDA. The analysis from the test showed this was not some easily fixable workmanship problem. It was not a manufacturing process that could be done differently in the future, or addressed with a new widget. It was the Track Gate Anomaly that had been observed in the past. It was high frequency vibrations causing the system's navigation and tracking to shift off target as it rocketed through space. Except it was no longer an anomaly; now it was a failure mode. MDA and Raytheon had tried to design fixes for it, but those changes appeared to have made it worse. Now they had a systemic engineering problem to solve.

O'Reilly ordered a halt to deliveries of the next-generation interceptors, and said he would not accept any more until they could be proven with a successful intercept. MDA and Raytheon's engineers went to work, with Michael Griffin leading a red team to review the failed test and second-guess any design changes. The ten next-generation interceptors that had already been delivered would have to wait for the engineered fixes. They would have to be retrofitted with a working kill vehicle.

Anthony Ray Montoya—the young noncommissioned officer whose first day at Greely was spent visiting Dale Titus, the bear attack victim—made a smart but counterintuitive career move. He had served on several battalion missile crews in several roles, but had transferred to the MP company to lead a platoon. Though much colder work, it would add leadership experience to his résumé.

Montoya knew the battalion crew jobs well. He had been on Alpha crew, Bravo crew, and Echo crew. He had been a communications operator and a weapons operator, then went to Officer Candidate School and came back on crew as a lieutenant and a sensors operator. Montoya had married, and then taken advantage of the Storknesting program in Fairbanks when his wife gave birth to their first child. To keep his promising career moving, he needed leadership time as an officer.

The fifty soldiers in the MP company's 1st Platoon were given to Montoya. He was a quick learner and smart enough to tread carefully around the platoon sergeant, who was older, more experienced, and just a few months earlier had been two ranks senior. Now the platoon sergeant reported to Montoya.

Most things in Alaska were somewhat different than in the Lower 48, and leading soldiers was too. Montoya had to worry about his platoon's mission of guarding the Missile Defense Complex, but he also had to worry about his platoon's safety. As soon as they stepped off Greely, they became part of the food chain. One of Montoya's soldiers rolled his car driving through icy conditions, another had to be airlifted to the hospital in Fairbanks after a snowmobile accident. He warned them to travel in groups, have a plan, learn how to use a snowmobile before riding one into the mountains, learn how to ice fish before cutting a hole in a frozen lake.

Montoya, a New Mexico native who was not especially fond of the cold, was sent to an elite army cold-weather training course at the Northern Warfare Training Center, fondly known as Black Rapids, in the heart of the Alaska Range mountains south of Delta Junction. He learned to ski and snowshoe and bivouac, to survive and lead soldiers in the wilderness at forty below.

15

USEFUL FAILURES

THE DECEMBER 15 GMD test was a failure, but it was a tremendously useful failure from an engineering standpoint. Raytheon developers, MDA engineers, and Griffin's red team were working on the Track Gate Anomaly around the clock at the Space Factory in Tucson and at MDA's facilities in Huntsville, Alabama. Data from the December test was beginning to frame the problem more clearly. It pointed to the possibility of an unstable thruster on the next-generation kill vehicle. The kill vehicles had been upgraded with a more sensitive navigation system (specifically, it was a component known as the inertial measurement unit—a collection of gyroscopes and accelerometers). The system's sensitivity made it more accurate, but also more susceptible to excessive vibrations from the unstable thruster.

Data from the failed test, viewed along with data from previous times the anomaly had been detected in space, was giving the engineers something to work with, something they couldn't get from computer simulations or ground testing.

O'Reilly was called to the Senate to justify his budget request, and was asked to explain why these issues could not be reckoned with on the ground, why they had to be studied during intercept tests that cost hundreds of millions of taxpayer dollars. Thanks to his new sets of data, he knew exactly why:

> To the greatest extent possible, we replicate the performance of the missile components on the ground as if they were flying. We do that hundreds of times. It occurs in very severe environments. That's our first confidence level that these components work right. In our latest GMD test, we did find we had a failure mode that could not be replicated on the Earth and that's why I am going to request an additional test to verify we fixed it.
>
> The Earth's gravitation is one problem with testing it on the ground, and literally the rotation of the Earth. These are very sensitive items and you must be in flight testing, and the frequencies and shocks that we can replicate on the ground are limited, even with our best capabilities, our best facilities.

Finally having a better understanding of their challenge, MDA and Raytheon engineers set out for a solution. There would be no silver bullet or new widget that would solve the problem. They would have to painstakingly develop new software, design a special cradle to mount the fragile navigation system, add new instrumentation, restructure the thrusters, and conduct hours upon hours of vibration tests.

A new high-frequency test bed was being built by Boeing to help solve the ground-testing problem that O'Reilly had noted. Raytheon designed and manufactured the kill vehicle, Orbital provided the boosters, and Northrop Grumman wrote much of the software for the missile crews—but Boeing managed the overall homeland missile defense program, so the company's test and evaluation business stepped in to set up the high-frequency test bed at its facility in Huntington Beach, California.

Across the beach from old oil rigs and famous surfing spots, Pat Rogers, Boeing's Environmental Lab technical lead engineer, and Ali Mandvi, Boeing's lead mechanical systems engineer for GMD, developed the test bed specifically to mimic the same high-frequency vibrations plaguing the kill vehicle's navigation system.

At the Pentagon, far from surf city, O'Reilly's management techniques had raised real concern. By March 2011, about halfway through his tenure, there was talk that he might be fired. The Defense Department's inspector general opened an investigation as top personnel at MDA were quitting in droves. John Daniels, the program director for sensors, said he "could no longer support O'Reilly." Albert Hemphill, director for operations, said he "was fed up and had enough and had to get out." Patricia Gargulinski, program director for target and countermissions, and Randy Stone, director of quality, safety, and mission assurance, both said they would have stayed at the agency if not for O'Reilly. All of them quit. On September 13, Pentagon investigators interviewed MDA's general counsel to get her impression of the allegations and the senior staff exodus. She told the investigators that she was quitting too. And, yes, it was "100 percent" because of O'Reilly's "abusive management style."

The feelings about O'Reilly were strong, but not universally shared. Katrina McFarland, MDA's acquisitions chief, had quit to become president of the Defense Acquisitions

University and then on to other top-ranking Pentagon jobs. McFarland was a sort of weapons development wunderkind, so her departure was seen as an alarming casualty of O'Reilly's directorship, but when the investigators inquired, she defended O'Reilly and was adamant that he had nothing to do with her leaving. Rick Lehner, MDA's longtime director of public affairs, defended O'Reilly too. He'd heard stories but had never seen O'Reilly yell at anybody and found the general to be a good boss, though perhaps lacking certain social graces.

Still, MDA was demoralized. The agency's nearly eight thousand employees—working across fourteen time zones with about three hundred of its top managers now out at Fort Belvoir in Virginia, and the lion's share in Huntsville, Alabama—were largely unhappy. The budget cuts and the mandated office relocations and the repeated testing failures weighed heavily.

Michalski had just come off crew and was assigned as the unit's logistics and budget officer, known as the brigade S4, a far cry from his longtime role as a homeland missile defender. Bowen asked Michalski to pull together a budget briefing for Lieutenant General Richard Formica, the new head of Army Space and Missile Defense Command, so Michalski prepared a slide deck for Bowen to present that explained for the general how the brigade was dealing with increasingly scarce funding.

Midway through Bowen's briefing to Formica, he came to a noticeable mistake on one of Michalski's slides. Formica,

Bowen, Michalski, and anyone else in the room who could do basic math saw it. The numbers clearly—embarrassingly—did not add up.

"Sorry, sir," Bowen told Formica, "obviously this is an oversight and will be corrected for the next briefing." He moved on. Bowen could have easily deflected the blame to Michalski by simply glancing in his direction. But Bowen did not pause to ask for clarification, did not telegraph that the error was anyone else's, and did not bring it up with Michalski later. Bowen knew that Michalski would already be upset with himself, and that Michalski would not screw up twice. Bowen protected him.

Across town, at Fort Carson in Colorado Springs, Spriggs was retiring from the US Army. It was December 31, 2011, and he had been working at the 100th Missile Defense Brigade for eight years, as a trainer or a developer or a crew member, and it was time to try something different. Spriggs stood in the long out-processing line, thinking about maybe buying a hot dog cart or becoming a locksmith. His uniform was covered in the many badges he had collected throughout his army career: drill sergeant, jump wings, combat medic, and a large homeland missile defense badge.

An entire battalion of soldiers was there processing for a deployment, and a young private approached Sergeant First Class Spriggs.

"Pardon me, sir," the private said, standing up straighter upon seeing Spriggs's drill sergeant badge.

"What can I do for you, troop?"

"Um, what's that badge right there, sir?" the private asked, pointing to Spriggs's 100th Missile Defense Brigade badge. It had an eagle flying with a lightning bolt gripped in its claws, above an Earth with mountains on top. The eagle had two semicircles around it pointing to a star.

"That, son, is the NASA HALO badge," Spriggs said. "Remember when the space shuttle blew up? Well right after that, they decided to design a way for people to parachute out of the shuttle, and I was on the test board. See, I've got my 82nd Airborne badge, but then we jumped out of the space shuttles, too. So this is my NASA HALO badge."

"Wow, thanks sir!"

After the private walked away, a wiser noncommissioned officer standing behind Spriggs asked what it *really* was. Spriggs told him it was from the 100th Missile Defense Brigade, but the NCO, even though he was also in the Colorado Army National Guard, and was also based in Colorado Springs, had never heard of the unit or its mission. It was easier for Spriggs to pretend he did high-altitude/low-opening parachute jumps from space than it was for him to explain GMD.

Spriggs grew out his hair, grew out his beard, and spent the next year operating a hot dog stand and a lock-picking service in town. The next year, he heard of a job opening at Army Space and Missile Defense Command, to work as a civilian training soldiers for the missile crews. Spriggs wanted back in. He cut his hair, shaved his beard, bought some ties, and went to work again with the brigade.

The brigade and its mission were still largely shrouded—even from other army soldiers, and even soldiers in Colorado Springs—but many of the unit's members were sticking around or returning, so a solid bench of homeland missile defense veterans was forming. The missile crews no longer had to learn their craft only from contractors who had never sat for a shift. They could be taught by veterans like Spriggs, who had experienced the excitement and boredom, the conflict and comradery, the fun and tedium of life on crew.

A few days before Spriggs left the army, Kim Jong-il, who had ruled North Korea for seventeen years, died of a heart attack. The successor was the second son, Kim Jong-un, believed to be about twenty-eight years old but otherwise a mystery. North Korea's nuclear and missile programs ramped up as suddenly as Kim Jong-un took power. North Korea kicked off an unprecedented run of missile tests and announced it would celebrate founder Kim Il-sung's April 2012 centennial birthday by, of course, blasting a satellite into space.

Bowen and Meakins were soon leaving the 100th. Bowen would be off to a senior role at Army Space and Missile Defense Command. Meakins would go on shift again, but this time as a missile defense officer at Northern Command. What might have been a pleasant tour of "hails and farewells" for the popular officers, however, was overshadowed by the looming threat of another big North Korean launch. The brigade was receiving intelligence that North Korea was getting ready to fire, so Bowen and Meakins focused the crews on understanding the situation and what their actions would be for a slew of contingencies. Bowen ordered training scenarios to be run more often, and to be focused specifically on defending against a weapon akin to the Taepodong-2.

The crews all wanted to be on duty for the launch. There could be no better bragging right in the air defense community than to have destroyed an intercontinental missile. Northern Command and the 100th for days had been watching the North Koreans prepare to launch the missile out of Sohae on the west coast. Pyongyang called it an Unha-3, in its guise as a satellite launch vehicle, but it used much of the same technology as an ICBM. The Pentagon sent intelligence assets into the western Pacific. Navy destroyers with the SPY-1 radar, intelligence-collecting aircraft, and satellites were all deployed to watch and analyze the North Korean missile's performance.

It was 5:39 A.M. on April 12 when the Quick Alert sent Major Matt Pollock's Echo crew into action at Schriever Air Force Base. Pollock was a workhorse. He had been with the brigade three years and he loved training for intercepts. His intensity—and his constant training runs—rubbed some other crew members the wrong way. Not everybody wanted to work on Pollock's crew. He did not take his job lightly, and certainly not during a missile launch, but Pollock knew, based on where the North Koreans were launching from, on the west coast and firing due south, that it was unlikely to be a threat anyway. The North Koreans would not normally launch from there, clear across their own country, toward the United States. Pollock already had an idea of where that missile was *not* going; he got an even clearer idea when the ninety-ton rocket exploded within seconds.

Two days later, North Korea paraded what appeared to be six road-mobile ICBMs, calling this new weapon the Hwasong-13. In a series of goodbye speeches and exit interviews the previous summer, Secretary of Defense Robert Gates had been quietly warning about a forthcoming road-mobile threat that could reach the United States. Now here it was, parading around

Pyongyang as a posthumous one-hundredth birthday gift to Kim Il-sung. It looked to be a three-stage design, possibly using solid fuel. It was unclear if these were mock-ups or early proto-types, but they did not appear to be operational. Still, it was a bad sign. The Taepodong-2 missiles or the Unha-series launch vehicles had all been assembled and fueled on the launchpad, and it took an hour to transfer the liquid fuel, so Northern Command and the 100th were always aware when a threat loomed, and could sometimes even approximate the time of a launch within minutes. A road-mobile, solid-fuel missile would present an entirely different challenge.

At MDA, O'Reilly's time was finally up. The Pentagon in-spector general concluded his leadership was too toxic, and recommended that the secretary of the army "consider ap-propriate corrective action," but O'Reilly was nearing retire-ment anyway. He was allowed to retire with the benefits of a three-star general, but with a letter of reprimand. Some at the agency disagreed with the reprimand, believing that O'Reilly was exactly the sort of driving force needed to corral and lead an endeavor as complex as developing, delivering, and upgrading missile defenses. His intimidation ensured everyone was prepared and had their facts straight. His people were making strides in tackling the Track Gate Anomaly. It all appeared to be a short-term gain, however. An annual "Best Places to Work" survey by the Partnership for Public Service ranked MDA number 223 of 224 smaller federal gov-ernment operations.

On November 19, 2012, the agency was turned over to

Vice Admiral James Syring, a Naval Academy graduate and engineer from Muncie, Indiana. For the most part, he was the opposite of his predecessor. O'Reilly was a micromanager with decades of missile defense experience. Syring could at times be aloof, delegated authority, and had limited experience using missiles to shoot at other missiles. O'Reilly was a socially awkward general with a temper. Syring was a polite admiral with the appearance and temperament of a network news anchor. The admiral lacked O'Reilly's specific expertise, but he didn't lack O'Reilly's brainpower. Syring was chosen for his experience running highly technical, risky, and enormously expensive military projects—he had managed the navy's newfangled Zumwalt-class destroyer program, and handled the navy office in charge of developing all weapons for ships.

Syring's immediate challenge was to prepare for a flight trial to examine fixes to the Track Gate Anomaly.

It was Wednesday, December 12, and Pollock's Echo crew was again on shift. And they were again prepared for a North Korean launch. Another satellite vehicle was fueling up at Sohae, doubling as an ICBM test bed. This time, however, Pollock watched his console as the Unha-3 rocket lifted off, climbed into space, and deployed its Kwangmyongsong-3 satellite. Because it was a space launch, the missile flew directly up into space, and never within range for Pollock to take a shot. The satellite was tumbling uselessly in orbit, but the launch itself was a frightening leap for North Korean missile technology.

Pollock had spent his first ten years in the army as an

enlisted active-duty soldier doing satellite communications. It felt like important work—he had been on the comms team for General Wesley Clark, the supreme allied commander for Europe during the Bosnian War—but his absences and constant moving around had been hard on his family. Eventually, Pollock stumbled across the 100th Missile Defense Brigade, where he found the best of both worlds, staying in the army but also staying in one place. As a crew director, he was handling billions of dollars of military equipment, thirty fifty-five-foot-tall interceptor missiles, command-and-control facilities, communications terminals, satellites, radars, and fire control computers—tied together through a twenty-thousand-mile fiber optic network. And he was directly charged with defending the United States. Not US interests abroad, but the United States itself.

Pollock was a "curve breaker." He did more than the other crew members, and some of them wanted him to tone it down so they didn't look lazy in comparison. The crews were full of overachievers, but even the overachievers would not make detailed recommendations to the brigade commander unless asked. Pollock did it regularly.

Pollock was also lucky. He had been with the brigade since 2009 and had already seen considerably more action than most crew members. The crews wanted to be on shift for any big event, to see enemy missile behaviors and the GMD system's reactions, even though being on shift for the launches meant the added burden of what they called "administrative recovery": hours of annotating screenshots, recording details of the launch, and then phone calls and meetings to discuss it all. But it came down to fortuitous scheduling. Pollock had now seen two big launches within six months. He had mixed feelings about those launches. On the one hand, it was good to see the North Koreans fail, but on the other hand the soldiers had thousands of hours of training that they wanted to put to use. Pollock had also just come off a stint as the unit's intelligence officer, so he was happy to collect real-world data from the successful North Korean satellite launch. The data helped the crews understand what their adversary could do.

Kiraly was still checking in, occasionally, on developments in North Korea, but his focus was on his immediate task: senior combat adviser for two Afghan National Army battalions. He had deployed to western Afghanistan, leading a team of twelve Colorado guardsmen partnered with sixty-two Slovenian soldiers.

The team was returning from a mounted combat patrol, coming back through a dusty afternoon to the main gate at Forward Operating Base Farah, when Kiraly spotted an Alaskan state flag flying on the base. He dismounted and walked over to see if he recognized any soldiers from his days at Fort Greely. The sergeant of the guard was Mark Scott. Four years earlier, Kiraly and Scott had fallen out over the sale of the Kiralys' Greely house to the Scotts. Scott, a mechanic at heart, wanted the garage rewired so he could hook up more power tools, and found an electrician who said the wiring needed to be replaced. Kiraly then found another electrician who said the wiring was fine. Now in Farah, Afghanistan, of all places, they were happy to make amends.

Scott a few years earlier had been promoted to staff sergeant and given a squad of MPs at Greely. Scott's squad had four of the platoon's five female soldiers, which at first Scott thought was because the platoon sergeant was out to get him. It turned out the platoon sergeant, who was also female, was out to mentor Scott. She was giving him a chance to learn to talk to and lead soldiers. He got the message, handled the squad well, and was sent to the army's Senior Leader Course to learn how to be a sergeant first class. Scott was sent to airborne school to jump out of airplanes at thirty years old, and then ultimately went to Afghanistan with a unit running security for the base at Farah.

When Scott returned to Greely in 2013, he had calmed down and become a better leader. Still, he was struggling to escape his reputation as the high-strung marine, and his promotion to sergeant first class went nowhere while a series of army investigations into his unit's leadership at Farah ran for nearly two years. All the investigations came back unfounded. A year after returning to Greely, Scott got his promotion and was put in charge of processing new MPs and running the driver's school. He was what the army calls a "Master Driver," so it was a good gig for him.

Kiraly returned to Colorado Springs in June 2013 and went directly back as a crew director for the 100th Missile Defense Brigade. Things at the brigade had changed.

16

YEOMAN'S WORK

THE MISSILE DEFENSE AGENCY had been working toward a flight trial to examine fixes to the Track Gate Anomaly. An intercept attempt would not even be considered. This was to be strictly a flight test to ensure the second-generation kill vehicle's troublesome navigation system could now, thanks to firmware updates and a new cradle, withstand vibrations outside Earth's atmosphere. There would be no target, just a series of planned maneuvers in space. Although it was only a flight test with no flashy intercept, the stakes were especially high. The second-generation interceptor was now more than three years delayed, and the program was dealing with a serious and systemic engineering challenge.

Syring was at the test site at Vandenberg in California on January 26, 2013. It was around 2:00 P.M. and there was a thick layer of fog along the coast. The interceptor, armed with the newly modified kill vehicle, blasted out of its silo and quickly disappeared into the hazy sky. The booster flew to its planned spot and then deployed the kill vehicle, which flew its controlled maneuvers while strapped with instruments measuring vibrations, roll, pitch, yaw, acceleration, and more.

After hours spent reviewing the collected data, MDA determined the flight was a success. The navigation system was no longer being overloaded because of vibrations. Still, vibrations caused by firing the thrusters, the four small engines that steer the kill vehicle in space, remained a concern. Syring ordered the program to move ahead with modifying the navigation systems so he could try an intercept test with the revamped kill vehicle, and then ordered another project to begin designing new thrusters to ease the in-flight vibrations. MDA was finally demonstrating progress again, but so was North Korea.

Jeffrey Lewis, the open-source analyst in Monterey, received an email from the US Geological Survey on February 12, alerting its subscribers to a shallow 4.9 body-wave magnitude tremor near North Korea's Punggye-ri Nuclear Test Site (the magnitude was soon updated to 5.1). It appeared that North Korea had just successfully detonated another nuclear weapon. This was not a dud like the first test in 2006, or a small bomb like the test in 2009. Lewis estimated it was likely several kilotons.

In response, a few weeks later, on an otherwise quiet Friday afternoon, newly confirmed Secretary of Defense Chuck Hagel walked into the Pentagon briefing room to announce the United States would deploy fourteen more interceptors for the GMD system, a striking reversal after his predecessor, Robert Gates, had cut that same number. It would cost about $1 billion for those weapons, and the new design had not yet scored a successful intercept. Questioned about the test record, Hagel admitted "there was an issue regarding our gyro guidance system," and said the Pentagon "certainly will not go forward with the additional fourteen interceptors until we are sure that we have the complete confidence that we will need."

Syring had to get it right, and he had to do it quick. It was a bad year to ask $1 billion for interceptors that weren't hitting their targets.

In March 2013, Congress and the White House had failed to reach a required deal on deficit reduction, and that failure triggered an $85 billion budget cut across many government programs, including the Pentagon and MDA. The political dysfunction then reached a nadir seven months later when the federal government shut down for sixteen days, including the Pentagon and MDA.

Political one-upmanship and its fallout with the budget and the shutdown was causing a sea of problems for the 100th Missile Defense Brigade. Michalski, still working as the brigade's logistics and budget officer, was knee-deep in it. The brigade's budget was not even a drop in the figurative bucket of Pentagon spending. Congress ultimately gave the Defense Department $614.8 billion to spend in 2013. Of that money, Army Space and Missile Defense Command then gave the brigade $3 million and the state of Colorado gave it $46,000. Much of the money paid for contractors such as security guards to help the MPs at Greely, mostly checking IDs at access control points (which cost about $1.25 million).

It paid for the brigade operations officer's five civilian contractors, the logistics and budget officer's one contractor, and all the other support needed to keep the small unit functioning.

Michalski and his fellow soldiers were not on the block for being cut, but their contractor support certainly was. It was the most immediate way of impacting the budget. Michalski managed not to furlough or lay off any contractors, but every week he found himself in a new meeting defending another funding line. Everything had to be justified and then justified again.

The crews had it bad too. Kiraly had returned to the brigade and was assigned as director of Alpha crew. It was good to be back, but not as good as before. MDA controlled the software that the crews used for their training runs, and this meant somebody from the agency had to be at work for the crews to train. Because of the budget cuts, MDA reduced training support to only weekday work hours. No more nights and weekends. The training runs, aside from keeping the crews sharp, were a great way to pass the time on the eight-hour shifts.

Staff Sergeant Patricia Young, now working as Kiraly's readiness operator, found the time was mostly passed with sports talk. Kiraly was a huge sports fan and the outcome of any big game could be debated for hours. Young was not a sports fanatic, but loved working on Kiraly's crew. He hosted them and their families for holidays at his home, he supported their continuing education, and, importantly, he aggressively protected their days off. And Kiraly was proud to have soldiers like Young on his crew. He called her "Backbone," because noncommissioned officers are said to be the backbone of the US armed forces. Young would remind the crew of whatever tasks it had upcoming, and Kiraly would say, "That's why you're the backbone. Backbone leads the way!"

Kiraly also liked to brag that Young was the first female soldier in the brigade to certify as a future-operations officer. The brigade and battalion had a fair number of female soldiers—indeed several women were founding members and several more were honor graduates of the GMD Qualification Course—but in 2011 Young was the first to certify for the crews' most intense position. Day to day, that role was relatively easy and mostly administrative. In the middle of a fight, though, it was by far the most stressful. It was the future-operations officer's job to key in the director's launch orders, to ensure everything at Fort Greely was working, to ensure the interceptor launched.

Pollock was off crew and had been assigned as the brigade's intelligence chief, but he still pulled shifts twice a month to maintain proficiency. Nobody liked training runs as much as he did, and Pollock was horrified by the idea that he could not train on weekends for a job that was supposed to be 24/7. He had no interest in watching movies in the node on Saturday and Sunday. He would rather work and train—it made the time pass quicker and more productively.

Over the course of several long meetings with MDA and the contractors, the crews negotiated to get training support sixteen hours each weekday. Access to the MDA's simulation program could now last from 6:00 A.M. to 10:00 P.M. Weekdays only. They eventually negotiated a quarterly "surge" in training support too so they could prepare for their certification tests.

Pollock also began lobbying hard for the brigade's soldiers to be able to manage their own training runs, at least on the weekends. Why not? Pollock figured maybe MDA or the contractors thought the soldiers would break the system, or make some jobs redundant, or perhaps a combination of the two. He encountered strong resistance.

Things seemed amiss at the brigade in Colorado, but they were out of control at the battalion in Alaska. It started with the "calendar scandal," which was about much more than the calendar. Lieutenant Colonel Joe Miley's wife had worked on, and posed for, a 1950s-pinup-girl-style calendar with pictures of women in lingerie. The images were suggestive but not lewd. There was no nudity. The calendars were sold as a charity fund-raiser to benefit the American Cancer Society. Miley, however, was the commander of the 49th Missile Defense Battalion, and concern was raised about his possible participation. An army investigation into the calendar put a spotlight on Fort Greely, and into that spotlight emerged a far more problematic issue. Complaints were raised that Miley was overlooking multiple inappropriate sexual affairs within the battalion.

The scandal was promptly on the front page of the *Army Times* newspapers sold in checkout lines at military commissaries across the country. The army ordered an inquiry and investigators came pouring into Greely—from Army Space and Missile Defense Command, Alaska Army National Guard, and Army headquarters. The battalion soldiers had generally been seen as charmingly incorrigible, but it had gone too far beyond that. Because of the investigations, the fun, wild west, us-against-the-world atmosphere at Greely was supplanted by a dark and suspicious milieu.

Miley was a plank holder, a founding member of the unit, an original at Greely's Diligent Sentry Officers Association. He had been the battalion crew director on that first-ever shift, working with Meakins's brigade crew across the country. But Miley's was a hands-off leadership style, and some soldiers recoiled when he did not address their grievances about adultery within the battalion. Miley had called a meeting in January to address allegations that a captain in the battalion was having an affair with another officer's wife, and that noncommissioned officers were sleeping with junior enlisted soldiers, but it ended with Miley sticking to his hands-off approach. It just wasn't his prerogative, he said.

Those were criminal offenses under the Uniform Code of Military Justice, but unless the soldiers were specifically on shift at Greely's Missile Defense Complex, then they were legally Alaska National Guardsmen and not bound by that code. Alaska National Guardsmen were subject only to the toothless Alaska Code of Military Justice, which conceded nearly all legal responsibility to local civilian authorities. (The next year, a National Guard Bureau review found no record of an Alaskan military court-martial since 1955, when the original code was passed.)

Miley's soldiers found no consolation in his legalese or his laissez-faire approach. They wrote directly to Miley's boss's boss: Lieutenant General Richard Formica at Army Space and Missile Defense Command. They said Miley's tolerance for sexual affairs made them afraid "for our wives and even our children in this toxic environment." As the investigations dug deeper, flummoxed Pentagon officials thought Miley was running the battalion "as if [sex] was the only thing to do" at Greely. On June 11, 2013, Formica announced that Miley had been suspended from his command.

Although Greely had fallen on dark times, it took no sheen off the Alaskan setting for Specialist Bethany Hendren. She had no frame of reference for what it was like before the scandals. Hendren landed at the Fairbanks airport on a Friday night. It was November 8, 2013, and a sergeant picked her up from the terminal and drove southeast down Route 2 along the Tanana River to Greely. The northern lights filled the driver-side windows of the government van. She had been in Alaska less than an hour and was enamored.

Hendren had been an MP in the Missouri National Guard but was looking for a full-time army job. The government shutdown had delayed her application, but once it reopened she was accepted into the 49th Missile Defense Battalion and flew immediately up to Greely. She hadn't thought to pack linens or warm clothes, so she layered up on sweatshirts the next morning when she set out to explore her new home. But it was minus 10°F and windy and she was freezing. Hendren bummed a ride back up to Fairbanks to outfit herself with cold-weather gear, and then embraced everything about life on the remote post.

The Better Opportunities for Single Soldiers program, or BOSS, was established to keep soldiers without families occupied and happy. Hendren was soon the BOSS vice president at Greely, and then president. The program offered classes in winterizing vehicles, outdoor survival, swift-water rescue, and firearms safety. It sponsored camping and kayaking and hiking trips. In the winter, it hosted sushi nights or game nights or bowling nights—and held them in the fort's brand-new community activity center, known as the CAC.

The center was built on Greely's parade grounds. It had a large parking lot with power outlets in each space to plug in engine block heaters. Soldiers and their families walked into the CAC through a massive foyer with a large stone fireplace that led up through the vaulted ceiling. To the left was the eight-lane bowling alley, and to the right were multipurpose rooms for families or committees or programs like BOSS, or rooms to occupy toddlers for an hour or two. In a massive open center area was a stage and seating and a food counter serving hot dogs, hamburgers, and gigantic fried chicken wings. Toward the back was an adult's game room with a small bar and high-top tables and billiards, and a kid's game room with no bar but air hockey, ping-pong, a handmade foosball table, and four TVs each connected to an array of gaming systems.

The CAC hosted free movies at six thirty on Friday and Saturday nights, but the soldiers and their families mostly used the facility during the week or for large gatherings. The weekend was for outdoor activities or for driving up to Fairbanks for dinner or entertainment. There was, after all, plenty to do in Alaska that didn't violate the Uniform Code of Military Justice.

MDA was driving toward an intercept test for its redesigned version of the new interceptor, but meanwhile Syring wanted to test a series of upgrades that had been done to the original first-generation interceptors. There were twenty of these, and they were the only interceptors deemed "operational" since all the newer interceptors were still being fixed. Much of the technology in the first-generation weapons, however, was from the 1990s, and the upgrades were meant to carry them into the twenty-first century. Again defending his budget in Congress, Syring said the agency had made "24 or 25 improvements to the current [first-generation] fleet that I will demonstrate in flight within the next month."

The agency was under pressure to explain why the homeland missile defense system could be relied upon to protect the United States—and why it should be allowed to buy fourteen more interceptors—when it had failed its last two tests. The standard riposte had been that the problems were with the new second-generation interceptor, and not the proven first-generation system. Asked specifically about this at his budget hearing, Syring responded, "There is the older version of interceptors that are in the ground today that have successfully flown three of three times, and that those continue to be at the forefront of the combatant commanders' stable . . . of interceptors to use in case of conflict."

On July 5, 2013, Syring intended to prove that the first-generation weapons worked, and the improvements had only made them better. This time, one would destroy a "complex target," meaning some decoys would be present. The first-generation interceptor would be launched from Vandenberg to strike down a target flying from Kwajalein.

The target missile launched, the radars and sensors tracked it, and the interceptor boosted off from Vandenberg. Then, once again, the kill vehicle did not separate from its booster. The test was a complete loss. The control room at Vandenberg, the nodes at Greely and Schriever, MDA's headquarters at Fort Belvoir—all were silent. *What the hell happened this time?*

Once again, the engineers set to work ferreting through reams of data to find what went wrong. Once again, they discovered a seemingly minor issue had caused the failure. A leak in the kill vehicle's battery disabled its delicate electronics. Syring would later explain to his congressional overseers that, while the interceptor was flying, "a voltage shift caused by battery electrolyte leakage shut down the flight computer," which meant this kill vehicle could not separate from its booster.

The Pentagon's testing directorate was less certain and criticized MDA for not duplicating the battery failure during ground tests to ensure it was the definitive cause of failure. Regardless, the agency planned to go back and fix the batteries in all interceptors, and to develop new software for all the first-generation kill vehicles to address the problem.

Lieutenant Colonel Dave Meakins, though no longer in the brigade, had not strayed far from the homeland missile defense world. He was working as a missile defense officer at the shared headquarters of Northern Command and NORAD. The Cold War–era NORAD and 9/11-era Northern Command were charged with defending the United States and Canada from external threats—this meant everything from illegal fishing, Russian aircraft, and hurricanes, to North Korean missiles. The wide-ranging mission had been coordinated from the joint command center under Cheyenne Mountain, but in 2008 it was moved to newer facilities at Peterson Air Force Base on the other side of Colorado Springs.

Cheyenne Mountain was all 1950s charm, but Peterson was more like a setting in a modern spy movie. The command center there, though windowless, was bright and sanitary, surrounded by large glowing screens and buzzing with personnel steeped in their mission. The center was manned by 179 people divided into five crews, which ranged from twenty-eight to thirty-two crew members. The crew was larger during a "period of interest," such as when intelligence officers said something like a North Korean missile launch may happen soon.

Crew members were situated around large screens at the room's front, and each operator had a bank of their own screens, several phones, and massive books of checklists. Aside from the books, everything else about the command center looked futuristic and clean. Emergency action controllers sat in the back, ensuring all the right people at the command center were on the phone with the right decision makers. If the event was urgent enough, the four-star officer leading Northern Command would sit in the far back of the room with the emergency action controllers, a few steps away from a large conference room with glass walls that can snap from transparent to opaque so the commander could jump in for a private, secure meeting if necessary.

The missile defense officer at the command center had access to GMD's software algorithms and would listen in as the crews at Schriever and Greely talked through intercept scenarios. The officer would let the Northern Command boss know if an inbound missile could be intercepted. If so, he called out "the missile is engageable" and then awaited orders to pass along to the crew director at the 100th Missile Defense Brigade.

As a backup to the modern command center at Peterson, Northern Command kept its original command center hidden deep inside Cheyenne Mountain's granite twenty miles away. The Mountain was used about once a month to keep it in "warm standby," in case the unthinkable happened. The more spacious command center at Peterson got far more use.

Meakins was pulling a shift in the Mountain as the missile defense officer for Northern Command on Thursday, September 12. He liked the job but hated the hours. Northern Command was doing twelve-hour shifts and the schedule took a toll. Still, it was a different perspective of the same mission. Meakins was regularly on the phone with the crew directors that he had known for years.

It was raining torrentially that day, and had been for some time, when Meakins arrived for his shift. He got there two hours early to refresh his expired PINs and passwords. Only four or five of the other twenty-eight crew members were there that early. The command director walked in. He wasn't exactly shaken—the command directors seemed to thrive on stress—but was excited to tell the crew that he had nearly been killed by a boulder as he was waiting for the shuttle at the Mountain's main entrance. Now, the command director reported, the Mountain's entrance was blocked by a landslide and the corridors were flooding. The facility would be sealed off to keep more water from coming in, and it wasn't safe to leave anyway because there could be more deadly boulders tumbling down.

An estimated fourteen inches of rain had fallen in a matter of hours, causing literal tons of debris and boulders to slide down the steep mountain and cover the entrance road with an eerie moonscape. An estimated five hundred thousand gallons of water had to be pumped from the facilities. Meakins and the bare-bones crew were stuck there for another twenty-four hours.

17

FLIGHT TEST GROUND-06B

SYRING TRAVELED TO A frozen Fort Greely in late February 2014. The Missile Defense Agency, its contractors, and the battalion had been working overtime for the past year to prepare Greely's missile fields for the fourteen additional interceptors that the Pentagon wanted. This was a direct response to North Korea's nuclear testing. Despite an ongoing budget fiasco in Washington, Greely was coming alive again, like the heady days of the mid-2000s, albeit with more oversight and less partying. Syring was pleased to find everything on schedule for adding the new interceptors—as long as they could score a successful test with the second-generation weapon first.

The next week, at the Pentagon, Syring announced to reporters that he was planning to finally return to intercept testing that summer. The agency called it Flight Test Ground-06b. It would be a retry of the December 2010 test that failed because of the Track Gate Anomaly, which itself was a retry of the January 2010 test that failed because somebody forgot to install a small lockwire part. Production of the new interceptors had been in limbo since the end of 2010. There had not been a successful intercept in nearly six years. Morale was suffering at MDA, at Raytheon, at the brigade, and at the battalion.

The second-generation interceptors were almost four years behind schedule, but Syring was trying to steer the program onto a slower, more traditional development path. The homeland missile defense system had been rushed into operation, and Syring believed that this was a sound decision at the time based on concern about North Korean missiles. However, it meant "the system engineering cycle was cut short."

Frank Kendall, the Pentagon's chief of development and procurement, and Syring's boss, said it less diplomatically: "The root cause was a desire to field these things very quickly and really cheaply," Kendall said. "The detailed engineering that should have been applied to these early designs wasn't there . . . We are seeing a lot of bad engineering, frankly, and it is because there was a rush." To meet rigid deadlines, to field *some* defense, MDA had to buy untested equipment. Now, although the Obama administration wanted fourteen more interceptors at $75 million each, that order would not be filled until the weapons could be proven to work in space.

MDA also wanted to fund a new program to develop a more reliable "redesigned kill vehicle," and to build a big new radar in Alaska to help the interceptors distinguish an enemy warhead from decoys or debris. Success in Syring's summer test would mean more second-generation interceptors, and it would mean the whole homeland missile defense enterprise could move forward. Failure would mean everyone went back to the drawing board, again.

Patricia Young had been inducted into the Sergeant Audie Murphy Club, an organization for the army's top 10 percent of noncommissioned officers. The elite group was named for a superlatively decorated World War II soldier who became an early advocate for treating post-traumatic stress disorder. Acceptance in the club required a series of three interview panels (which the army calls boards), and each panel had three sergeants major asking questions about leadership, regulations, ethics, and community service. As a reward for Young's acceptance, another first for the unit, she was sent to watch the test interceptor blast off from Vandenberg Air Force Base on the morning of June 22.

The interceptor was to fly westward and strike a target launching out of Kwajalein Atoll in the Pacific Ocean. Young had been working on the system for eight years and was thrilled to watch it launch in person. She joined a delegation of senior military and contractor personnel on a hill just above Vandenberg, at the Ronald Reagan Memorial Viewing Site.

Richard Michalski, now a lieutenant colonel, had ended his two-and-a-half-year tour as the brigade's logistics and budget officer in January. He was back as the director of Charlie crew and would lead the June 22 intercept test mission. Marcus Kent, now a warrant officer, was on the crew as well. The brigade would no longer use whichever crew happened to be on shift for the tests. The real-world missile threat from North Korea had grown too concerning and needed to be monitored at all times, so this would be the first event for which two crews would be used: Bravo crew on a regular shift watching the real world in one node, and Charlie crew conducting the test in the other node on the opposite side of the fishbowl conference room.

Behind Charlie crew, the conference room was packed. Contractors and officers had been milling in and out of the node. The temperature was rising, figuratively from the nervousness but also literally from the extra body heat. Michalski noticed the air conditioner kicking on more often to keep all the electronics cool. He knew firsthand that the failures were bad for morale—he had been the director on the first test to fail because of the Track Gate Anomaly—and he wanted to give his crew the huge motivational boost of a success. But he was not especially nervous or worried about another failure either.

The developers would take it hard if their baby failed to do what it was supposed to do. The crews trained for that constantly though. Managing failures was one of their most important functions. They spent hours every shift practicing what to do if an interceptor flopped, or communications were lost, or one or more operator consoles went down. And Michalski and Kent had now been doing this for a decade.

The target, a forty-five-foot-long intermediate-range ballistic missile, fitted with simple countermeasures, was launched from the test site on Kwajalein Atoll on a trajectory toward open ocean northeast of Hawaii. The target was designed to imitate a weapon that could travel as far as 5,500 kilometers. Guided missile destroyer USS *Hopper* was positioned near Kwajalein, and its onboard SPY-1 radar acquired the target and sent the tracking data back to the brains of the GMD system. The system's computers then developed a plan of attack using the tracking data from the navy ship.

Michalski ordered the system to "go weapons free."

The plan of attack was transmitted to the launch equipment at Vandenberg. About six minutes after the target had been detected, Patricia Young saw the silo doors swing open at Vandenberg, the rocket exhaust came blazing out of the silo, and then the second-generation interceptor climbed up through the atmosphere. It looked like a thick, dark pencil riding into space atop a streaking fireball.

The GMD computer also generated and sent a cue to the Sea-based X-band Radar vessel, positioned southwest of Hawaii, so the huge radar could find the target. It found it, and then provided in-flight reports to guide the kill vehicle through space and help it discriminate the warhead from the chaff.

A launch technician called out stage updates, and the air conditioner was still humming, but otherwise the node was silent. The kill vehicle separated from the booster. It acquired the target. Two of MDA's High Altitude Observatory aircraft, highly modified Gulfstream jets, flying northwest of Hawaii, trained their electro-optical and infrared sensors on the target and the kill vehicle. Everyone in the conference room looked to the television screen displaying infrared imagery of the target, a small dot flying against a deep blue background. The blue display flashed red and yellow as the kill vehicle collided with and destroyed the target.

The test was a success. Finally.

It had taken years, teams of experts, and $1.981 billion, but the Track Gate Anomaly appeared to be solved, and the program was getting into what Syring called a better "system engineering cycle."

About two months after the successful intercept test, at a conference in Huntsville, Alabama, Syring made his first public comments about the Track Gate Anomaly and what it took to solve it. He noted that it was common for space vehicles to have combustion and vibration issues, which can be worked out through test flights.

"If you go back and study the history, it takes years sometimes to work through these issues," he said. "It can get so bad you can have a booster failure at launch or a booster failure in flight." Syring noted that the anomaly was observed as early as 2001, when it was incorrectly thought to be from electromagnetic interference, but it had never caused any real trouble until the more sensitive navigation system was installed in 2006. "It all makes sense today. All that was many years of engineering to get to that conclusion, but it makes sense in terms of what happened."

MDA's original plan had been to first test the second-generation interceptor in early 2008, before sending them into the field. But delays in the testing, and constant pressure to meet deadlines, had meant the interceptors were bought and deployed to Fort Greely before they could be tested.

Syring and MDA were solving extraordinarily complex technical problems, but this required the added costs of failure review boards and supplementary tests, and then going back to fix the equipment that had already been bought, and testing it again. This also added years to the overall evolution of homeland missile defense. There was supposed to have been a more realistic "salvo test" with multiple interceptors fired against one target in early 2009, but that would ultimately be delayed by nine years.

On February 2, 2015, Syring was sitting in the Pentagon briefing room, announcing his agency's plans for the upcoming year. He maintained his ever-somber tone, and kept his hands folded on a small desk, always displaying the three bright-yellow rank insignia bars on his sleeve. He said nothing about the successful intercept. He said resources would be redirected to examine all the interceptors and subcomponents to determine reliability and help the 100th's missile crews better understand how many shots they must take to ensure an incoming warhead was destroyed. He announced plans to begin designing the new tracking radar in Alaska and the more reliable kill vehicle. He then revealed that the 100th would, for the first time, test the homeland defense system against an ICBM-range target in 2017.

The success of the June 2014 test lifted morale for the missile crews. Pollock joked that Michalski finally hadn't missed. They were in good spirits when they got the bad news: the crews would start pulling twelve-hour shifts instead of eight-hour shifts. It would be eight days of working two daytime shifts, then two midnight shifts, then four days off—but everyone was half dead by the end of the second midnight shift and spent at least one of the days off asleep or wandering around like a zombie. The idea was to get the missile crews on the same schedule as Northern Command's watch crews, and to get the missile crews more time off between rotations so it would be easier to fit in new training or other tasks.

For the most part, the crews were heartbroken. Michalski

loved the eight-hour shifts. He could run four to six training scenarios per day. Each run took about forty-five to sixty minutes, and that left about two hours for administrative work, and then they were done. But *twelve*? The battalion crews at Greely had done twelve-hour shifts on and off for a few years; it helped them further stretch their limited manpower. Meakins was pulling twelve hours as a missile defense officer for Northern Command, and he loathed the longer shifts.

At Schriever, where the two nodes were separated by an admin area and the glass-walled conference room, Michalski would lead his training runs and then allow the five-soldier crew to spread out across the space. When they could not train, he let them study for continuing education, or he let them exercise. Sometimes they dragged in a stationary bike or a rowing machine. Sometimes it was just push-ups and sit-ups.

It was up to the crew director how much time to spend on training, VIP visits, maintenance, and so on, and how much time to give the crew to just hang out and be ready. They had access to cable television, and the node had over a thousand movies on DVD that had been donated over time, mainly from the $5 bin at Walmart. Kent didn't like the longer shifts but figured it was a great time to catch up on movies, to read, or to study. He had completed a bachelor's degree while at the brigade and was now working on his master's degree.

Kent, however, was single and didn't have children. Young had a family and the new shifts were terrible. She came home from a midnight shift, took a nap, hung out with the kids before school, went to sleep for a few hours until the kids got home, and then went back to work.

Michalski and Kiraly, who also both had families, *really* didn't like the shifts. They took their grievance to Colonel Tim Lawson, the brigade commander, who deferred to the two officers as the unit's elder statesmen. The commander agreed to ease off the twelve-hour shifts and order them only sparingly. But Lawson would only be there another year and their mission wasn't getting easier.

The crews were also mired in a protracted campaign to get two computer monitors at the operating consoles. For about five years they had been pushing to get each crew member a dual-monitor setup, instead of the old single monitors. It meant hardware and software changes, which meant winning the assent of too many organizations. MDA, Army Space and Missile Defense Command, Northern Command, Boeing, and Northrop Grumman had little urgency to address a small issue that impacted only the fifty soldiers on crews at the brigade and battalion.

Pollock was happy to be a squeaky wheel on the subject of dual monitors. He was off crew and working on a team doing research and development for the GMD system. The crews were behind him, mostly.

Kiraly put it bluntly: "Here I am trying to guard the fucking world, and I have two monitors at my desk at home when I play *Call of Duty* on one screen and look at Facebook on the other. Why don't I have two screens when I'm trying to launch a ballistic missile?"

Meetings with representatives from all the GMD stakeholders—normally more than fifty people—were held weekly. Adding the dual monitors had been an "action item" in those meetings since around 2010. The crews had been making progress until one crew member, a senior officer who was only with the brigade a short time, mentioned during a development meeting that he could do intercepts without the second monitor. It was more bluster than anything else. He was bragging about how good he was. But that was all the industry developers and government money managers needed to hear. The dual-monitor requirement was dropped, and the crews had to start all over again. At the time, Pollock had been baffled. "Well, yeah, you *can* do it with one. But why wouldn't you want to do it better with two?!"

Now, Pollock was on the system development team and could push things forward. If his assertiveness upset the program managers from Boeing or the software developers from Northrop Grumman, then so be it. He was the operator. They were not. The Boeing reps found Pollock especially troublesome. He clashed with them on all sorts of issues, including some difficult conversations about adding classified training scenarios to simulate the GMD system's behavior more realistically. It lost him a few friends, but he was at peace with that.

On January 6, 2016, North Korea detonated a weapon that it claimed was a powerful hydrogen bomb. This was an unlikely claim. Hydrogen bombs, also known as thermonuclear weapons, use a two-phase explosion that is technologically challenging to create—only the United States, Russia, France, and China had demonstrated such a weapon. Still, the nuclear device appeared to have about a 10-kiloton yield and was North Korea's biggest so far, akin to the Little Boy bomb that decimated Hiroshima.

Jeffrey Lewis argued that, though it was too small to have been a hydrogen bomb, the development was nonetheless quite bad. He and many other analysts believed it was likely a boosted fission weapon that could be used to produce smaller, lighter warheads. The kind that didn't require a significant amount of fissile material. The kind suitable for arming a fleet of intercontinental ballistic missiles.

North Korea had long conducted nuclear or missile tests on specific anniversaries or to coincide with world events, meant to garner as much attention as possible and typically done in a cycle of provocation and condemnation: Washington and Seoul lead efforts to isolate or pacify North Korea (via proposed sanctions or military exercises), North Korea responds with a defiant act meant to deter its enemies (via nuclear or missile tests), then UN Security Council members react (via statements and maybe even sanctions), and then North Korea responds again.

The January 2016 test, Lewis thought, seemed different. It seemed like the focus was mainly on advancing North Korean nuclear weapon technology to a point that it could go into production. North Korea's official Korean Central News Agency said, "The nuclear test finally examined and confirmed the structure and specific features of movement of nuclear warhead that has been standardized to be able to be mounted on strategic ballistic rockets of the Hwasong artillery units." The Korean Central News Agency was not exactly considered a journal of record, but its rhetoric was worth parsing. And it was bad news that they were talking about a standardized design for nuclear weapons.

18

PYONGYANG A GO GO

A SMALL MEDICAL CLINIC had finally opened at Fort Greely. No longer did the soldiers need to make the long drive to Fairbanks if they or their kids got sick.

Mark Scott was making that drive most days anyway, not because his kids were sick but because one of them had made it big in the Alaskan youth hockey scene. Scott, who had never played hockey or even learned to skate, had become a goalie coach so he could support his youngest daughter. Her vague interest in ice hockey had grown into a serious youth career— she was the goalie on an all-boys Competitive League team. Outside of his day job, Scott basically lived at an ice rink in Fairbanks.

He had finally been promoted and taken over as platoon sergeant for the MPs' 2nd Platoon, leading about fifty soldiers. He then led 3rd Platoon, where a soldier didn't like the former marine's style and lodged an official complaint. Scott was again subjected to what turned out to be another unfounded investigation. In the meantime, he was shuffled out from his leadership role in the MP unit. A new battalion headquarters was built at Greely in 2016, so Scott was moved to a physical security job, helping to outfit the battalion's new facilities with security measures. He took it all in stride. He had other things to care about now.

Scott's fellow Alaskan-born soldier, Jeanette Padgett, took a relatively smoother ride. She had completed Officer Candidate School and was commissioned as an air defender. Padgett spent time on the battalion staff before being assigned to a crew, and then was placed on a team that evaluated the crew's readiness.

Bethany Hendren's career was rolling too. She had proven an outstanding MP and was selected for the GMD Qualification Course. She graduated in 2015 but twice turned down the possibility of switching from the MP unit to join a crew. She wanted to first log leadership time as a sergeant, which she could only do out on patrol.

The next year, Hendren joined Alpha crew as the communications operator. She grew to like working on crew, wielding an enormous weapon from the warmth of the control node, but she missed spending time outside.

Hendren didn't miss the cold, but guarding the missile fields had felt like real soldiering—kitting up with cold-weather gear, loading a rifle and a sidearm. She could look back fondly on when the arctic heater in the back of the Humvee broke, and her teammate placed the short end of an orange safety cone against the blower in the front to siphon the hot air into the back of the vehicle. She missed regularly seeing the northern lights, or a sunrise or sunset, while on patrol. She missed shooting at the range in minus 40°F, wearing arctic gloves and wondering how useful she would really be in a firefight while dressed like the Michelin Man.

At Greely's missile fields, Raytheon and Boeing were delivering interceptors again. The successful test had cleared the contractors to continue building the second-generation weapons and lowering them into silos. Still, Syring decided it would be best to replace the entire thruster system on the newest kill vehicles, so none of the past issues with vibrations or the Track Gate Anomaly would resurface. Engineers from Raytheon, teamed with Aerojet Rocketdyne, had built a new thruster system, but Syring would not put it on the interceptors until after a flight test to evaluate the new design.

On January 28, 2016, the Missile Defense Agency tested the new thrusters in space. There was a target, but the plan was not to hit it. The kill vehicle was to merely fly near the target, using the new divert thrusters to maneuver around in space until it was out of fuel. The test was announced as "successfully evaluating [the] performance of alternate divert thrusters for the system's Exoatmospheric Kill Vehicle." But Syring was holding something back.

Like Obering with the "glancing blow" in 2006, Syring was telling the truth, although not the whole story. The new thruster system *did* work, and they could consider the redesign a success. But a circuit board, which was not technically part of the new system, shorted out during the flight and could not control one of the four thrusters. Syring ordered a review to study what had happened. The agency concluded that "foreign object damage" was the most likely culprit, meaning something had shaken loose within the kill vehicle and fallen onto the circuit board. The glitch might have caused the kill vehicle to miss on a real intercept.

Syring, nevertheless, was satisfied with the new design and ordered production to start, with a new manufacturing process to better protect the circuit boards on the newest kill vehicles. MDA did not plan to go back and fix the circuit boards on its older interceptors. It was a risk, but a risk they felt comfortable taking. The agency would field eight fully upgraded second-generation interceptors. These would be added to the sixteen partially upgraded second-generation interceptors and twenty first-generation interceptors that were already deployed.

A week after the thruster test, at 5:30 P.M. on Super Bowl Sunday, Northern Command and the 100th Missile Defense Brigade got a Quick Alert. They were waiting for it. Satellites had been watching North Korea's Sohae Satellite Launching Station for about a month. A three-stage Unha-series rocket blasted off and succeeded in dumping its Kwangmyongsong-4 meteorology satellite into space. It appeared to be a repeat of the December 2012 launch. Northern Command officials at first took solace that the satellite appeared to have missed its trajectory and was tumbling in orbit, but then intelligence reports estimated the satellite weighed twice as much as the one launched four years earlier. North Korean nukes were getting lighter and more powerful, while North Korean rockets were launching heavier payloads (though not launching them accurately).

On April 14, 2016, the indications and warnings were flowing in again. This time, however, North Korea was attempting its first test launch of a new road-mobile Musudan intermediate-range ballistic missile. There was no pretension that the Musudan was a peaceful satellite launch vehicle like the Unha. The Musudan was a weapon designed to reach Japan or US forces on Guam. American and South Korean intelligence assets had seen the missile being moved near Wonsan, by a bay on North Korea's east coast. The next day, Lieutenant Colonel Michael Strawbridge and his Delta crew were on shift for the brigade.

Strawbridge had joined the unit in 2009, become a deputy director three years later, then took over Delta crew two years after that. He was intense and charismatic and led the most excitable of the five battalion crews.

As a deputy director, Strawbridge had worked for Lieutenant Colonel Chad Witt, who believed his soldiers needed to really sound off, to be able to tune out—or drown out—all outside noise during a mission. For training runs, Witt had played episodes of *The Jerry Springer Show* on the television at top volume. Then, for crew certifications or real-world events, he would keep the television off. If the crew could function with ridiculous background noise, they could certainly do the job without it. Strawbridge carried that on and kept his crew excited and loud. To him, watching Michalski's laconic Charlie crew was like sitting in church.

On downtime, especially for midnight shifts, Strawbridge allowed Delta crew to play card games or watch sports. He tried to keep the job fun for his soldiers, especially as the training runs were getting tougher and the North Korean threat was getting scarier.

Susan Rice, Obama's national security adviser, was in Colorado Springs for a speech at the Air Force Academy and for briefings from Northern Command, Strategic Command, and the 100th Missile Defense Brigade about North Korea's missiles and the brigade's ability to defend against them. As the North Koreans appeared closer to launching the Musudan, Rice and Admiral Cecil Haney, the Strategic Command chief, were shuttled from Peterson Air Force Base, a few miles down the road, to the missile crew nodes at Schriever Air Force Base.

Lieutenant Colonel Mike Tobey walked into the node to tell Strawbridge that Rice was coming, and that she might be dropping in to see a crew in action. Maybe, if there was time, they would do a demo run to give her an idea of how the system worked?

Tobey had been in the original big class of thirty students at the GMD Qualification Course. Tobey's wife, Geneen, had been in that big class too, and shared the distinguished honor graduate title with Michalski. Now Geneen worked on Boeing's GMD team, often quarreling with Pollock, and Mike still worked at the brigade. The Tobeys were deeply experienced in homeland missile defense, and Mike Tobey knew how big a deal it was to have the national security adviser popping in to learn about the mission. While Strawbridge and Tobey discussed Rice's visit, an updated intelligence report came in, and now projected the North Koreans would launch at any moment.

Colonel Tim Lawson, the brigade commander, was down the hall waiting to receive Rice and Haney. Tobey ran out to warn Lawson. "Quick, go get them, and get your ass in here!" Tobey said. Urgency eclipsed decorum, but Lawson understood and ran outside to find Rice and Haney, and brought them into the node.

Strawbridge was ready, but was also sweating into his uniform. He had been on crew for a North Korean test launch the previous year, but never with the president's national security adviser and a combatant commander peering over his shoulder. Strawbridge could hear Rice and Haney asking lots of questions. Then he heard the piercing *beep, beep, beep* of the Quick Alert, and he went to work.

Strawbridge knew that North Korea had not yet tested a reentry vehicle to carry a nuclear warhead up to space and back down to Earth, so this launch was likely just a test. This was in the back of his mind, though, and not something he considered until after afterward. Delta crew's soldiers were dialed in, prepared to do their jobs. Working their mission was second nature, like speaking an acquired language or driving with a stick shift. Still, Strawbridge could hear Rice and Haney asking questions, because part of the job was listening to many conversations simultaneously, and crew members typically developed an expanded auditory perception. They all needed to have total awareness—this was how Meakins and the original crews developed the operating procedures—so they constantly trained to overhear one another's conversations, which sometimes made dinner at a crowded restaurant interesting.

Delta crew worked up a sweat for the Musudan launch, and gave Rice and Haney a lively real-world demonstration, but the soldiers did not have to do more than collect data. North Korea's test ended quickly in what the Pentagon called "a fiery, catastrophic attempt at a launch." The Musudan exploded not far from its launchpad.

Across town from Schriever, at Northern Command headquarters, US Air Force General Lori Robinson took command. On May 13, 2016, she became the first female officer to lead a unified combatant command and, therefore, the highest-ranking woman in the US military's 240-year history. As a commander, she seemed almost laid-back, but it was more of an affectation, a Chuck Yeager style that she honed early in her career as an air weapons controller, the calm voice on the radio talking pilots through combat missions. Robinson was ambitious and an incisive leader.

She and her husband, David, had both been active-duty air force officers in the mid-1990s. The Pentagon was moving her to Japan and him to South Korea, and in most military families that would mean the wife would leave the service and join her husband. Instead, he took an airline job, and she ascended to become a four-star general. And she did it fast. Between June 2012 and October 2014, she climbed from a two-star general at Air Forces Central Command to a four-star leading Pacific Air Forces. Now she was the Northern Command chief, managing the Pentagon's expansive homeland defense and civil support missions. If North Korea launched a missile in anger, the missile crews could only shoot at it under her authority.

Dr. John Schilling, an aerospace engineer and a long-time North Korea watcher, was not especially alarmed by the

Musudan missile, but a less publicized North Korean test that same month had caught his attention. The week before the Musudan launch ended in "fiery, catastrophic" failure, the North Koreans had conducted a ground test of a big liquid-fuel engine, and published images to prove their acumen. Schilling, rather conveniently, was that day attending a conference of American rocket experts, some of whom had worked on the United States' old liquid-fuel ICBMs. Schilling studied the images and polled his colleagues. The consensus was not good.

North Korea's new rocket engine represented a huge technological leap. Pyongyang had traditionally used a mix of kerosene and nitric acid to power its rockets, based on outdated Scud missile technology that gave them only a limited reach. The large engine, however, appeared to use high-energy propellants, which would mean Kim Jong-un's missiles could potentially deliver nuclear warheads to New York or Washington. Schilling concluded that "flight tests of a North Korean ICBM could begin in as little as a year."

Jeffrey Lewis agreed with Schilling. The new engine was a troubling development. Lewis had been flippant about North Korea's early nuclear program, but he was no longer joking or laughing. He began writing a series of op-eds arguing that it was time to stop considering North Korea as a punch line. The cover of *The New Yorker* earlier that year depicted Kim as a toddler playing with toy missiles. The country seemed bizarre and isolated and easy to lampoon, but its dictator was brutal and his missiles were real.

The North Korean tests pressed on. There was a quick succession of failed Musudan tests. The launches were done so quickly—three tests in April, one in May, and two on June 22—that it did not appear the North Koreans were taking time to study their failures and improve the missile. Still, one of the two Musudans that was launched on June 22 managed to travel four hundred kilometers and reach over one thousand kilometers altitude. Schilling remained unimpressed with the Musudan, but felt it was time to worry about North Korea's longer-range missiles. North Korean ICBMs used the same ex-Soviet engine as the Musudan, albeit in a clustered and multistage setup, and they had now used one of those engines successfully.

In August North Korea notched a successful test of a solid-fuel submarine-launched ballistic missile. Then, on September 9, they detonated an atomic bomb more powerful than the A-bomb used at Hiroshima.

19

ICBM-RANGE

JARROD CUTHBERTSON WAS NOW a young officer with a family. He'd received an online bachelor's degree with the GI Bill, passed the GMD Qualification Course, completed Officer Candidate School, and joined a battalion crew at Fort Greely. As a lieutenant, the best career move would have been to transfer back to the MP unit so he could get leadership time, but he wanted more opportunities for his family. He loved Fort Greely, but Delta Junction could only offer so much, and Colorado Springs offered plenty.

He was able to swap places with a lieutenant in Colorado Springs who wanted to try Alaskan life. Cuthbertson was sent directly to Echo crew at the brigade as the sensors operator. He already had a top secret clearance and was fully certified for crew work. It was a seamless move.

In September 2016, as Cuthbertson was settling into life in the Lower 48, Colonel Kevin Kick took command of the 100th Missile Defense Brigade. Kick had a background of command experience, but strategic missile defense was new to him. He immediately flew to Greely to learn more about the battalion there. "Readiness" was on his mind. The brigade and battalion missile crews had obligations to the army, to the National Guard, to their families, to their mission—and the mission was growing more complex as more interceptors were introduced and more North Korean missiles had to be addressed. His job was to ensure they were ready for it all.

At Greely, the crews and staff told Kick that it was a strain to provide five battle-ready crews, each with five proficient soldiers, filling three shifts a day. They lacked the manpower and often had to fill shifts with alternate crew members. If somebody was sick or on a training exercise or otherwise unavailable, their seat would be temporarily occupied by another certified crew member. This wasn't ideal because the crews functioned best as experienced teams to coordinate the swift execution of many tasks.

The battalion's manpower issue was punctuated with an exclamation mark in early 2017. A few months after Kick arrived at the brigade, Lieutenant General James Dickinson took over Army Space and Missile Defense Command. Dickinson ordered a no-notice crew evaluation at Greely. It did not go well. A crew, encumbered by too many alternates, had struggled to work cohesively, and it showed.

Kick needed no more convincing. No-notice crew evaluations would become the norm. Alternate crew members would become the exception. And the brigade in Colorado and battalion in Alaska would both go to twelve-hour shifts. The plan was for the crews to pull a month of day shifts and then a month of midnight shifts, followed by two weeks of "reset." The two weeks were meant to give the soldiers time for vacations, medical appointments, army obligations, or whatever else might take them off shift.

But during that month of midnight shifts, the soldiers' families were not living the same vampiric life, and one parent's sudden absenteeism could create friction at home. In many cases, though, it meant the soldier on midnight shifts simply tried to stay awake to be with their family for a few hours during the day, wandering around at home in a sort of daze, forgetting where they put the car keys or unable to find the glasses they were still wearing. Michalski and Kiraly worried that those crew members, trying to lead both a professional and family life, might not be at the top of their game by the time they went back to work.

The two officers drove across town to Peterson Air Force Base, where a medical clinic had done sleep studies for airmen on shift work. They asked doctors there to review the crews' schedules. The conclusion was that eight-hour shifts were ideal. It didn't fly with Kick though. North Korea was shooting off missiles too regularly—all the crews had to be fully manned, certified, and ready, and Kick felt the best way to do that with a limited pool of soldiers at Greely was to use twelve-hour shifts.

Crew members were typically asked to work eighteen to twenty-four months before being offered another assignment in the brigade. Those assignments would allow them to rest with a nine-to-five-type job, such as managing resources or running readiness evaluations or working in the intelligence shop. But for the more senior-ranked deputy directors and directors, there were fewer assignments available. They simply could not get burned out. Neither Michalski nor Kiraly asked to come off crew.

The soldiers were, at least, on the cusp of notching a

major win. The Missile Defense Agency and the contractors and all the organizations that claimed a share of the enterprise had, finally, committed to giving each crew member dual computer monitors. Pollock was in a position to push it forward too. His development team flew out to Huntsville, Alabama, to take the new hardware and software for some test runs, and immediately began writing new procedures for using their expanded real estate.

When the monitors arrived in the nodes, it was like Christmas morning. Kick asked everyone how they liked it, and nearly everyone was ecstatic. Michalski was the exception. *What am I going to fill this other monitor with? Shouldn't the monitors be stacked vertically instead of side-by-side? What if some information falls outside my peripheral vision?* Michalski did not voice his misgivings. He did not want to ruin the crews' big triumph.

Kiraly's Alpha crew was asked to help plan the upcoming test of the homeland missile defense system against an ICBM-range target. It would be held in the spring, and be the longest and highest-speed intercept yet attempted. Patricia Young was thrilled. She'd watched the interceptor launched by Michalski in 2014, and would now get to help plan the tactics, techniques, and procedures for the new test mission, and then be on the crew that launched it. Kiraly was pleased as well. Alpha crew, by simple bad luck, had not been on shift during any of the North Korean launches, so at least they would get to fire off one of the redesigned, second-generation interceptors. Alpha crew put in hours and hours of prep work and training for it. The test was scheduled to occur on the last day of Alpha crew's "reset" period, before they went back to starting their regular rotation of shifts. Then word came that the test would be pushed back by one day.

Instead, Echo crew would be brought in from its day off to run the test from the second node. Kiraly, Young, and the others were crushed. After all their work for the test, Echo crew would get to stroll into the second node, fire off the interceptor, and go home. Michalski, Strawbridge, Pollock, and the other directors felt bad for Kiraly. He'd been around since the beginning, worked hard, and knew the system as well as anybody, but the schedule acted against him.

To the MDA folks, it seemed a miracle that the ICBM-range test was happening at all. Syring had begun holding meetings for the event in the summer of 2016. The meetings were several hours long, several times a week, and typically ran through PowerPoint decks with several hundred slides. The engineers, including Syring, were reviewing every single component on the target missile, every single component on the interceptor, all of the telemetry data they were expecting, and all of the aircraft and all of the satellites that would be flying to collect still more data. If something appeared to be out of order by a micron, Syring would stop the meeting and it would be investigated. There was no room for error. Nothing could be left to chance.

Every few days, some issue arose that caused the discussion to shift toward scrubbing the test. But, every time, the issue was solved and they pushed on until the next issue cropped up.

The week of the test came, and somehow they had cleared each hurdle. Syring and his MDA leadership team flew out to Colorado Springs so they could watch from the conference room behind the brigade node at Schriever. Everyone at the facility on Schriever was tense. Suddenly all the bosses were around all the time, and ushering each of them through the base's layer upon layer of security checkpoints was brutal. *I don't have any more security badges to hand over! Doesn't it help that my picture is on the damn wall?!*

Chris Johnson, MDA's chief of public affairs, had not slept in days. All of the agency's previous tests of the homeland missile defense system had been preceded by a series of announcements about the event. The Pentagon wanted to show it had nothing to hide, and wanted to avoid freaking out the city of Los Angeles by unexpectedly blasting a fifty-five-foot missile interceptor up the coast. Johnson had planned to do the usual media blitz and was scheduling interviews and inviting a press pool, but a few weeks before the test he was told to put a lid on it. Now it was secret.

An official from the Pentagon's Joint Staff had called Syring and told him no more publicizing the tests, not even the date. Syring demurred. He worried that—aside from possibly frightening some Californians—the abrupt secrecy would cause suspicion among the media and then possibly among Congress, as though the test was being hidden so they could skew the results. The Joint Staff didn't budge. The test had to be secret. They were worried that if certain foreign countries knew when the test would happen, then those countries could more easily spy on it. There were even exclusion windows for when the test could not happen because unfriendly Chinese satellites were known to be overhead in that time frame.

All the reporters covering the Pentagon knew it was coming anyway, and the day before the test they were all calling Johnson, every few minutes, all day long, to confirm it. He could not tell them anything.

At six the next morning, Johnson was driving to Schriever when he got another phone call, this time from Rear Admiral Jon Hill, MDA's deputy director. Hill said Secretary of Defense James Mattis had just called Syring, and Mattis was angry to have woken up that morning and read in the news that there was going to be a big missile defense test today. It was supposed to be a secret, but it was the first story in the Pentagon's Early Bird morning news roundup.

The reality was that hiding this sort of event was unreasonable. The FAA had to publish a "notice to airmen" so no aircraft accidently flew into the path of the target or the interceptor. The Coast Guard had to publish a "notice to mariners" so no vessels were chugging along in the Pacific when the first stage of a booster rocket dropped out of the sky and ruined some sailor's day. If journalists monitored those notices, then surely curious foreign countries did too.

Still, getting an earful from Mattis was not a good way to start an already stressful day, so Syring was in a lousy mood as his entourage crowded into the 100th Missile Defense Brigade's conference room between the two nodes. The space was like a version of the conference room from *Dr. Strangelove*, with a big round conference table and big television monitors overhead. On Tuesday, May 30, it was saturated with almost one hundred engineers and generals and admirals. The most important of them had seats at the table, with everyone else lining the back and side walls. For the crowd, there was nothing to do but wait. Nobody was allowed to bring in mobile phones, so it was all hand-wringing and nervous murmuring.

The countdown began, the murmuring stopped, and the target launched.

Echo crew went to work, methodically moving through the checklists that Kiraly's Alpha crew had created and soaking in the data at their consoles. One radar reported tracking the target, the next radar reported tracking the target.

In the conference room, it felt like an hour had passed between when the target launched and when the interceptor launched. It was less than twenty minutes. The order was given to "go weapons free," and the GMD system would launch its interceptor at any moment.

Strawbridge's crew had won a "best crew" competition that year, so he'd been invited to watch the launch from the Ronald Reagan Memorial Viewing Site, above Vandenberg. Strawbridge had thought it was too cloudy and the test would be scrubbed, but the clouds broke. Then Amtrak's Pacific Surfliner had come chugging past Vandenberg, as it did several times a day, but it only delayed the test briefly. So Strawbridge stood there in the pleasantly cool weather and watched as the silo's clamshell doors swung open and the second-generation weapon, with its new navigation and thruster equipment, lifted off into a clear California sky.

At Schriever, the wait between when the interceptor was launched and when it was supposed to make impact felt like several hours. It was actually less than ten minutes. The conference room was completely silent. Syring, the pragmatic and reserved navy engineer, was visibly uneasy.

Johnson had sat in on many of the planning meetings

and knew the system, but he was a public affairs officer and not a technical person. He had only a vague idea of what was happening. A young engineer sitting next to Johnson had a much more detailed understanding of the test. The engineer had explained some details on an information sheet, showing what each of the stages meant, how much time between each stage, and so on.

The information sheet said the interceptor should have reached the target by now. It was several seconds beyond the intercept point and there was still no report, so Johnson turned to ask the engineer. The young man had his head in his hands. He was crying. Johnson's blood pressure sky-rocketed. *Oh shit it failed and now there are so many reporters to call back.*

A few more seconds passed, and then somebody wearing a headset called out that it was an intercept. Johnson, con-fused, looked up to the overhead screen showing an infrared image of the target, and a second or two later the screen flashed bright yellow and orange as the interceptor collided with and destroyed the warhead. Johnson turned again to the young engineer.

"What the fuck man?!"

"Yeah, sorry," the engineer said, "I guess the target feed just lagged a few seconds behind."

Syring stood up. The normally dour admiral was ebullient. Heartfelt, full-bodied handshakes were exchanged all around. The oppressive tension had blown out of the room, but only temporarily. Now they had to wait for all the telemetry data to confirm that the intercept was a success, and not a "glancing blow" or worse. The interceptor had hit something. Was it the target? The data collected from the test was transmitted to MDA, and then had to be digested through computer algorithms, the algorithms had to create the hydrocode analysis, and then it had to be vetted by the engineers.

Syring was pacing up and down the long hallway outside the node. Johnson now had his phone and every time he got off a call with one reporter, it would ring with another. Syring, who had never shown much interest in the media, was walking up to Johnson every few minutes to ask what the reporters were saying.

It didn't just feel like the analysis took hours, it actually did take hours. About three. Eventually, all the engineers came back into the conference room to announce that they each agreed: the test met all its objectives. The radars had all tracked the target and communicated properly, the target had released countermeasures and the interceptor had seen and dismissed them, and the target was destroyed. It was a success. The mock ICBM launched from Kwajalein and traveled about 5,500 kilometers toward the West Coast.

The White House called seeking recorded video of the test, in case they wanted to publicize it. Syring spoke briefly with the president and then that was it. Enough. Syring said he was going to sleep and went back to his hotel around 5:00 P.M.

The next morning, Johnson went to 7-Eleven and bought all the store's copies of *USA Today*, which had the test on its front page. He met Syring and they called into the Pentagon pressroom to brief the media there on the event. The briefing was a disappointment for Syring and Johnson. They felt they had just achieved a major accomplishment, based on years of hard work. The last year especially had been difficult, and the last week almost sadistic. But the reporters, naturally skeptical and now doubly so because of the clumsy attempt to hide the test, had some questions.

A week later, Syring was sitting before the House Armed Services Committee for more questions. He had twenty-eight pages of testimony but requested instead to show a two-minute video from the intercept. He gave a solemn narration of the dramatic footage. Though proud of the accomplishment, the admiral took no victory lap and was quick to express concern for the future.

"I would not say we are comfortably ahead of the threat," Syring lamented. "The last six months have caused great concern to me in the advancement of and demonstration of technology, of ballistic missiles from North Korea." He warned that North Korea was improving its missiles and countermeasures at an alarming rate, so he hoped the homeland missile defense system could be made more capable.

But Syring's time at MDA was up. The next week, he retired.

The brigade's crews were happy with the test result, but their focus was squarely on North Korea. Kim Jong-un had been testing medium- and intermediate-range missiles nonstop, and it appeared he might soon test an ICBM. Probably a mobile missile too. The sort of weapon that could be hidden, driven anywhere, and then launched.

By June, the intelligence community was reporting that a test was likely. By July, they were operating under a "period of interest." General Lori Robinson ordered Northern Command to add crew members to its watch shifts. At Greely, Boeing was working to get the last of the forty-four interceptors into silos, but much of those activities had to be suspended in case the interceptors already in the ground needed to be launched against a North Korean ICBM.

20

24/7/365

ON JULY 4, INTELLIGENCE showed significant movement around North Korea's Panghyon Aircraft Factory, in a bucolic valley in the country's west. Around 4:20 P.M. spy satellites could see a two-stage, liquid-fueled Hwasong-14 ICBM being readied on its mobile launcher. North Korean scientists were fueling and inspecting it, and Kim Jong-un was in attendance.

At Fort Greely, Bethany Hendren's Alpha crew was on shift. They were lucky. Most of the other crew members wanted this mission. There had been much talk about who would get to sit on crew for it, who might get to make history. Hendren wasn't exactly nervous, but there was a new sort of excitement among Alpha crew. Somewhere in their minds, they were aware that they might not get authority to shoot, and that even if they did, there were plenty of scenarios in which an intercept could not happen. But these weren't scenarios they worried much about.

At 5:30 P.M. the Quick Alert sounded—the flashing white light and shrill *beep, beep, beep.* Alpha crew was at their consoles. They were prepared for it, but the alert was eternally startling. On the center overhead television screen in the node, a globe whirled around and displayed a red dot near

Panghyon, and soon a red threat fan showing the missile's trajectory flying up toward the Sea of Japan. *How far will it go?*

Hendren was the communications operator. It was her job to notify the MPs to clear the missile fields in case interceptors were to be launched. There were scripts for those warnings in the big books of procedures that the crews kept at each console. Hendren had memorized the warnings over hours upon hours of training runs.

Her adrenaline began moving with the first note of the Quick Alert and she was on the phone instantly. "Stand by," she said, and began looking for her book. She could not find it. "Stand by." Hendren looked for three long seconds before her mind shifted into procedural-memory mode. As a matter of course, from rote memory, she started giving her alerts and updates, and firing up the sirens that warn everyone away from the missile fields at Greely. The sirens could be heard throughout Delta Junction.

Hendren was also certified as a weapons operator, and she listened carefully to the whole mission. Her screens were set up so she could do the weapons operator job too, or help with parts of it, if she really had to.

The red threat fan updated to show the missile's trajectory was highly lofted—it was flying almost straight up in the air and not on a flatter trajectory that could take it over neighboring Japan or toward the United States. The missile reached 2,802 kilometers up into space (the International Space Station orbits about 400 kilometers above Earth). It flew for thirty-seven minutes and splashed into the Sea of Japan 934 kilometers from its launch site, but never came within range for an intercept.

According to Pyongyang's official Korean Central News Agency, Kim Jong-un, after seeing his first-ever successful ICBM flight test, said, "I guess they are not too happy with the gift package we sent them for the occasion of their Independence Day. We should often send them gift packages so they won't be too bored." The news agency noted that Kim made his comment "with a guffaw." The news agency also said the Hwasong-14 was capable of striking the "heart of the United States" with "large heavy nuclear warheads." This was a bit of an exaggeration, but only a bit. If North Korea wanted to, it could likely use the Hwasong-14 ICBM to deliver a three hundred kilogram nuclear warhead to Alaska or Seattle.

In early 2017 Major Matt Pollock was again assigned as director for the brigade's Bravo crew. The crews had all taken to giving themselves nicknames, and Pollock thought Bravo Battle Crew was the lamest of the five nicknames. He solicited the crew to come up with something better, and Aaron Coons, a young lieutenant on the crew, asked his cousin to draw a new graphic for their insignia. Coons gave the new design to Pollock; it was a muscular soldier punching a North Korean missile in half. They adopted the unofficial insignia and renamed themselves the Bravo Brawlers. There was also the Alpha Assassins, Charlie Rock Crew, Delta Destroyers, and Echo Eliminators.

Before returning as a director, Pollock had made some gains in his efforts to ensure the crews could train as much as they wanted (or as much as he wanted). After about three years of arguing and lobbying, a program was put in place to teach the crew members how to operate the training software so the crews could run their own training scenarios without relying on the Missile Defense Agency's schedule. It would take several more months to get it all sorted, but the trainer program would eventually help to productively pass the hours on shift.

Even Pollock admitted the twelve-hour shifts were hard. He'd done shift work as a regular active-duty soldier, working almost nonstop throughout his tour on the communications team for the Supreme Allied Commander during the Bosnian War. Those were short spurts though.

Nonetheless, Pollock felt shift work near home was better than the nonstop work when he was deployed. He had missed his oldest son's first T-ball season during the Bosnian War, but now for his youngest he was only missing a game or two. The shifts were exhausting, but the mission felt too important. He might have wandered around the house in a daze that afternoon, but once he stepped into the node, the conditioned air and the familiar consciousness rushed back.

After the July 4 test, the crews were even more wired-in for their shifts. Any notable missile launch triggered a Quick Alert. Space launches were common and not too affecting for the crews. Training launches in China or elsewhere were similar. Russian ICBM tests could be a little nerve-wracking because, for a brief time, it seemed like the missile was heading across the Arctic toward the United States. Shorter-range missile launches in Syria or Yemen were frequent in 2017 and were more surreal and distressing to watch. *Someone at the other end of this is probably dying,* Pollock thought.

No matter how many training runs or how many real-world events a crew sat through, no matter how much a pending event was discussed, and no matter how much certainty about the launch time, everybody still got a jolt from the Quick Alert.

Pollock and the Bravo Brawlers were expecting a big jolt on July 28. The intelligence community had been reporting that the next North Korean ICBM test was likely. The missile's transporter-erector-launcher vehicle was spotted on the move near Kusong, not far from the Panghyon Aircraft Factory where the first ICBM had been tested earlier that month. Around July 18 it was clear that another test launch was coming, not at the Panghyon Aircraft Factory but at North Korea's No. 65 Factory, which built the transporter-erector-launcher vehicles.

On July 27, satellite imagery showed the North Koreans had begun preparations for the launch, which included constructing a viewing area near the site for Kim Jong-un. On July 28 the intel analysts knew almost to the minute when the launch would occur. It would, for a change, be during the North Korean night. It would also be during Bravo crew's shift.

The Hwasong-14 ICBM was launched from the No. 65 Factory at 11:41 P.M. local time. Pollock's Bravo crew could tell early on that it would be a successful flight. Their experience was that most failures happened as the missile boosted. They tracked this one for forty-seven minutes. It flew on a lofted trajectory up to 3,700 kilometers into space, and traveled about 1,000 kilometers from the launch site. It was a higher-performance flight than the first test, and Pyongyang said the unusual launch time and location were meant to demonstrate "the capability of making surprise launch of ICBM in any region and place any time."

Bravo crew was not itching to shoot the North Korean missile down, and they couldn't have anyway given its lofted trajectory, but they did desire a feeling of readiness. They wanted to know that they and their equipment were well prepared if called upon. They wanted to see their system work faultlessly, even if it was just tracking a missile. It had worked, but Pollock was convinced that it could have worked better. He again set out agitating for changes to the home-land missile defense system after he'd observed how it re-acted to the ICBM launch, and observed what the system could and could not see. The changes this time were made quickly. New procedures were written and adopted based on the crews' experiences on July 4 and July 28, and radar data would be used more efficiently.

On September 3, the North Koreans detonated a nuclear device. They said it was a hydrogen bomb that could be car-ried by an ICBM. It was not clear if the weapon could really be carried by a missile, but the blast was enormous. Jeffrey Lewis and a team of nuclear weapons and satellite imagery experts studied synthetic aperture radar imaging of North Korea's Punggye-ri Nuclear Test Site as an Airbus satellite had captured imaging of the precipitous Punggye-ri before and after the test. The experts found the device was powerful enough to have reshaped the mountain under which it was detonated. Several of the higher-end estimates placed the weapon's yield at around 250 to 300 kilotons—or more than sixteen times the explosive energy of the bomb dropped on Hiroshima.

The timing wasn't great. The United States and North Korea were engaged in an especially heated, if somewhat repetitive, repartee. US president Donald Trump said North Korean threats would "be met with fire and fury like the world has never seen." Kim Jong-un then specifically threatened "enveloping fire at the areas around Guam with medium-to-long-range strategic ballistic rocket Hwasong-12 in order to contain the US major military bases on Guam."

Secretary of Defense Jim Mattis could not abide a threat against the seven thousand US military personnel who were deployed at two bases on Guam, so he issued his own warning: "Any threat to the United States or its territories, including Guam, or our allies, will be met with a massive military response—a response both effective and overwhelming." Mattis then clarified by adding: "We are not looking to the total annihilation of a country, namely North Korea, but as I said, we have many options to do so."

The Hwasong-14 ICBM tests had been lofted upward and never traveled more than one thousand kilometers away from North Korea. They were never in range for an intercept. It was expected that North Korea wanted to test reentry vehicles, however, and a lofted trajectory was not ideal for that because the stresses experienced would be quite different. Their likely solution was to test reentry vehicles on intermediate-range missiles with a normal, flatter trajectory that took them well out into the Pacific. On August 28, North Korea launched over Japan a Hwasong-12 missile, possibly to test a reentry vehicle. North Korean rockets had overflown Japan a handful of times before, but this was the first time they did it with a missile designed to carry a nuclear weapon. It caused international outcry, and considerable anger among the Japanese.

By mid-September, the North Koreans were again poised to launch a Hwasong-12, and were doing so amid specific threats to aim the missile at or near Guam. The 210-square-mile island was 3,200 kilometers southeast of the Korean peninsula, and was now a favorite object for Kim's antagonism.

The intelligence reports suggested North Korea's missile would fly over Japan, and the rumor mill suggested that if it did fly over Japan, and was in range for an intercept, then the crew on shift would be ordered to destroy it.

Michalski's Charlie crew had been about to go on shift when a general from the Colorado National Guard, visiting Schriever to meet soldiers in the 100th Missile Defense Brigade, dropped by. He asked Michalski how long he'd been in the unit. "Fourteen years, sir."

"Fourteen years?! Then how have I never heard of you?" the general asked. Michalski, the calmest and quietest of the 100th's crew directors, was livid. *How have you never heard of me? Interesting question, sir, because I've never heard of you either.*

"Sir, you may not have heard of me, but the missile defense community has," he said, politely. The general was surprised that Michalski had not ventured into other units or other specialties. After all, that was how the army built a well-rounded soldier. That was how a soldier became a general. But that wasn't why Michalski was there. Michalski, who left active service as soon as he could after West Point, who was marked in Meakins's Illinois National Guard unit as "a junior officer with a bad attitude," had specifically made homeland missile defense his calling. He had no interest in another job.

"Sir, if this actually were to happen tomorrow," Michalski asked, "if North Korea launches, wouldn't you want the most seasoned guy—who's been on the system for fourteen years and has seen all there is to see—to be on the console for that event?"

On September 14, Michalski's Charlie crew was on the consoles. Michalski was nervous before the shift. It reminded him of his time as an Olympic tennis hopeful. He would walk around before a big match feeling anxious and a little queasy, but as soon as he walked out on the court, the nerves were gone. And the moment he walked into the node and sat in the director's chair, his nerves were gone. He was ready. Not just to sit and take screenshots of a North Korean missile flight, but to destroy that missile. *We're going to engage the threat*, Michalski thought to himself, matter-of-factly.

Just before 4:00 P.M., the Quick Alert shifted Charlie crew into gear. Michalski was fully committed to launching interceptors in combat for the first time in history. It was a responsibility he wanted. If everything went right, it would be the crew's success. If anything went wrong, it would be Michalski's failure.

Charlie crew saw the threat fan extend from Pyongyang's Sunan International Airport, far over Hokkaido, Japan, and into the Pacific. Suddenly, the GMD system reported that it had "weapons access." For Michalski, this meant his crew could input launch commands, if they were given the authority.

The threat fan showed the missile was heading not to Guam but out toward open ocean well north of Hawaii. It was projected to fly about 3,700 kilometers (conspicuously just a few hundred kilometers farther than the distance to Guam).

Michalski was briefing the missile defense officer at Northern Command, every thirty seconds, about how much more time they'd have weapons access. He read off the weapons engagement times—how long before it would be too late to launch an interceptor. "Two minutes to engagement." He waited for his authorization. "Minute and a half to engagement."

Michalski was watching a little blue bar recede across his monitor that indicated the interceptor launch window was closing. He was waiting to give the order to "go weapons free." The missile defense officer at Northern Command did not necessarily need updates every thirty seconds. The officer was fully aware of how much time was left in Charlie crew's window to shoot, but Michalski knew there were perhaps hundreds of others, including the country's key decision makers and commanders, like General Lori Robinson, listening to his reporting. He wanted to make the situation clear.

Robinson could hear everything on the Ops Loop, and could see what Charlie crew was seeing. She was also on another command net, updating Mattis in what the secretary would later praise as her "steady, clipped voice on the net giving updates."

Getting weapons release authorization as early as possible was crucial for the crews. The GMD software—and its millions of lines of code and algorithms—could determine when was the best time to launch the interceptors. If authorized to launch before the "weapons access" window opens, the director can choose to let the system decide, or it can be held back, constrained, until a time of the director's choosing. If that authorization comes late, all the crews can do is let the system launch as soon as possible, and not necessarily at the ideal time.

In his last thirty-second update, Michalski added, "If we're going to engage this, we have to do it now." He did not get a launch order, and the blue bar ran out. The window closed.

Two months later, Bravo crew was ready to see if the tweaks to the system worked. There were some new procedures and, Pollock hoped, there would be some new radar data too. There was also finally a full complement of forty-four interceptors—the last one had been lowered into its silo three weeks earlier.

The intelligence reports once more indicated a North Korean ICBM test was on the schedule during Bravo crew's shift. This one was expected to be a different missile. Unlike its predecessors, the Hwasong-15 was not shown publicly in North Korea before its launch. It was much bigger too, 70.5 feet long and 6.5 feet in diameter.

Intelligence reporting on the Hwasong-15's launch had become clearer in early November. Preparations at a new position near Pyongsong, nineteen miles from Pyongyang, were noticed about three days before the launch. This time, the North Koreans were not building the obvious observation platform for Kim Jong-un. To be sneakier, he was using a new mobile trailer. Despite the North Korean efforts at stealth, around 9:00 A.M. on November 28, the intelligence reports noted work was being done on the Hwasong-15's launchpad. Around 10:00 A.M. the ICBM was stood up on its firing table.

At 12:17 P.M. Pollock and Bravo crew were snapped into action by the Quick Alert. The big Hwasong-15 boosted into the early North Korean morning. It flew for nearly fifty-four minutes, about 4,500 kilometers into space, and again the lofted trajectory took it only about 960 kilometers from its launchpad. Assessments differed as to whether the test payload, which sat in place of what would be a nuclear warhead, had survived reentry into Earth's atmosphere. The weapon's reentry vehicle might not have worked. There was general agreement, however, that the vehicle appeared roomy enough to house large or multiple warheads, or even decoys to try to fool the US homeland missile defense system.

The North Korean Central News Agency said the Hwasong-15 ICBM was capable of carrying a "super-large heavy warhead" and "striking the whole mainland of the US." Kim Jong-un said his country had finally completed its nuclear force. Indeed, the Hwasong-15 had shown itself to be capable of reaching anywhere in the United States.

The good news, at least, was that the changes made to the missile defense system had worked exactly as Pollock had hoped. He was pleased. It was, at times, difficult to deal with multiple contractors and bureaucracies, and to stay motivated through long hours, but the crews all found it thoroughly gratifying to see their input bear fruit.

The Bravo Brawlers had been on shift for five North Korean missile launches in 2017. "Kim Jong-un must have Bravo crew's schedule," Kick, the brigade commander, would say the next year during Pollock's promotion to lieutenant colonel. Some crews weren't on for any. Kiraly's Alpha crew, on top of getting bumped from his test intercept, had missed all of the North Korean launches.

During weekend shifts, while Pollock was still waiting for the ability to manage his own training runs, Bravo crew sometimes sat around and discussed what it would be like if they really did destroy an inbound nuclear warhead in space.

What kind of person would you then become?

Would you want to be on the cover of Time *magazine because you just saved Los Angeles?*

Or would you want to keep working and remain invisible?

The majority of Bravo crew said they would want to remain invisible. Pollock agreed.

EPILOGUE

THE MISSILE DEFENSE ADVOCACY ALLIANCE sponsors a series of discussions on various approaches to the missile problem. The events are normally quiet affairs to mull over new ideas or the current state-of-the-art. On November 2, 2017, the alliance held an event on the top floor of the Hart Senate Office Building, in a sunny room with expansive views of Washington. About twenty young, well-dressed congressional aides were there to take notes for their bosses, plus a few older engineers who follow these issues, and a handful of reporters. Riki Ellison founded the alliance and runs its panel discussions. Ellison is a broad, tough-looking man with close-cropped salt-and-pepper hair. He's friendly and always sharply dressed, but looks like he can still easily pull four-hundred-pound dead lifts—before he took an interest in missile defense, Ellison won three Super Bowls as a linebacker for the San Francisco 49ers.

The discussion topic was boost-phase missile defense: destroying missiles while they were first launching. It was to include MDA's amiable deputy director, Rear Admiral Jon Hill, and Tom Lawhead, a top air force civilian working at the F-35 Lightning II fighter aircraft office, who was there to talk about airborne sensors. At the last minute, Duncan Hunter, a former marine and outspoken Republican member of the House Armed Services Committee, joined the panel. He arrived in the middle of Hill's remarks, which generally updated on why boost-phase intercepts were so difficult and on the agency's plans to eventually test lasers based on unmanned vehicles.

Hunter sat at the end of the panel table, next to Admiral Hill, and launched right in.

"We can shoot AMRAAMs off F-35s in the first three hundred seconds that it takes a missile to go up in the air," he said. The AIM-120 Advanced Medium-Range Air-to-Air Missile was widely deployed among the United States and its allies. It was designed to shoot down enemy aircraft. "You can use an F-35 with AMRAAMs to shoot down ballistic missiles, it's that simple.

"I'm working with guys at Los Alamos and Livermore, and what I've come up against is a brick wall called the Missile Defense Agency," Hunter continued. "We're only $10 million away and two years from getting it right" if the Pentagon and MDA, he added, would acquiesce; otherwise North Korea's nuclear force cannot be contained.

"I've got all the numbers, they're open source . . . but I've come up against a brick wall called the Missile Defense Agency," Hunter repeated.

A physicist at Lawrence Livermore National Laboratory, Dr. Gregory Canavan, had shown Hunter a study suggesting this intercept scheme was possible. Canavan, a retired air force colonel and longtime missile defense engineer, had worked on the White House Science Council for Reagan and helped start the Strategic Defense Initiative. He was also credited with establishing the space-based interceptor program, better known as Brilliant Pebbles.

"One reason we're not doing it, is because it's not a billions-of-dollars program, that's one reason no one's interested," Hunter said. It was a scandalous charge: the Pentagon, MDA, and industry were purposefully sandbagging ideas like Dr. Canavan's.

"I don't care what the MDA says . . . everybody that does missile defense right now is in the box, especially if you've got twenty-five years in the military, you're in the box," Hunter said. "It might not be a $10 billion program that takes five years, and a big contractor gets that job, it's doable right now . . . but that makes nobody happy, there's no retired general that works for, name-a-company, who says I would like to do that thing that costs no money, that doesn't get me a contract. No one says that . . . That has stopped us from doing boost-phase shoot down."

Ellison tried to steer the discussion toward MDA's more traditional programs and asked for questions about all the Pentagon's intercept programs, but nobody dared change the subject.

Hill, a polished thirty-two-year navy veteran, launched into a careful defense of his agency. "Congressman, I love your passion. First of all, I'm not a Ph.D., but I do have a master's in physics and I have looked at Dr. Canavan's math, and it's very intriguing . . . I've personally gone through and looked at the equations Dr. Canavan laid down, and I'll tell you, there's a lot of assumptions in there." Specifically, Hill said the plan required unrealistically good indications and warnings of missile launches, and took a wildly optimistic view of the AMRAAM's abilities.

"That's a pretty short-range missile, and its seeker is not designed for those targets and those velocities," the admiral said. "I'm a missileer, I've spent my career designing and firing missiles at sea, and I'll tell you if you go to the farthest range that missile will shoot, it's out of gas and there's no maneuverability capability in it."

Hunter did not question Hill's physics skills, but did question MDA's fitness to solve problems such as boost-phase missile defense. "We have been let down tragically by DoD and all of our smart guys that do missile stuff, because the time is now and there is no answer now," the congressman said. "The MDA did not fix this, they've done multiple programs, they've stopped, they've started, we should have had a solution for this and we don't—it's time to come at this from a different angle."

Hill jumped in. "You wouldn't say you don't have confidence in the system to take down whatever North Korea throws at us today?"

"I have confidence in the system for us to shoot down a limited number of ICBMs," Hunter said, referring to the GMD homeland defense system.

"Okay, that's fair."

"So what's going to happen is, once they get more than a limited number of ICBMs, this conversation is done, it means nothing, this is all for fun. We have a window, and we weren't ready to take advantage of this window," Hunter said.

"We don't want to live in that world either," Hill said, "but I'll say again, our requirements come from the combatant commanders, driven a lot by what [Congress] directs us to do." But at this point Hunter and Hill had begun talking past each other. The Missile Defense Agency was trying to solve ridiculously hard problems at the intersection of military operations and physics, but was taking too long for Hunter's liking.

"I've been here ten years. You've been at MDA for how long?" Hunter asked.

"Nine months."

"For nine months. I've seen guys come and go . . . they all have great thoughts but nothing gets done because you get two years in your job and then you're off. And we still haven't gotten there yet and, according to you, it's still pie in the sky."

"I never said it was pie in the sky."

Ellison again tried to move on to other aspects of missile defense, but Hunter jumped back into his polemic, now ripping into the MDA's preference for trying lasers, or directed energy systems, for boost-phase intercepts. The enemy, he suggested, would just use tougher materials that are harder to destroy with lasers. "Then when you go to solid-state rocket fuel . . . it's much faster."

Hill interrupted, now more animated. "We'd have, like, zero indication or warning with solid rocket fuel! You don't see it refueling, so now you've got that problem, again, of not knowing where they're going to launch or when they're going to launch. And, again, are aircraft gonna be there?"

"You'll always get pushback on anything that's not their idea or that they bought into," Hunter told the audience.

"I hear what you're saying, but to be fair here, it's an

incredibly complex part of the missile launch phase," Hill said. "You're over enemy territory, you don't know where they're launching from. You said liquid and solid-state rockets? There are different indications and warnings for those. This is not an easy problem and I don't think there's an easy answer."

"Your answer is: there's no answer."

After the conversation wrapped up, MDA spokesman Chris Johnson swept Hill out of the room—off to another appointment. An aide came to remind Hunter he had to leave as well. "What is it? A hearing? Yeah, well, I don't need to sit through another hearing on the Jones Act. This is too important."

Hunter stuck around as long as there was somebody to talk to. He collected a business card from an adviser to Lawrence Livermore National Laboratory and told his aide to schedule a meeting with the man. He debated Bloomberg's Tony Capaccio about whether North Korea was an existential threat to the United States. He told Reuters' Mike Stone that the F-35 missile defense idea was being considered by Secretary of Defense Jim Mattis; that maybe it would be a good project for the Pentagon's Strategic Capabilities Office, or maybe for the Defense Advanced Research Projects Agency. "Either way, I don't want to be sitting here next year saying 'let's do directed energy,' or the year after that."

In August 2018 Hunter was indicted for wire fraud, falsifying records, campaign finance violations, and conspiracy—he was nonetheless reelected to the House of Representatives three months later. In June 2019 Hill was promoted and took over as director of the Missile Defense Agency.

Hunter and Hill's argument was largely civil, no tempers were lost, but it showcased a key problem for MDA, even among those who support missile defense. And Hunter was indeed a supporter. Hunter wanted a technological solution to containing nuclear-armed countries such as North Korea and perhaps, eventually, Iran. Intercepting missiles in space with the GMD homeland defense system, or even with some new technology on the horizon, is generally limited to addressing small numbers of rudimentary ICBMs that do not carry advanced countermeasures. That technology was extraordinarily hard to achieve. Boost-phase intercepts are even harder. They would have to successfully meld some new technology solution with highly accurate intelligence and surveillance reports, precise attack operations, and total air superiority over and around the target. It may not be "pie in the sky," but it was supposed to be a high-flying drone carrying a heavy laser weapon in the sky. At least that was MDA's plan, until the idea was shelved in 2020.

The agency is also planning upgrades and an expansion of the crew's GMD system.

On March 25, 2019, the first-ever salvo test for the system hit its target. The test fired two interceptors from Vandenberg against one ICBM-class target that was launched from Kwajalein Atoll in the Marshall Islands. "The GBI-Lead destroyed the reentry vehicle, as it was designed to do," the Missile Defense Agency said. "The GBI-Trail then looked at the resulting debris and remaining objects, and, not finding any other reentry vehicles, selected the next 'most lethal object' it could identify, and struck that, precisely as it was designed to do." All previous intercept tests had used one interceptor against one target. A salvo, though, is more realistic to the "shot doctrine" used by the 100th Missile Defense Brigade and the 49th Missile Defense Battalion, which would launch multiple interceptors at each incoming target.

In the future, MDA and Raytheon hope the kill vehicles could be able to communicate with each other. Dr. Mitch Stevison, Raytheon's vice president for strategic and naval systems, believes this could help differentiate an enemy warhead from countermeasures or debris, or could help perform "kill assessments" to determine if an intercept was successful.

MDA and lead contractor Boeing installed the last of the original forty-four GBIs in November 2018 (forty of which are at Fort Greely). Another twenty interceptors were then ordered for a planned total of sixty-four. These were to be fitted with a more reliable and more communicative Redesigned Kill Vehicle, but that program was then terminated.

Dr. Michael Griffin, the former head of NASA whom Lieutenant General Patrick O'Reilly had tapped to help solve the Track Gate Anomaly problem, since February 2018 had been serving as the undersecretary of defense for research and engineering. On August 14, 2019, Griffin decided to nix the new kill vehicle program and cancel the government's contract with Boeing and Raytheon. Eight months earlier, MDA had delayed a design review for the new kill vehicle after it discovered "the failure of certain critical components to meet technical requirements," the agency said. "The technical design problems were so significant as to be either insurmountable or cost-prohibitive to correct," it added. "Research and testing accomplished prior to the program's end will inform development of the next-generation interceptor, which will include a new kill vehicle."

The Pentagon's goal had been to field the twenty additional, more reliable interceptors by around 2023. That goal then slipped to 2025. MDA's five-year plan, beginning in 2021, includes $4.9 billion for a Next-Generation Interceptor program ($1.2 billion had been spent on its cancelled processor). The new interceptor could potentially be fielded around 2027 or 2028. That time frame could be problematic. In a February briefing, Hill noted that by the mid- to late 2020s the current technology was likely to fall behind adversary technology. Since a higher-performance interceptor may not be ready, he said MDA is hoping it can augment homeland missile defenses with the navy's Aegis interceptors and possibly the army's Terminal High Altitude Area Defense interceptors to add more layers.

Staff Sergeant Caroline Domenech was the weapons operator for Delta crew at Fort Greely. If there was an order to launch an interceptor to destroy a nuclear warhead, she would be the soldier on her crew to input the order. She would do it without hesitation, but with significant heartache for what would happen next.

Domenech joined the 49th Missile Defense Battalion from a National Guard unit in her native Puerto Rico. She flew up to Alaska in September 2009 for a three-year tour and hated it immediately. It was about 90°F when she left San Juan and about 40°F at Greely. The temperature would soon drop another eighty degrees, and she was ready to go home. Slowly, she started to like her new unit, and by year three she was willing to stay. The MP patrols were not for her though; she wanted something mentally challenging. In April 2014 Domenech was allowed to try the GMD Qualification Course in Colorado Springs. She passed, and came back to Greely that June to join a crew.

Domenech was on shift as Delta crew's weapons operator for North Korean missile launches in 2015, 2016, and 2017. Each time she was on for a North Korean test, she felt as though she might have to launch an interceptor. The feeling followed her off post too. Domenech lived in Delta Junction, but her house was close enough to Greely that whenever North Korea launched, and the missile fields at Greely went "red" in response, she could hear the God Voice ordering the fields cleared for a possible launch. She would hate for that to ever happen, whether it be her or somebody else to launch an interceptor in combat, because she knew what that would mean. Even if the mission was successful and the incoming warhead was shot down, it could portend war—possibly nuclear war.

On October 30, 2017, US Strategic Command began its annual "Global Thunder" war game, a ten-day event to exercise every piece of the US nuclear enterprise. The scenario begins as a conventional conflict somewhere in the world, which then escalates into nuclear war. As the men and women of Strategic Command fight that war, they must work with increasingly sketchy information and degraded communications, as the nuclear exchange quickly destroys the US military's resources. Toward the end of the exchange, Strategic Command has an aircraft that can still fly around to execute the president's orders. Buried under Strategic Command's headquarters in Omaha, Nebraska, is also still a "battle deck" where a commander can operate.

Greg Bowen, now a brigadier general at Strategic Command, was for this exercise playing the role of night shift commander, leading the fight from the battle deck. During the final exchange of nuclear missiles, there is a countdown clock on the deck ticking down to when Omaha becomes a smoking hole in the ground. That's how nuclear war ends, so that's how the war game ends. When that clock hits zero, all the screens on the battle deck shut down and the lights dim. Bowen and everyone on the deck sit in silence for a minute, thinking about what just happened.

The war game and Bowen's work at Strategic Command were focused on Russia and China more than North Korea. But by the end of 2017, North Korea had become a nuclear power. They had demonstrated a nuclear warhead and demonstrated an intercontinental ballistic missile.

One year after the sobering war game, Bowen was back for a visit to the 100th Missile Defense Brigade in Colorado Springs. He was there for the unit's fifteenth anniversary. Meakins was there too. He'd since retired from the army and was working for a contractor in Huntsville, but he was still doing work on the homeland missile defense program. Kiraly couldn't make it because he'd just moved to Huntsville. He was still in the army but now working for Army Space and Missile Defense Command. Young was there. Spriggs was there, and like Meakins was dressed in a tie and jacket because he was also now working on the program as a contractor. Meakins and Spriggs, unbound by army regulations, both had goatees, but Spriggs's was fantastically robust, like that of a wise sensei. Michalski and Pollock were there in uniform, relatively well shaven. Pollock had just finished a midnight shift a few hours before the event.

For soldiers who had been involved in this single and unique enterprise for so long, the anniversary was a welcomed event. Many of them, though, were really there in deference to Bowen. A conference room was being named "the Bowen Room" to recognize his efforts in creating a brigade from nothing. Bowen was sincerely honored. He was also a little surprised, or worried, to receive a commemoration that was usually bestowed posthumously. Places aren't typically named for living people. Bowen also wasn't so sure about having a conference room named for him. Would anyone enjoy sitting through PowerPoint briefings in the Bowen Room? Or getting dressed down by their commander in the Bowen Room? "At least name a happy place after me," he said, "maybe the bathroom."

ACKNOWLEDGMENTS

This book would have been very different and far less interesting without the cooperation offered to me by soldiers—past and present—in the 100th and 49th. None of them had any obligation to speak with me, yet many of them did despite difficult schedules. I am incredibly grateful for their time. I'd also like to thank Jenn Staton and Zach Sheely, who are two of the best army public affairs officers I've worked with. They are not mentioned in the book but were indispensable for the interview process.

I'd especially like to thank Rich Michalski, Mark Kiraly, and Matt Pollock for their time and patience. They collectively spent double-digit hours being interviewed by me, either on the phone or in person, and often between their twelve-hour shifts. It could be that I'm an utter joy to speak with, but it's more likely that they're dedicated professionals who wanted to explain a challenging mission.

Huge thanks are due to my agent, Jim Hornfischer, who helped take this from a research project to a coherent narrative, and to my editor, Marc Resnick, who was thoughtfully understanding as I promised to deliver, and then retracted, batches of chapters throughout the process. I'd also like to thank Hannah O'Grady and all the pros at St. Martin's Press and Macmillan—it's been a pleasure.

Most important, I'd like to profusely thank my wife. Many interviews and much of the writing occurred at odd hours on nights and weekends during an incomparably eventful year for our family (and a year in which I spent her birthday in Colorado with the 100th). Thank you!

NOTES

1: The 300

7 *to take out the army's interceptor:* This scenario is based on demonstration of the GMD system as well as analysis from: Laura Grego and David Wright, "Incremental Progress but No Realistic Capability: Analysis of the Ground-based Midcourse Missile Defense Test FTG-15 (May 30, 2017)," Union of Concerned Scientists, January 2018, 5–6, https://s3.amazonaws.com/ucs-documents/global-security/missile-defense-test-white-paper-1-24-18v4.pdf.; also based on MDA Director Vice Admiral Jim Syring's comment that a May 2017 intercept was "an operational scenario that we're concerned about."

8 *1.3 million active-duty servicemen and women:* "Department of Defense (DoD) Releases Fiscal Year 2017 President's Budget Proposal," US Department of Defense, press release, February 9, 2016, https://www.defense.gov/News/News-Releases/News-Release-View/Article/652687/department-of-defense-dod-releases-fiscal-year-2017-presidents-budget-proposal/.

2: Weekend Warriors

11 *eight hundred or so residents of Delta Junction:* Padgett interview, November 14, 2018; David Rennie, "Star Wars work begins in Alaska," *The Telegraph*, June 15, 2002, https://www.telegraph.co.uk/news/worldnews/northamerica/usa/1397378/Star-Wars-work-begins-in-Alaska.html.

12 *a ground-breaking ceremony at Fort Greely:* James Walker, Lewis Bernstein, and Sharon Lang, "Seize the High Ground: The U.S. Army in Space and Missile Defense," Historical Office, U.S. Army Space and Missile Defense Command (2003): 243–44, https://history.army.mil/html/books/070/70-88-1/cmhPub_70-88-1.pdf.

13 *digging out silos for Missile Field One:* Bowen interview, August 17, 2018; Linda James, "GMD test bed construction ahead of schedule," *Boeing Frontiers* 1, No. 7, November 2002, https://www.boeing.com/news/frontiers/archive/2002/november/i_ids4.html.

13 *The prefabricated silo shells weighed 130,000 pounds:* Walker, Bernstein, and Lang, "Seize the High Ground," 243.

14 *Digging in a glacial basin is unpredictable:* Bowen interview, August 17, 2018; Kiraly interview, November 27, 2017; Scott interview, November 15, 2018.

14 *the immediate deadline was October 2003:* Bowen interview, August 17, 2018.

14 *In-Flight Interceptor Communications System Data Terminal:* Walker, Bernstein, and Lang, "Seize the High Ground," 240.

16 *the scariest experiences of his army career:* Bowen speech, October 25, 2018, 100th Missile Defense Brigade Command Headquarters, Colorado Springs, Colorado.

17 *worried that he'd get kicked out of the unit:* Meakins interview, March 1, 2019.

19 *civilian engineers be used as developer-operators:* Kadish interview, February 23, 2018.

21 *The December 2003 GMD Qualification Course:* Michalski interview, January 11, 2018; Frobe-Recella interview, January 29, 2019; Meakins interview, March 1, 2018; Simpson interview, January 8, 2019. Frobe-Recella's GMD Operator Advanced Course Graduation Ceremony program, March 19, 2004.

24 *Frobe knew she'd get a job:* Frobe-Recella interview, January 29, 2019.

24 *"tabletop" drill:* Michalski interview, December 8, 2017; Meakins interview, March 1, 2019.

24 *"gray beard" conferences:* ibid.

26 *their comments were becoming military requirements:* Meakins interview, March 1, 2019; Kiraly interview, January 9, 2018.

3: Island of Misfit Toys

28 *ignoring a lieutenant colonel:* Bowen speech.

28 *none of them had driver's licenses:* Kiraly interview, November 27, 2017.

29 *carrying only a stick:* Bowen speech.

30 *a "hard-nosed realist":* Kadish interview, February 23, 2018.

31 *the agency's director was given executive power:* Walker, Bernstein, and Lang, "Seize the High Ground," 234.

31 *"little or no warning" before facing ICBM threats:* "Executive Summary of the Report of the Commission to Assess the Ballistic Missile Threat to the United States" (known as the Rumsfeld Commission), July 15, 1998, Federation of American Scientists, https://fas.org/irp/threat/bm-threat.htm.

31 *CIA director George Tenet was warning the Senate:* "The Worldwide Threat in 2003: Evolving Dangers in a Complex World," DCI's Worldwide Threat Briefing, February 11, 2003, https://www.cia.gov/news-information/speeches -testimony/2003/dci_speech_02112003.html.

32 *"Don't fuck it up":* Obering interview, November 3, 2017.

4: The Old Fort

33 *the border guards opened his humidor:* Kiraly interview, January 9, 2018.

34 *caribou dying en masse:* "Caribou Deaths Near Army Base Puzzle Alaskans," *New York Times,* July 31, 1972, https://www.nytimes.com/1972/07/31/archives /caribou-deaths-near-army-base-puzzle-alaskans.html?_r=0.

34 *Blueberry Lake:* "Survey of Reported Chemical and Biological Contamination at the Fort Greely Gerstle River Test Center," US General Accounting Office, November 30, 1979, https://www.gao.gov/assets/130/128242.pdf.

35 *red digital countdown clock:* Kiraly interview, January 9, 2018; Obering interview, January 18, 2018.

36 *shutting down much of Alaska Route 4:* off-the-record interview.

36 *moose walking around the airstrip:* Scott interview, November 15, 2018.

37 *pulling cable with the MDA guys:* Bowen interview, August 17, 2018; Kiraly interview, January 9, 2018.

38 *the dishwasher was making $20 an hour:* Bowen speech.

39 *The houses had red lights in the window:* Kiraly interview, January 9, 2018; Scott interview, November 15, 2018.

39 *"a surface-to-air missile on steroids":* Bowen interview, August 17, 2018.

39 *an immediate schism between the two groups:* Bowen speech.

41 *Greely would be turned into a prison:* Padgett interview, November 14, 2018.

43 *"SPC Scott: Thanks for your service":* Scott interview, November 15, 2018.

44 *"This is where we're going to work":* Michalski interview, October 25, 2018.

5: Going Live

45 *get five interceptors in silos by the end of 2004:* Kadish interview, February 23, 2018.

45 *Holly's digital countdown clocks:* Obering interview, January 18, 2018.

46 *National Missile Defense Act of 1999:* National Missile Defense Act of 1999, Public Law 106–38, 106th Congress, July 22, 1999, https://www.congress .gov/106/plaws/publ38/PLAW-106publ38.pdf.

47 *It missed its target by seventy meters:* Bradley Graham, *Hit to Kill: The New Battle Over Shielding America from Missile Attack* (New York: PublicAffairs, 2003), 199.

47 *something obstructed its flow:* Graham, *Hit to Kill,* 200.

48 *CBS News' Dan Rather was there:* Kadish interview, February 23, 2018; Coyle interview, March 29, 2018.

48 *a small pin had broken:* Graham, *Hit to Kill,* 390; "Defense Acquisitions: Missile Defense Agency Fields Initial Capability but Falls Short of Original Goals," US Government Accountability Office, March 15, 2006, https://www.govinfo .gov/content/pkg/GAOREPORTS-GAO-06-327/html/GAOREPORTS -GAO-06-327.htm.

49 *His stakeholders' meeting:* ibid.

50 *speech to the Carnegie Endowment for International Peace:* Philip E. Coyle III, "The Problems and Prospects of the New Alaska Missile Interceptor Site: Ten Fallacies About Missile Defense," remarks to the Carnegie Endowment for International Peace's Non-Proliferation Roundtable, September 20, 2004, http://carnegieendowment.org/files/finCoyleCarnegieMissileDef.pdf.

51 *the official first shift would begin at 6:00 A.M. on October 1, 2004:* Meakins interview, March 1, 2019; Simpson interview, January 8, 2019; Frobe-Recella interview, January 29, 2019; Kent interview, October 24, 2018; Spriggs interview, October 25, 2018.

53 *no secret of his ambitions:* Kiraly interview, January 9, 2018.

54 *Bowen had grown concerned:* Bowen interview, August 17, 2018.

55 *"You'll have to get an A on every test":* ibid.

56 *The brigade was proving peculiar . . . The crews were odd too:* Meakins interview, March 1, 2019; Kent interview, October 24, 2018; Spriggs interview, October 25, 2018.

57 *Michalski began to think seriously:* Michalski interview, October 25, 2018.

6: Origin Story

59 *a thirty-two-foot crater on Staveley Road:* Richard Hollingham, "V2: The Nazi rocket that launched the space age," BBC, September 7, 2014, accessed April 18, 2017, http://www.bbc.com/future/story/20140905-the-nazis-space-age-rocket.

59–60 *antiaircraft guns to shoot missiles down:* Donald R. Baucom, *The Origins of SDI, 1944–1983* (Lawrence: University Press of Kansas, 1992), 2–3.

60 *"Monty beat us to it":* Jeremy Stocker, *Britain and Ballistic Missile Defence, 1942–2002* (London: Frank Cass, 2004), 22–24.

60 *Moscow controlled the original V-2 factory:* Hollingham, "V2."

60 *modify its Nike air defense system:* Baucom, *Origins of SDI*, 7–8.

61 *Bell reported that destroying a ballistic missile was possible:* "History of U.S. Missile Defense Efforts 1945–Present: Nike Zeus, The U.S. Army's First Antiballistic Missile," US Missile Defense Agency, October 20, 2009, 2–3, https://www.mda.mil/global/documents/pdf/zeus.pdf.

61–62 *Nike Zeus could possibly work against one incoming warhead:* Fred Kaplan, *The Wizards of Armageddon* (New York: Simon and Schuster, 1983), 343–344.

63 *McNamara called the Pentagon a "jungle":* Tim Weiner, "Robert S. McNamara, Architect of a Futile War, Dies at 93," *New York Times,* July 6, 2009, http://www.nytimes.com/2009/07/07/us/07mcnamara.html?pagewanted=all.

64 *McNamara decided not to field it:* Kaplan, *Wizards of Armageddon,* 346.

64 *he favored a national fallout shelter program:* Ernest J. Yanarella, *The Missile Defense Controversy: Technology in Search of a Mission* (Lexington: University Press of Kentucky, 2002), 110–112.

65 *surprisingly ambitious plan:* Walter S. Poole, "The Joint Chiefs of Staff and National Policy: 1965–1968," Office of Joint History, Office of the Chairman of the Joint Chiefs of Staff, 2012, 32, https://www.jcs.mil/Portals/36/Documents/History/Policy/Policy_V009.pdf.

65 *the gulf between missile defense's supporters and opponents:* ibid., 34–36.

66 *allowing a minimalist program to address China:* Baucom, *Origins of SDI*, 32–33.

66 *"I'd go down fighting":* Poole, "Joint Chiefs of Staff," 36.

67 *"Defense is moral, offensive is immoral!":* Nova/Frontline Special Report, "Visions of Star Wars," originally broadcast on PBS on April 22, 1986. Transcript provided by WGBH Educational Foundation, 12; Kaplan, *Wizards of Armageddon,* 346.

67 *three-to-one advantage over the Soviet arsenal:* Robert S. Norris and Hans M. Kristensen, "Global Nuclear Weapons Inventories, 1945–2010," *Bulletin of the*

Atomic Scientists 66, no. 4 (July/August 2010): 81, http://journals.sagepub.com /doi/abs/10.2968/066004008.

67 *a strikingly conflicted September 1967 speech:* Morton H. Halperin, "The Decision to Deploy the ABM: Bureaucratic and Domestic Politics in the Johnson Administration," *World Politics* 25, no. 1 (October 1972): 62–64, https://doi.org /10.2307/2010431.

68 *"a kind of mad momentum":* ibid.

68 *hide those comments in an appendix:* Kaplan, *Wizards of Armageddon,* 348.

69 *The Vietnam War also started to weigh heavily:* Yanarella, *Missile Defense Controversy,* 176; Baucom, *Origins of SDI,* 68.

69 *ABM deployment was stalling:* Baucom, *Origins of SDI,* 55–59.

69 *Safeguard would be deployed:* Yanarella, *Missile Defense Controversy,* 173.

70 *fifty yeas and fifty nays:* Baucom, *Origins of SDI,* 62–63, 66–67.

70 *The Chappaquiddick scandal:* Jenna Russell, "Conflicted Ambitions, then, Chappaquiddick," *Boston Globe,* February 17, 2009, http://archive.boston.com /news/nation/articles/2009/02/17/chapter_3_chappaquiddick/.

71 *Agnew cast the deciding fifty-first vote:* Baucom, *Origins of SDI,* 72–73.

71 *Bell was being critical:* Memorandum from Kissinger to Nixon, "Contractor Doubts About Safeguard," April 15, 1970, attached to memorandum from Laurence Lynn to Kissinger, "Bell Labs on Safeguard," April 14, 1970, 1–2. Location of original: National Archives, Nixon Presidential Materials Project, National Security Council Files, Box 840, ABM System vol. III, http:// nsarchive.gwu.edu/NSAEBB/NSAEBB36/docs/doc06.pdf.

71 *bargaining chip for arms control:* Kaplan, *Wizards of Armageddon,* 354.

72 *the SALT I agreement and Anti-Ballistic Missile Treaty:* Treaty Between the United States of America and the Union of Soviet Socialist Republics on the Limitation of Anti-Ballistic Missile Systems (ABM Treaty), US Department of State Bureau of Arms Control, Verification and Compliance, May 26, 1972, accessed March 12, 2017, https://2009-2017.state.gov/t/avc /trty/101888.htm.

72 *a paltry one hundred interceptors:* Baucom, *Origins of SDI,* 178.

72 *cost about $5.7 billion:* John W. Finney, "Safeguard ABM System to Shut Down; $5 Billion Spent in 6 Years Since Debate," *New York Times,* November 25, 1975, http://www.nytimes.com/1975/11/25/archives/safeguard-abm -system-to-shut-down-5-billion-spent-in-6-years-since.html.

72 *cost about $10 billion:* Baucom, *Origins of SDI,* 182.

73 *"We're engaged right now"*: Ronald Reagan, "Address to the Nation on National Security (Star Wars Speech)," March 23, 1983, Reagan National Library Archives, https://reaganlibrary.gov/research/speeches/32383d.htm.

75 looked like a mean-machine: Kadish interview, February 23, 2018.

76 *Boeing disqualified itself*: Graham, *Hit to Kill*, 181–185; Graham Spinardi, "Technical Controversy and Ballistic Missile Defence: Disputing Epistemic Authority in the Development of Hit-to-Kill Technology," *Science as Culture*, 2013, 25–26, https://www.research.ed.ac.uk/portal/files/14789822/SPINARDI _Technical_Controversy_and_Ballistic_Missile_Defence.pdf.

76 *awkwardly negotiated a subcontract*: Graham, *Hit to Kill*, 183–85.

7: Fail

77 *The one-million-square-foot eyesore*: Steve Vogel, "Navy Annex being razed after 70 years of service," *Washington Post*, December 30, 2012, https://www .washingtonpost.com/politics/navy-annex-being-razed-after-70-years-of -service/2013/01/05/fe1c05ce-50a0-11e2-8b49-64675006147f_story.html; Rick Lehner interview, January 24, 2018.

77 *he wanted to sit at headquarters*: Obering interview, November 3, 2017.

77 *no novice at launching big rockets*: "Booz Allen Hamilton Leadership Biography," Booz Allen Hamilton Inc, https://www.boozallen.com/d/bio/leadership/trey -obering.html; "Lieutenant General Henry A. 'Trey' Obering III," U.S. Air Force, updated December 2008, https://www.af.mil/About-Us/Biographies /Display/Article/106099/lieutenant-general-henry-a-trey-obering-iii/.

80 *"Why haven't you fired yet?!"*: Meakins interview, March 1, 2018; Spriggs interview, October 25, 2018.

81 *no gap in coverage while she took two months of maternity leave*: Frobe-Recella interview, January 29, 2019.

81 *The crews were also learning new lingo*: Meakins interview, March 1, 2018.

82 *Bowen stood out there in the cold, undetected*: Bowen speech.

84 *"When that lamp is off, you can air your grievances"*: Kiraly interview, November 27, 2017.

85 *a requirement based on intelligence estimates*: Obering interview, November 3, 2017.

85 *The software had run unnecessarily precise checks*: off-the-record interview.

86 *rusted in the silo on Kwajalein*: Obering interview, November 3, 2017.

87 *his big beach party*: Bowen interview, August 17, 2018.

88 *The first email that left Fort Greely's housing*: ibid.

8: Anomaly

89 *Obering was briefed on the unhappy findings:* Ashley Roque, "Obering: MDA May Not Meet Congressionally Mandated Testing Date," *Inside Missile Defense* 11, no. 8 (2005): 1–9, https://www.jstor.org/stable/24784524?seq=1/subjects; Wade Boese, "More Testing Urged for Missile Defense," *Arms Control Today,* April 2005, https://www.armscontrol.org/act/2005–07/more-testing-urged-missile-defense.

89 *a prioritized list of recommendations:* Obering interview, January 18, 2018.

90 *as if the device were blinking its eye:* ibid.

90 *Specialist Jarrod Cuthbertson had enjoyed a few beers:* Cuthbertson interview, October 25, 2018; Robinson interview, October 24, 2018.

93 *the Seat Belt Police:* ibid.

94 *the Interceptor Storage Facility:* Cuthbertson interview, October 25, 2018; Scott interview, November 15, 2018; Bowen speech.

95 *moose came in and out of the complex regularly:* Cuthbertson interview, October 25, 2018; Robinson interview, October 24, 2018; Scott interview, November 15, 2018.

95 *he got "scope bite":* Cuthbertson interview, October 25, 2018.

96 *skin will go numb and then freeze:* Linton Weeks, "Quick Question: Can It Feel Any Darn Colder?" NPR, January 29, 2014, https://www.npr.org/sections /theprotojournalist/2014/01/29/267598179/quick-question-can-it-feel-any -darn-colder.

96 *keeping too warm could be a problem:* Elvin Montes interview, November 14, 2018.

97 *they felt the need to begin forming some history:* Bowen interview, August 17, 2018; Kiraly interview, January 9, 2018.

98 *their own distinctive unit insignia:* Sharon Watkins Lang, "SMDC History: 49th Missile Defense Battalion (GMD) heraldry approved," Army.mil, August 17, 2015, https://www.army.mil/article/154008/smdc_history_49th _missile_defense_battalion_gmd_heraldry_approved.

98 *Then they were in the club:* Bowen interview, August 17, 2018; Kiraly interview, January 9, 2018.

99 Robert's Rules of Order: Kiraly interview, January 9, 2018.

99 *NUDET award:* Kiraly interview, January 9, 2018.

100 *A stinging government audit:* "Missile Defense Agency Fields Initial Capability but Falls Short of Original Goals," US Government Accountability Office, March 2006, https://www.gao.gov/assets/250/249310.pdf.

100 *"quality control weaknesses":* ibid.

9: Icefog

102 *Mark blew through the red light:* Kiraly interview, January 9, 2018.

103 *He'd had to wait two years:* ibid.

104 *Montoya was in it too:* Montoya interview, November 14, 2018.

105 *"Deviate. Defend Washington with all interceptors":* Pollock interview, August 6, 2018.

106 *hidden deep inside Cheyenne Mountain's tunnels:* author tour with Steven Rose, Cheyenne Mountain's deputy director, November 16, 2017.

107 *fourteen students passed:* Sara Storey and Laura Kenney, "Major GMD players graduate from GTEC's Operator Course," *The Eagle,* U.S. Army Space and Missile Defense Command/U.S. Army Forces Strategic Command 13, No. 5, May 2006, 11, https://ufdcimages.uflib.ufl.edu/AA/00/06/14/39/00078/05-2006.pdf.

107 *like learning how to* constrain *the system:* Kiraly interview, January 9, 2018.

108 *handing over leadership of the 49th: Warriors: Quarterly Magazine for the Alaska Department of Military and Veterans Affairs,* Summer 2006, 10.

108 *an air defense artillery officer:* Benjamin Crane, "Changing of the guard: 100th soldiers say farewell to Col. Bowen and welcome in Col. Hildreth," Army.mil, July 31, 2012, https://www.army.mil/article/84669/changingoftheguard100th soldiers_sayfarewelltocolbowenandwelcomeincolhildreth.

109 *"he just got attacked by a bear":* Montoya interview, November 14, 2018.

109 *Titus had been out with his rifle:* Montoya interview, November 14, 2018; Cuthbertson interview, October 25, 2018; Kiraly interview, March 7, 2018.

111 *"axis of evil":* "President's State of the Union Address," Office of the Press Secretary, Washington, DC, January 29, 2002, https://georgewbush-whitehouse.archives.gov/news/releases/2002/01/20020129-11.html.

111 *six-party talks:* "The Six-Party Talks at a Glance," Arms Control Association, June 2018, https://www.armscontrol.org/factsheets/6partytalks.

111 *Intelligence reports differed:* Philip Maxon, "Official Estimates of the Taepo Dong-2," 38 North, January 28, 2011, https://www.38north.org/2011/01/estimates-of-taepodong-2/; Missile Defense Project, "Taepodong-2 (Unha-3)," *Missile Threat,* Center for Strategic and International Studies, August 8, 2016, last modified June 15, 2018, https://missilethreat.csis.org/missile/taepodong-2/; "North Korea Missile Capabilities," Nuclear Threat Initiative, May 1, 2010, https://www.nti.org/analysis/articles/north-korea-missile-capabilities/.

10: Taepodong-2

112 *The closest NASA lets civilians get:* Brad Scriber, "Why NASA Blew Up a Rocket Just After Launch," *National Geographic,* October 31, 2014, https://news.nationalgeographic.com/news/2014/10/141030-first-person-rocket-explosion-antares/.

113 *one-hundred-foot-tall three-stage rocket:* Missile Defense Project, "Taepodong-2 (Unha-3)."

114 *Kiraly was brought in:* Kiraly interview, January 9, 2018.

114–115 *disavowed their long-range missile test moratorium:* "North Korea Test-Fires Several Missiles," *New York Times,* July 4, 2006, https://www.nytimes.com/2006/07/04/world/asia/04cnd-korea.html.

115 *had finished fueling the missile:* "Nations press North Korea on missile," CNN, June 19, 2006, https://web.archive.org/web/20060623140645/http://www.cnn.com/2006/US/06/19/nkorea.missile/index.html.

115 *Meakins and Kent had been ordered to stay at Vandenberg:* Meakins interview, March 1, 2018; Kent interview, October 24, 2018.

118 *"You all need to leave":* Spriggs interview, October 25, 2018.

118 *Spriggs froze in his seat:* ibid.

118 *and then turned to his task like a robot:* Kiraly interview, April 8, 2019.

119 *As the countdown to the* Discovery's *launch ticked toward liftoff:* Meakins interview, March 1, 2018.

119 *but Northern Command could not get Rumsfeld on the phone:* off-the-record interviews; Kiraly interview, November 27, 2017.

120 *"a letdown":* William Yardley, "A Missile Defense System Is Taking Shape in Alaska," *New York Times,* December 10, 2006, http://www.nytimes.com/2006/12/10/us/10greely.html.

123 *"I want to see it happen":* Secretary of Defense Donald Rumsfeld and Director of the Missile Defense Agency Lt. Gen Henry "Trey" Obering III, Department of Defense transcript, August 27, 2006, http://archive.defense.gov/Transcripts/Transcript.aspx?TranscriptID=3705.

123 *"The word 'frustrated' is not one that is appropriate":* ibid.

124 *"Go Cubs":* Kiraly interview, January 9, 2018.

11: Glancing Blow

125 *Obering wanted to launch interceptors from the real site at Vandenberg:* Obering interview, November 3, 2017.

126 *especially vocal about simplifying the tests:* Obering interview, January 18, 2018.

126 *Senator Carl Levin dug in to Obering's testing plan:* Hearing of the Strategic Forces Subcommittee of the Senate Armed Services Committee, Fiscal Year 2007 Defense Authorization Request for Missile Defense Programs, April 4, 2006, https://play.google.com/store/books/details?id=DRVeGAXBsrkC&rdid =book-DRVeGAXBsrkC&rdot=1.

127 *at 10:39 A.M., an interceptor launched:* "Missile Defense Exercise and Flight Test Successfully Completed," US Missile Defense Agency, September 1, 2006, https://www.mda.mil/global/documents/pdf/06news0020.pdf.

127 *hydrocode analysis that generates an animation:* Obering interview, November 3, 2017.

128 *Obering walked into the Pentagon pressroom:* Missile Defense Agency Director Lt. Gen. Henry "Trey" Obering III, Department of Defense transcript, September 1, 2006, http://archive.defense.gov/Transcripts/Transcript.aspx ?TranscriptID=3710.

128 *"a hit, but not a kill":* Hearing of the Strategic Forces Subcommittee of the House Armed Services Committee, Fiscal Year 2013 Defense Authorization Request for Missile Defense, March 6, 2012, https://www.govinfo.gov/content /pkg/CHRG-112hhrg73437/pdf/CHRG-112hhrg73437.pdf.

129 *North Koreans announced they would detonate their first atomic bomb:* "North Korea pledges to test nuclear bomb," CNN, October 4, 2006, http://www .cnn.com/2006/WORLD/asiapcf/10/03/nkorea.nuclear/index.html.

129 *"North Korean nuclear scientists are now officially the worst ever":* Jeffrey Lewis, "NORK Data: It Was a Dud," *Arms Control Wonk*, October 9, 2006, https:// www.armscontrolwonk.com/archive/201230/nork-data-it-was-a-dud/.

130 *In March 2007 the Pentagon allowed:* Terry Moran, *Nightline*, aired on April 25, 2007, available at https://www.youtube.com/watch?v=UV4JGIpUH3Q.

131 *He was thinking of his crew's reliance:* Kiraly interview, January 9, 2018.

132 *A potent radar is necessary for this:* George Lewis, "The LRDR: (Not) The Best Discrimination Money Can Buy?," *Mostly Missile Defense*, January 30, 2019, https://mostlymissiledefense.com/2019/01/30/the-lrdr-not-the-best -discrimination-money-can-buy-january-30-2019/#_ftnref6; https://www.gao .gov/assets/700/696076.pdf; "Missile Defense: Air Force Report to Congress Included Information on the Capabilities, Operational Availability, and Funding Plan for Cobra Dane," US Government Accountability Office, December 2010, https://www.gao.gov/assets/250/241487.pdf; *Making Sense of Ballistic Missile*

Defense: An Assessment of Concepts and Systems for U.S. Boost-Phase Missile Defense in Comparison to Other Alternatives, National Research Council 2012 (Washington, DC: The National Academies Press), 138, https://www.nap.edu/read/13189 /chapter/7#138.

133 *which required an X-band radar:* "Missile Defense: Actions Being Taken to Address Testing Recommendations, but Updated Assessment Needed," US General Accounting Office, February 2004, https://www.gao.gov/assets/250 /241487.pdf.

133 *Rumsfeld had on his desk the same newspaper:* Kadish interview, February 23, 2018; Stephen Buckley, "Giant Brazilian Oil Rig Sinks, Begins to Leak," *Washington Post,* March 21, 2001, https://www.washingtonpost.com/archive /politics/2001/03/21/giant-brazilian-oil-rig-sinks-begins-to-leak/737135ef -e67e-47a8-b235-3c2588f4ee9b/?utm_term=.1b7d69ec8c8f.

134 *In early 2003 MDA bought a semisubmersible fifty-thousand-ton seagoing platform:* "A Brief History of the Sea-based X-band Radar-1," US Missile Defense Agency, n.d., https://www.mda.mil/global/documents/pdf/sbx_booklet.pdf.

134 *originally supposed to be there by the end of 2005, but problems abounded:* Jonathan Karp, "A Radar Unit's Journey Reflects Hopes, Snafus in Missile Defense," *Wall Street Journal,* November 28, 2006, https://www.wsj.com/articles /SB116468133449434113.

135 *Mark Scott was hunting by himself:* Scott interview, November 15, 2018.

136 *Fort Greely was becoming somewhat more comfortable:* Kiraly interview, November 27, 2017; Bowen interview, August 17, 2018.

12: Bad Vibrations

137 *Raytheon in 2002 had opened its Space Factory:* "Inside the Space Factory: Lab Gears Up for Next Missile-Destroying 'Kill Vehicle,'" Raytheon, June 14, 2014, last updated October 14, 2018, https://www.raytheon.com/news/feature /rms14_space_factory; "The Warhead Hunters: Meet Some of the Engineers Behind an Amazing Missile Defense System," Raytheon, November 14, 2014, last updated December 11, 2017, https://www.raytheon.com/news/feature /warhead-hunters.

138 *"That is ab-so-lute bullshit":* Obering interview, January 18, 2018. This is Obering's retelling. Raytheon several times declined the author's requests for interviews, facility visits, or materials.

138 *The test was a dud:* "FY 2007 Annual Report for the Office of the Director, Operational Test & Evaluation," Office of the Director of Operational

Test & Evaluation, December 2007, https://www.dote.osd.mil/Publications/Annual-Reports/2007-Annual-Report.

139 *"We're the 300, defending 300 million!":* Meakins interview, March 1, 2018; Simpson interview, January 8, 2019.

140 *something akin to an astronaut:* Simpson interview, January 8, 2019.

141 *MDA mounted a camera on the target looking aft:* Obering interview, November 3, 2017.

141 *target missile traveled southeast for about seventeen minutes:* "GMD Flight Tests of Operationally-Configured Interceptors," *Mostly Missile Defense,* May 9, 2012, https://mostlymissiledefense.com/2012/05/09/gmd-flight-tests-of-operationally-configured-interceptors-may-9-2012/; "Flight Test FTG-03a-9/28/07 Narrated Overview," US Missile Defense Agency, posted May 7, 2009, https://www.youtube.com/watch?v=E1WXFfZ89rg.

141 *The target did not use countermeasures:* "GMD Flight Tests of Operationally-Configured Interceptors."

142 *North Korea would not have anything more complex:* Obering interview, January 18, 2018. The Pentagon's independent testing directorate said of the September 28, 2007, event: "Several aspects of the engagement were representative of an unsophisticated threat, such as lacking specific target suite dynamic features and intercept geometry. Several other aspects were realistic of a particular engagement, but relatively unchallenging, such as closing velocity and fly out range." "FY 2007 Annual Report," Office of the Director of Operational Test & Evaluation.

142 *But the Clearwater Lodge:* Kiraly interview, November 27, 2017; Captain Jason Brewer interview, October 24, 2018; author visit.

145 *Xichang Space Launch Center:* "Xichang Space Launch Center," Nuclear Threat Initiative, June 7, 2013, https://www.nti.org/learn/facilities/883/.

145 *destroy an inoperable Fengyun-1C weather satellite:* Brian Weeden, "2007 Chinese Anti-Satellite Test Fact Sheet," Secure World Foundation, November 23, 2010, https://swfound.org/media/9550/chinese_asat_fact_sheet_updated_2012.pdf.

146 *specifically chosen because of their test record:* "One-Time Mission: Operation Burnt Frost," US Missile Defense Agency, n.d., https://web.archive.org/web/20120214031001/http://www.mda.mil/system/aegis_one_time_mission.html.

147 *he had been flying in and out of Brussels:* Obering interview, January 18, 2018.

148 *By August 2008 a deal was reached:* Thom Shankar and Nicholas Kulish,

"U.S. and Poland Set Missile Deal," *New York Times*, August 14, 2008, http://www.nytimes.com/2008/08/15/world/europe/15poland.html.

148 *A gigantic SBX radar would be shipped to Europe:* Steven A. Hildreth and Carl Ek, "Long-Range Ballistic Missile Defense in Europe," Congressional Research Service, September 23, 2009, available at https://fas.org/sgp/crs/weapons/RL34051.pdf.

148 *About $3.9 billion:* ibid.

148 *expected Michalski to be running the operation in Poland:* Michalski interview, October 25, 2018.

149 *John Robinson was at his house on Fort Greely:* Robinson interview, October 24, 2018; Cuthbertson interview, October 25, 2018.

150 *"Don't fuck it up":* Obering interview, January 18, 2018.

13: The Culling

151 *Bailey walked from his house on Fort Greely to the Missile Defense Complex:* Bailey interview, January 25, 2019.

153 *cost more than $210 million:* "Defense Acquisitions: Missile Defense Transition Provides Opportunity to Strengthen Acquisition Approach," US Government Accountability Office, February 2010, https://www.gao.gov/assets/310/301067.pdf.

153 *preparing each handmade interceptor was a major undertaking:* "Flight Test FTG-03a," US Missile Defense Agency.

154 *one big step in each test:* "Defense Acquisitions: Production and Fielding of Missile Defense Components Continue with Less Testing and Validation Than Planned," US Government Accountability Office, March 2009, https://www.gao.gov/assets/290/287097.pdf.

156 *Yowell and Kiraly learned this by looking up:* Kiraly interview, April 8, 2019.

156 *about two thousand miles from the launch site:* Michael Elleman, "North Korea Launches Another Large Rocket: Consequences and Options," 38 North, February 10, 2016, https://www.38north.org/2016/02/melleman021016/; Craig Covault, "North Korean rocket flew further than earlier thought," Spaceflight Now, April 10, 2009, https://spaceflightnow.com/news/n0904/10northkorea/.

156–157 *"We will not increase the number of current ground-based interceptors":* Robert Gates, "DoD News Briefing with Secretary Gates from the Pentagon," Department of Defense, April 6, 2009, http://archive.defense.gov/Transcripts/Transcript.aspx?TranscriptID=4396.

157 *more than 2 kilotons:* Lian-Feng Zhao, Xiao-Bi Xie, Wei-Min Wang, and Zhen-Xing Yao, "Yield Estimation of the 25 May 2009 North Korean Nuclear Explosion," *Bulletin of the Seismological Society of America* 102, no. 2 (April 1, 2012): 467–78, https://pubs.geoscienceworld.org/ssa/bssa/article-abstract/102/2/467/349540/yield-estimation-of-the-25-may-2009-north-korean?redirectedFrom=fulltext; Jonathan Medalia, "North Korea's 2009 Nuclear Test: Containment, Monitoring, Implications," Congressional Research Service, November 24, 2010, available at https://fas.org/sgp/crs/nuke/R41160.pdf. The best analysis appears to be that this was a nuclear device. The seismic measurements were consistent with a nuclear test and similar to North Korea's "dud" test in 2006. However, as far as is known to the unclassified world, there was no radioactive fallout detected, which makes it difficult to confirm.

157 *fire off two missiles:* Sam Kim, "N. Korea Monday fired two missiles, not three: ministry," Yonhap News Agency, May 27, 2009, https://en.yna.co.kr/view/AEN20090527005000315.

157 *O'Reilly was moving to revamp the agency:* "Report of Investigation Concerning Lieutenant General Patrick J. O'Reilly, US Army, Director, Missile Defense Agency (Report No. H1O116727365)," Inspector General, United States Department of Defense, May 2, 2012, https://media.defense.gov/2018/Jul/25/2001946766/-1/-1/1/O'REILLYROI.PDF. As of April 2019, O'Reilly was a Nonresident Senior Fellow at the Atlantic Council, and numerous attempts to reach him through the Atlantic Council, by phone and email, went unanswered. This book's descriptions of his thinking and actions are based on his official comments to the DoD inspector general, witness accounts provided to the DoD inspector general, and several off-the-record author interviews with O'Reilly's former colleagues.

158 To *his bosses, O'Reilly appeared to be an outstanding director:* off-the-record interview.

159 *Griffin had a bachelor's degree:* "Michael D. Griffin," U.S. Department of Defense biography, https://dod.defense.gov/About/Biographies/Biography-View/Article/1489249/michael-d-griffin/.

159 *O'Reilly called and asked if he'd come to Huntsville:* off-the-record interview.

159 *a "red team review" trying to solve the Track Gate Anomaly problem:* Obering interview, January 18, 2018.

160 *Gates instead that day revealed a new plan:* DoD News Briefing with Secretary Gates and Gen. Cartwright from the Pentagon, Department of Defense transcripts, September 17, 2009, https://archive.defense.gov/transcripts/transcript.aspx?transcriptid=4479.

161 *O'Reilly stepped in to defend the new plan:* "Patrick O'Reilly, Missile Defense in Europe," Atlantic Council transcript, October 7, 2009, https://www.atlanticcouncil.org/news/transcripts/transcript-missile-defense-in-europe-patrick-o-reilly.

161 *The move was criticized by many Republicans:* Peter Baker, "White House Scraps Bush's Approach to Missile Shield," *New York Times,* September 17, 2009, http://www.nytimes.com/2009/09/18/world/europe/18shield.html.

162 *The culture shock of coming to or leaving from Greely:* Major Michael Long interview, November 14, 2018.

162 *families had been hoping for a mild winter:* Robinson interview, October 24, 2018.

14: Management by Blowtorch and Pliers

164 *Patricia Young had never heard of the 100th Missile Defense Brigade:* Young interview, October 25, 2018.

165 *Another detachment would soon be sent to Shariki:* Bowen interview, August 17, 2018.

166 *entire US army contingent at Shariki:* Teri Weaver, "Tiny base assimilates into Japanese town: To allay locals' health fears, housing built close to radar," *Stars and Stripes,* Pacific edition, Monday, October 8, 2007, https://www.stripes.com/news/tiny-base-assimilates-into-japanese-town-1.69654.

167 *Raytheon engineers at first thought:* "Missile Defense Test Conducted," US Missile Defense Agency, news release, January 31, 2010, https://www.mda.mil/news/10news0001.html.

167 *hadn't installed a small part, known as a lockwire:* "Missile Defense: Opportunity Exists to Strengthen Acquisitions by Reducing Concurrency," US Government Accountability Office, April 2012, 74, www.gao.gov/assets/600/590277.pdf.

167 *$236 million:* ibid., 75.

168 *Pentagon's $712 billion budget:* Todd Harrison, "Analysis of the FY 2011 Defense Budget," Center for Strategic and Budgetary Assessments, June 29, 2010, https://csbaonline.org/research/publications/fy-2011-defense-budget-analysis.

169 *"I want you to tell me that you 'fucked up'":* This exchange was based on multiple witness interviews by DoD inspector general, including O'Reilly. "Report of Investigation Concerning Lieutenant General Patrick J. O'Reilly," Inspector General.

169 *hunting its target in space about seventy seconds earlier:* "A Three-Stage Two-Stage GBI Interceptor," *Mostly Missile Defense,* February 2, 2016, https://

mostlymissiledefense.com/2016/02/02/a-three-stage-two-stage-gbi-interceptor
-february-2-2016/.

169 *a viable boost vehicle*: "The FY2010 Annual Report for the Office of the
Director, Operational Test & Evaluation," Office of the Director of Operational Test & Evaluation, December 2010, available at https://www.dote.osd
.mil/Portals/97/pub/reports/FY2010/pdf/bmds/2010gmd.pdf.

170 *mostly profane screaming*: "Report of Investigation Concerning Lieutenant
General Patrick J. O'Reilly," Inspector General.

170 *"management by blowtorch and pliers"*: ibid.

15: Useful Failures

175 *It pointed to the possibility of an unstable thruster*: Obering interview, January
18, 2018.

175 *a component known as the inertial measurement unit*: Vice Admiral James Syring, presentation at BMDS Symposium, Huntsville, Alabama, August 13,
2014, available at https://mostlymissiledefense.files.wordpress.com/2015/05
/syringaugust2014smdctranscript.pdf.

176 *"a failure mode that could not be replicated on the Earth"*: Lieutenant General Patrick O'Reilly Testimony Before the Senate Armed Services Strategic Forces
Subcommittee, April 13, 2011, available at https://www.govinfo.gov/content
/pkg/CHRG-112shrg68090/html/CHRG-112shrg68090.htm.

177 *developed the test bed specifically to mimic the same high-frequency vibrations*: Guy
Norris, "Missile Defense Flight to Follow Boeing Test Innovation," *Aviation
Week*, December 3, 2012, https://aviationweek.com/awin/missile-defense-flight
-follow-boeing-test-innovation.

177 *top personnel at MDA were quitting in droves*: "Report of Investigation Concerning Lieutenant General Patrick J. O'Reilly," Inspector General, 16.

178 *had never seen O'Reilly yell at anybody*: Lehner interview, January 24, 2018.

178 *eight thousand employees—working across fourteen time zones*: Justin Creech,
"Missile Defense Agency completes realignment of headquarters building,"
Belvoir Eagle, August 18, 2011, https://www.army.mil/article/63799/missile
_defense_agency_completes_realignment_of_headquarters_building.

179 *Bowen could have easily deflected the blame to Michalski*: Michalski interview,
October 25, 2018.

180 *"That, son, is the NASA HALO badge"*: Spriggs interview, October 25, 2018.

182 *it was unlikely to be a threat anyway*: Pollock interview, December 13, 2017.

182 *Gates had been quietly warning about a forthcoming road-mobile threat*: John

Barry, "Robert Gates Exit Interview: Concerns About US Supremacy, Nuclear Proliferation, More," Daily Beast, June 21, 2011, https://www.thedailybeast.com/robert-gates-exit-interview-concerns-about-us-supremacy-nuclear-proliferation-more?ref=scroll.

183 *they did not appear to be operational:* Rachel Oswald, "North Korea Won't Have Operational Mobile ICBM Without Testing: Engineer," Global Security Newswire, March 22, 2013, https://www.nti.org/gsn/article/no-way-n-korea-has-operational-mobile-icbm-without-testing-engineer/.

183 *He was allowed to retire with the benefits of a three-star general:* Leada Gore, "Former MDA chief Lt. Gen. Patrick O'Reilly allowed to retire as three-star general despite findings he bullied subordinates," *Al.com,* January 4, 2013, https://www.al.com/breaking/2013/01/former_mda_chief_lt_gen_patric.html.

183 *"Best Places to Work" survey:* Al Kamen, "O'Reilly, still the boss," *Washington Post,* July 10, 2012, https://www.washingtonpost.com/politics/oreilly-still-the-boss/2012/07/10/gJQA7bZfbW_story.html?utm_term=.4519fb929a5f. Current year survey available here: https://bestplacestowork.org/rankings/overall/sub.

184 *tumbling uselessly in orbit:* "Crippled N. Korean probe could orbit for years," *Korea Herald,* December 18, 2012, http://www.koreaherald.com/view.php?ud=20121218000874.

185 a *twenty-thousand-mile fiber optic network:* "Boeing-led Missile Defense Team Completes GMD Flight Test," Boeing press statement, January 26, 2013, https://boeing.mediaroom.com/2013-01-26-Boeing-led-Missile-Defense-Team-Completes-GMD-Flight-Test.

186 *The data helped the crews:* Pollock interview, August 7, 2018.

186 *they were happy to make amends:* Kiraly interview, April 10, 2019.

187 *All the investigations came back unfounded:* Scott interview, November 15, 2018.

16: Yeoman's Work

189 *new thrusters to ease the in-flight vibrations:* "Missile Defense: Opportunities Exist to Reduce Acquisition Risk and Improve Reporting on System Capabilities," US Government Accountability Office, May 2015, 20, https://www.gao.gov/assets/680/670048.pdf.

189 *it was likely several kilotons:* Jeffrey Lewis, "North Korea's Big Bang," *Foreign Policy,* February 13, 2013, https://foreignpolicy.com/2013/02/13/north-koreas-big-bang/. Other estimates were similar; see James M. Acton, "Nuclear Defi-

ance out of North Korea," Carnegie Endowment for International Peace, February 12, 2013, https://carnegieendowment.org/2013/02/12/mythical-alliance-russia-s-syria-policy/ffry.

189 *the United States would deploy fourteen more interceptors:* Secretary of Defense Chuck Hagel; James Miller, Undersecretary for Policy, Department of Defense; Admiral James Winnefeld, Vice Chairman, Joint Chiefs Of Staff, DoD news briefing, March 15, 2013, https://archive.defense.gov/Transcripts/Transcript.aspx?TranscriptID=5205.

190 *that failure triggered an $85 billion budget cut:* Devin Dwyer and Mary Bruce, "Obama Signs Order to Begin Sequester Cuts After President, Congress Can't Reach Deal," ABC News, March 1, 2013, https://abcnews.go.com/Politics/OTUS/obama-signs-order-begin-sequester-cuts-president-congress/story?id=18628023.

190 *the federal government shut down for sixteen days:* Jonathan Weisman and Ashley Parker, "Republicans Back Down, Ending Crisis Over Shutdown and Debt Limit," *New York Times,* October 16, 2013, https://www.nytimes.com/2013/10/17/us/congress-budget-debate.html.

190 *$614.8 billion to spend:* Office of the Under Secretary of Defense (Comptroller)/Chief Financial Officer, "United States Department of Defense Summary of Performance and Financial Information Report: Fiscal Year 2013," Department of Defense, February 11, 2014, 4, https://comptroller.defense.gov/Portals/45/documents/citizensreport/fy2013/2013_report.pdf.

190 *Army Space and Missile Defense Command then gave the brigade $3 million:* Michalski interview, March 7, 2018.

192 *"Backbone leads the way!":* Kiraly interview, April 8, 2019; Young interview, October 25, 2018.

193 *a 1950s-pin-up-girl-style calendar:* Tim Ellis, "Army, Guard launch investigation into 'racy' Fort Greely calendar fund-raiser," KUAC, October 5, 2012, https://fm.kuac.org/post/army-guard-launch-investigation-racy-fort-greely-calendar-fund-raiser.

194 *no record of an Alaskan military court-martial:* "National Guard Bureau Office of Complex Investigations Report of Assessment of the Alaska National Guard," Appendix C-2, September 3, 2014, available at http://www.akleg.gov/basis/get_documents.asp?session=29&docid=65715. The Alaska Code of Military Justice was updated to better reflect the federal Uniform Code of Military Justice. The update was based largely on recommendations from the National Guard Bureau's report.

195 *afraid "for our wives":* Gopal Ratnam, "Alaska's Fort Greely called 'toxic environment' for condoning sexual affairs," Bloomberg News, May 27, 2013, available at https://www.adn.com/alaska-news/article/alaskas-fort-greely-called-toxic-environment-condoning-sexual-affairs/2013/05/28.

195 *"as if [sex] was the only thing to do":* Jim Miklaszewski and Courtney Kube, "'Open Season' for sex at Alaskan base, military officials say," NBC News, May 24, 2013, http://usnews.nbcnews.com/_news/2013/05/24/18477490-open-season-for-sex-at-alaskan-base-military-officials-say?lite.

195 *Miley had been suspended:* Leada Gore, "Battalion commander at SMDC's Fort Greely suspended following investigation into racy calendar, allegations of fraternization," *AL.com,* June 12, 2013, https://www.al.com/breaking/2013/06/battalion_commander_at_smdcs_f.html.

196 *Hendren was soon the BOSS vice president:* Hendren interview, November 14, 2018.

196 *the CAC:* author visit.

197 *"24 or 25 improvements":* Vice Admiral James Syring, Testimony before the Subcommittee on Strategic Forces of the House Armed Services Committee, US Government Printing Office, May 8, 2013, www.gpo.gov/fdsys/pkg/CHRG-113hhrg82459/pdf/CHRG-113hhrg82459.pdf.

198 *destroy a "complex target":* Tony Capaccio, "U.S. to Attempt First Missile Intercept Test Since 2008," Bloomberg News, July 2, 2013, https://www.bloomberg.com/news/articles/2013-07-02/u-s-to-attempt-first-missile-intercept-test-since-2008.

198 *"a voltage shift caused by battery electrolyte leakage":* Vice Admiral James Syring, Subcommittee on Strategic Forces of the House Armed Services Committee, US Missile Defense Agency, March 19, 2015, www.mda.mil/global/documents/pdf/ps_syring_031915_hasc.pdf.

198 *Pentagon's testing directorate was less certain:* Department of Defense Developmental Test and Evaluation, "FY 2014 Annual Report," Office of the Under Secretary of Defense for Acquisition and Sustainment, March 2015, 63.

199 *like a setting in a modern spy movie:* author visit and tour with Colonel Rich Timmons, a Command Center Director for the NORAD/NORTHCOM Command Center, known as the N2C2, November 16, 2017.

201 *the Mountain's entrance was blocked by a landslide:* Meakins interview, March 1, 2018.

201 *An estimated fourteen inches of rain:* Tom Roeder, "Workers still trying to

excavate underground base after epic storm, slide," *The (Colorado Springs) Gazette,* October 4, 2013, https://gazette.com/military/workers-still-trying-to -excavate-underground-base-after-epic-storm/article_424bea4f-2832-58cf -b907-b701f3417980.html.

17: Flight Test Ground-06b

203 *"the system engineering cycle was cut short":* Vice Admiral James Syring, "Missile Defense Agency Briefing," Pentagon Briefing Room, March 4, 2014, available at https://archive.defense.gov/Transcripts/Transcript.aspx?TranscriptID/5388.

203 *"We are seeing a lot of bad engineering":* Amy Butler, "Fiscal '15 Funds to Counter GMD 'Bad Engineering,'" *Aviation Week,* February 25, 2014, https://aviationweek .com/defense-space/kendall-fiscal-15-money-counter-bad-engineering-gmd.

203 *the Sergeant Audie Murphy Club:* Angie Thorne, "Sgt. Audie Murphy Club serves as elite organization for NCOs," *Fort Polk Guardian,* July 10, 2009, available at https://www.army.mil/article/24226/sgt_audie_murphy_club_serves_as _elite_organization_for_ncos.

205 *he was not especially nervous or worried about another failure:* Michalski interview, December 8, 2017.

205 *Guided missile destroyer USS* Hopper *was positioned near Kwajalein:* "MDA Report to Congress, Flight Test Ground-Based Midcourse Defense-06b (FTG-06b)," US Missile Defense Agency, July 11, 2014, 2–3, available at https://www .esd.whs.mil/Portals/54/Documents/FOID/Reading%20Room/MDA/15-F -0060_Flight_Test_Ground-Base_Midcourse.pdf?ver=2017-05-16-145850-200.

206 *About six minutes after the target had been detected:* "Target Missile Intercepted Over the Pacific Ocean During Missile Defense Exercise," US Missile Defense Agency, press statement, June 22, 2014, https://www.mda.mil/news/14news0005 .html.

206 *Two of MDA's High Altitude Observatory aircraft:* MDA Report to Congress. Additional information: L3 Technologies, "HALO-II and IV High Altitude Observatory #2 Gulfstream-IIB," https://www2.l3t.com/aeromet/Services /HALO-II-IV.htm.

206 *$1.981 billion:* "Missile Defense: Opportunities Exist to Reduce Acquisition Risk and Improve Reporting on System Capabilities," US Government Accountability Office, May 2015, 10, www.gao.gov/assets/680/670048.pdf.

207 *a more realistic "salvo test" with multiple interceptors fired against:* ibid.

210 *Kiraly put it bluntly:* Kiraly interview, January 9, 2018.

211 *It lost him a few friends, but he was at peace with that:* Pollock interview, December 13, 2017.

211 *technologically challenging to create:* Mary Beth D. Nikitin, "CRS Insight: North Korea's January 6, 2016, Nuclear Test," Congressional Research Service, January 7, 2016, available at https://fas.org/sgp/crs/nuke/IN10428.pdf.

212 *many other analysts believed it was likely a boosted fission weapon:* Josh Keller, Ford Fessenden, and Tim Wallace, "Why Experts Doubt That North Korea Tested a Hydrogen Bomb," *New York Times,* January 6, 2016, https://www.nytimes.com /interactive/2016/01/06/world/asia/north-korea-nuclear-bomb-test.html.

212 *suitable for arming a fleet of intercontinental ballistic missiles:* Jeffrey Lewis, "North Korea's Nuke Program Is Way More Sophisticated Than You Think," *Foreign Policy Magazine,* September 9, 2016, https://foreignpolicy.com/2016/09 /09/north-koreas-nuclear-program-is-way-more-sophisticated-and-dangerous -than-you-think/.

212 *"nuclear warhead that has been standardized":* Matt Clinch, "Here's the full statement from North Korea on nuclear test," CNBC, September 9, 2016, https://www.cnbc.com/2016/09/09/heres-the-full-statement-from-north -korea-on-nuclear-test.html.

18: Pyongyang a Go Go

213 *A small medical clinic had finally opened at Fort Greely:* Major Michael Long interview, November 14, 2018. The clinic opened in December 2015.

213 *Mark Scott was making that drive most days:* Scott interview, November 15, 2018.

214 *Padgett spent time on the battalion staff:* Padgett interview, November 14, 2018.

214 *Hendren's career was rolling too:* Hendren interview, November 15, 2018.

215 *"successfully evaluating [the] performance of alternate divert thrusters":* "Ground-based Midcourse Defense System Conducts Successful Flight Test," US Missile Defense Agency, news release, January 28, 2016, https://www.mda.mil /news/16news0002.html.

216 *"foreign object damage" was the most likely culprit:* Director of Operational Test and Evaluation, "Ground-based Midcourse Defense (GMD): FY 2016 DOT&E Annual Report," December 2016, 421–22, https://www.dote.osd.mil/Portals /97/pub/reports/FY2016/bmds/2016gmd.pdf?ver=2019-08-22-105348-463.

216 *did not plan to go back and fix the circuit boards:* David Willman, "There's a flaw in the homeland missile defense system. The Pentagon sees no need to fix it," *Los Angeles Times,* February 26, 2017, https://www.latimes.com/nation /la-na-missile-defense-flaw-20170226-story.html.

216 *The agency would field eight fully upgraded second-generation interceptors:* "Missile Defense: Delivery Delays Provide Opportunity for Increased Testing to Better Understand Capability," US Government Accountability Office, June 2019, 57, https://www.gao.gov/assets/700/699546.pdf.

217 *intelligence assets had seen the missile being moved:* Anna Fifield, "North Korea's missile launch has failed, South's military says," *Washington Post,* April 15, 2016, https://www.washingtonpost.com/world/asia_pacific/north-koreas-missile -has-failed-officials-from-south-say/2016/04/14/8eb2ce53-bc38-40d0-9013 -5655bed26764_story.html.

218–219 *"get your ass in here!":* Strawbridge interview, October 24, 2018.

220 *"a fiery, catastrophic attempt":* "North Korean missile test 'fiery, catastrophic' failure: Pentagon," Reuters, April 15, 2016, http://www.reuters.com/article /us-northkorea-missile-usa-pentagon-idUSKCN0XC28N.

220 *Between June 2012 and October 2014, she climbed from a two-star general:* "General Lori J. Robinson," U.S. Air Force biography, March 2017, https:// www.af.mil/About-Us/Biographies/Display/Article/108119/general-lori-j -robinson/.

220 *She and her husband, David, had both been active-duty air force:* "Lori Robinson Is the First Woman to Lead a Top-Tier U.S. Combat Command," *Time* magazine YouTube channel, November 22, 2017, https://www.youtube.com/watch?v =3sJPj09EdYA.

221 *"flight tests of a North Korean ICBM could begin in as little as a year":* John Schilling, "North Korea's Large Rocket Engine Test: A Significant Step Forward for Pyongyang's ICBM Program," 38 North, April 11, 2016, https://www .38north.org/2016/04/schilling041116/.

221 *Lewis agreed with Schilling:* Jeffrey Lewis, "New DPRK ICBM Engine," *Arms Control Wonk,* April 9, 2016, https://www.armscontrolwonk.com/archive /1201278/north-korea-tests-a-fancy-new-rocket-engine/.

222 *managed to travel four hundred kilometers and reach over one thousand kilometers altitude:* "Musudan (BM-25)," Missile Threat, Center for Strategic and International Studies, August 8, 2016, modified June 15, 2018, https://missilethreat .csis.org/missile/musudan.

222 *used the same ex-Soviet engine as the Musudan:* John Schilling, "A Partial Success for the Musudan," 38 North, June 23, 2016, http://38north.org/2016/06 /jschilling062316/.

222 *notched a successful test of a solid-fuel submarine-launched ballistic missile:* "Pukguksong-1 (KN-11)," Missile Threat, Center for Strategic and International

Studies, August 29, 2016, modified November 1, 2019, https://missilethreat
.csis.org/missile/kn-11/.

222 *an atomic bomb more powerful than the A-bomb used at Hiroshima:* Ralph Vartabe-
dian, "North Korea has made a nuclear weapon small enough to fit on a missile. How worried should the world be?," *Los Angeles Times,* August 9, 2017,
https://www.latimes.com/world/la-fg-north-korea-nuclear-bomb-20170809
-story.html; Lewis, "North Korea's Nuke Program." Author's note: The "Little
Boy" bomb used against Hiroshima was estimated to have a 15-kiloton yield.
North Korea's September 9, 2016, test was estimated at between 15 to 25
kilotons.

19: ICBM-range

223 *Delta Junction could only offer so much:* Cuthbertson interview, October 25,
2018.

224 *A crew, encumbered by too many alternates, had struggled to work cohesively:* Kiraly interview, April 8, 2019.

224 *the plan was for the crews to pull a month of day shifts:* Michalski interview, October 25, 2018; Kiraly interview, April 8, 2019; Pollock interview, October
25, 2018.

225 *The conclusion was that eight-hour shifts were ideal:* Michalski interview, October 25, 2018; Kiraly interview, April 8, 2019.

227 *Kiraly, Young, and the others were crushed:* Young interview, October 25, 2018;
Pollock interview, August 6, 2018.

228 *but a few weeks before the test he was told to put a lid on it:* Author experience;
Johnson interview, April 23, 2019.

228 *There were even exclusion windows for when the test could not happen:* Johnson
interview, April 23, 2019.

229 *Mattis was angry:* ibid.

229 *"notice to mariners":* Navarea XII Warnings, 22/2017, https://msi.nga.mil
/api/publications/download?key=16694429/SFH00000/UNTM/201722
/NtM_22-2017.pdf&type=view.

230 *Echo crew went to work:* Michalski interview, December 8, 2017; Kiraly interview, November 27, 2017; Pollock interview, December 14, 2017; Sergeant
Zachary Sheely, "In Their Words: Missile defense crew recounts intercontinental ballistic missile target flight test," Army.mil, December 18, 2017,
https://www.army.mil/article/198388/in_their_words_missile_defense_crew
_recounts_intercontinental_ballistic_missile_target_flight_test.

230 *Strawbridge had thought it was too cloudy:* Strawbridge interview, October 24, 2018.

233 *He warned that North Korea was improving its missiles and countermeasures:* "Fiscal Year 2018 Priorities and Posture of Missile Defeat Programs and Activities," House Armed Services Subcommittee on Strategic Forces, June 7, 2017, transcript available at https://www.govinfo.gov/content/pkg/CHRG-115hhrg26737 /html/CHRG-115hhrg26737.htm.

20: 24/7/365

235 *Around 4:20 P.M. spy satellites could see a two-stage, liquid-fueled Hwasong-14:* Ankit Panda, "Why Is Russia Denying That North Korea Launched an ICBM?," *The Diplomat,* July 11, 2017, https://thediplomat.com/2017/07/why-is-russia -denying-that-north-korea-launched-an-icbm/. Author's note: US intelligence officials said they observed the missile on its launchpad for about seventy minutes. They said this, presumably, to signal to North Korea that the United States could have destroyed that Hwasong-14 on the launchpad, if it were so inclined.

235 *Hendren wasn't exactly nervous:* Hendren interview, November 15, 2018. Other aspects of the July 4, 2017, launch were based on off-the-record accounts.

236 *Her adrenaline began moving:* Hendren interview, November 15, 2018.

236 *The sirens could be heard throughout Delta Junction:* Domenech interview, November 21, 2018.

236 *The missile reached 2,802 kilometers up into space:* Ankit Panda and Vipin Narang, "North Korea's ICBM: A New Missile and a New Era," *The Diplomat,* July 07, 2017, https://thediplomat.com/2017/07/north-koreas-icbm-a-new-missile-and-a -new-era/.

237 *According to Pyongyang's official Korean Central News Agency, Kim Jong-un:* Choe Sang-Hun, "U.S. Confirms North Korea Fired Intercontinental Ballistic Missile," *New York Times,* July 4, 2017, https://www.nytimes.com/2017/07/04/world /asia/north-korea-missile-test-icbm.html.

237 *to deliver a three hundred kilogram nuclear warhead:* Michael Elleman, "North Korea's Hwasong-14 ICBM: New Data Indicates Shorter Range Than Many Thought," 38 North, November 29, 2018, https://www.38north.org/2018/11 /melleman112918/.

237–238 *a program was put in place to teach the crew members how to operate the training software:* Pollock interview, August 6, 2008; Kiraly interview, April 8, 2019.

238 *Space launches were common and not too affecting:* Pollock interview, August 6, 2018.

239 *The missile's transporter-erector-launcher was spotted on the move near Kusong:* Ankit Panda, "North Korea May Test a Second Intercontinental Ballistic Missile Any Day Now," *The Diplomat,* July 25, 2017, https://thediplomat.com/2017/07 /north-korea-may-test-a-second-intercontinental-ballistic-missile-any-day-now/.

239 *another test launch was coming:* Pollock interview, August 6, 2018; Barbara Starr and Ryan Browne, "US intelligence shows North Korean preparations for a possible missile test," CNN, July 20, 2017, https://edition.cnn.com/2017 /07/19/politics/north-korea-possible-missile-test/index.html.

239 *constructing a viewing area near the site for Kim Jong-un:* Ankit Panda, "What the US Knew About North Korea's Second ICBM Launch Before It Happened," *The Diplomat,* July 31, 2017, https://thediplomat.com/2017/08/what-the -us-knew-about-north-koreas-second-icbm-launch-before-it-happened/.

239 *No. 65 Factory, which built the transporter-erector-launcher vehicles:* "North Korea's No. 65 Factory Is Not a Missile Base," 38 North, August 7, 2017, https:// www.38north.org/2017/08/no65factory080417/.

239 *On July 28 intel analysts knew almost to the minute when the launch would occur:* Pollock interview, August 6, 2018.

239 *was launched from the No. 65 Factory at 11:41 P.M. local time:* DoD News, "Pentagon Spokesman Comments on North Korean Missile Launch," Defense Media Activity, July 28, 2017, https://dod.defense.gov/News/Article/Article/1261474 /pentagon-spokesman-comments-on-north-korean-missile-launch/.

239 *It flew on a lofted trajectory:* "Hwasong-14 (KN-20)," Missile Threat, Center for Strategic and International Studies, July 27, 2017, modified November 5, 2019, https://missilethreat.csis.org/missile/hwasong-14/.

240 *"the capability of making surprise launch of ICBM":* Panda, "What the US Knew About North Korea's Second ICBM Launch Before It Happened."

240 *New procedures were written and adopted based on the crews' experiences:* Pollock interviews, August 6, 2018, and October 25, 2018.

240 *powerful enough to have reshaped the mountain under which it was detonated:* Jeffrey Lewis, "SAR Image of Punggye-Ri," *Arms Control Wonk,* September 13, 2017, https://www.armscontrolwonk.com/archive/1203852/sar-image-of -punggye-ri/.

240 *estimates placed the weapon's yield placed it at around 250 to 300 kilotons:* "North Korea's Punggye-ri Nuclear Test Site: Satellite Imagery Shows Post-Test

Effects and New Activity in Alternate Tunnel Portal Areas," 38 North, September 12, 2017, https://www.38north.org/2017/09/punggye091217/.

241 *"fire and fury like the world has never seen"*: Peter Baker and Choe Sang-Hun, "Trump Threatens 'Fire and Fury' Against North Korea if It Endangers U.S.," *New York Times*, August 8, 2017, https://www.nytimes.com/2017/08/08/world/asia/north-korea-un-sanctions-nuclear-missile-united-nations.html?module=inline.

241 *"enveloping fire at the areas around Guam"*: Christine Kim and Soyoung Kim, "North Korea says seriously considering plan to strike Guam: KCNA," Reuters, August 8, 2017, https://www.reuters.com/article/us-northkorea-missiles-usa-idUSKBN1AO2L9.

241 *against the seven thousand US military personnel*: Jim Michaels, "Tiny island of Guam is key U.S. military outpost now in North Korea's cross hairs," *USA Today*, August 9, 2017, https://www.usatoday.com/story/news/world/2017/08/09/guam-key-us-military-outpost/552770001/.

241 *Jim Mattis could not abide a threat*: Matthew Nussbaum, Bryan Bender, and Brent D. Griffiths, "Mattis warns of 'massive military response' if North Korea threatens attack," *Politico*, September 3, 2017, https://www.politico.com/story/2017/09/03/trump-north-korea-nuclear-242289.

243 *"wouldn't you want the most seasoned guy"*: Michalski interview, December 8, 2017.

243 *Just before 4:00 P.M.*: "North Korea fires second ballistic missile over Japan," BBC News, September 15, 2017, https://www.bbc.com/news/world-asia-41275614.

245 *"steady, clipped voice"*: Jim Mattis, May 24, 2018, comments at General Lori Robinson's retirement ceremony.

245 *"If we're going to engage this, we have to do it now"*: Michalski interview, October 25, 2018.

245 *a full complement of forty-four interceptors*: "Boeing Missile Defense Team Loads Milestone Missile into Silo," Boeing statement, November 7, 2017, https://boeing.mediaroom.com/2017-Nov-07-Boeing-Missile-Defense-Team-Loads-Milestone-Missile-into-Silo#assets_20295_130059-117.

245 *70.5 feet long and 6.5 feet in diameter*: Choe Sang-Hun, "North Korea's New Missile Is Bigger and More Powerful, Photos Suggest," *New York Times*, November 30, 2017, https://www.nytimes.com/2017/11/30/world/asia/north-korea-missile-test.html.

246 *clearer in early November*: Barbara Starr, "North Korea working on advanced

version of missile that could reach US, source Says," CNN, November 2, 2017, http://www.cnn.com/2017/11/01/politics/north-korea-missile/index.html.

246 *about three days before the launch:* Ankit Panda, "The Hwasong-15: The Anatomy of North Korea's New ICBM," *The Diplomat,* December 6, 2017, https://thediplomat.com/2017/12/the-hwasong-15-the-anatomy-of-north -koreas-new-icbm/.

246 *Around 10:00 A.M. the ICBM was stood up on its firing table:* ibid.

246 *At 12:17 P.M. Pollock and Bravo crew were snapped into action:* Michael Elleman, "North Korea's Third ICBM Launch," 38 North, November 29, 2017, https:// www.38north.org/2017/11/melleman112917/.

246 *only about 960 kilometers from its launchpad:* Zachary Cohen, Ryan Browne, Nicole Gaouette, and Taehoon Lee, "New missile test shows North Korea capable of hitting all of US mainland," CNN, November 30, 2017, http:// www.cnn.com/2017/11/28/politics/north-korea-missile-launch/index.html.

246 *Assessments differed:* Panda, "Hwasong-15"; Barbara Starr and Ray San-chez, "North Korea's new ICBM likely broke up upon re-entry, US officials says," CNN, December 2, 2017, http://www.cnn.com/2017/12/02/asia/north -korea-missile-re-entry/index.html.

246 *the vehicle appeared roomy enough:* "North Korea's New Missile"; Michael Elleman, "The New Hwasong-15 ICBM: A Significant Improvement That May be Ready as Early as 2018," 38 North, November 30, 2017, https://www .38north.org/2017/11/melleman113017/.

246 *finally completed its nuclear force:* Bahk Eun-ji, "North Korea says it has achieved goal of becoming nuclear state," *Korea Times,* November 29, 2017, https://www.koreatimes.co.kr/www/nation/2017/11/103_240097.html.

246 *capable of reaching anywhere in the United States:* Panda, "Hwasong-15"; Elle-man, "New Hwasong-15 ICBM"; Sang-Hun, "North Korea's New Missile."

247 *on shift for five North Korean missile launches:* Pollock interview, December 13, 2017.

Epilogue

248 *Missile Defense Advocacy Alliance:* Author in attendance, November 2, 2017, http://missiledefenseadvocacy.org/advocacy/events/congressional-round-table -events/boost-phase-missile-defense/.

253 *Hunter was indicted for wire fraud:* Morgan Cook and Jeff McDonald, "Rep. Duncan Hunter and wife indicted on fraud and campaign finance charges,"

San Diego Union-Tribune, August 21, 2018, https://www.sandiegouniontribune.com/news/watchdog/sd-me-hunter-indict-20180821-story.html.

254 *the idea was shelved in 2020:* "Department of Defense Press Briefing on the President's Fiscal Year 2021 Defense Budget for the Missile Defense Agency," Vice Admiral Jon A. Hill and Michelle C. Atkinson, February 10, 2020, https://www.defense.gov/Newsroom/Transcripts/Transcript/Article/2081326/department-of-defense-press-briefing-on-the-presidents-fiscal-year-2021-defense/source/GovDelivery/.

254 *"The GBI-Lead destroyed the reentry vehicle":* Daniel Wasserbly, "MDA: Homeland missile defence system's first salvo firing hits target," *Jane's Defence Weekly,* March 26, 2019, https://www.janes.com/article/87436/mda-homeland-missile-defence-system-s-first-salvo-firing-hits-target.

255 *kill vehicles could be able to communicate with each other:* Dr. Mitch Stevison interview, January 21, 2019.

255 *Griffin decided to nix the new kill vehicle program:* Bryan Pietsch, "Pentagon ends Boeing 'kill vehicle' contract, cites technical problems," Reuters, August 21, 2019, https://www.reuters.com/article/us-defense-boeing-kill-vehicle/pentagon-ends-boeing-kill-vehicle-contract-cites-technical-problems-idUSKCN1VB2IT.

256 *In a February briefing:* "Department of Defense Press Briefing on the President's Fiscal Year 2021 Defense Budget for the Missile Defense Agency," Vice Admiral Jon A. Hill and Michelle C. Atkinson, February 10, 2020, https://www.defense.gov/Newsroom/Transcripts/Transcript/Article/2081326/department-of-defense-press-briefing-on-the-presidents-fiscal-year-2021-defense/source/GovDelivery/.

256 *She would do it without hesitation:* Domenech interview, November 21, 2018.

258 *Bowen and everyone on the deck sit in silence for a minute:* Brigadier General Greg Bowen, "Remarks at DefenseOne Summit," November 9, 2017, available at https://www.youtube.com/watch?time_continue=336&v=hBleWQKbt38.

INDEX